Secrets of the Trading Pros

Founded in 1807, John Wiley & Sons is the oldest independent publishing company in the United States. With offices in North America, Europe, Australia and Asia, Wiley is globally committed to developing and marketing print and electronic products and services for our customers' professional and personal knowledge and understanding.

The Wiley Trading series features books by traders who have survived the market's ever-changing temperament and have prospered—some by reinventing systems, others by getting back to basics. Whether a novice trader, professional, or somewhere in between, these books will provide the advice and strategies needed to prosper today and well into the future.

For a list of available titles, visit our Web site at www.WileyFinance.com.

Secrets of the Trading Pros

Techniques and Tips That Pros Use to Beat the Market

H. JACK BOUROUDJIAN

John Wiley & Sons, Inc.

Published by John Wiley & Sons, Inc., Hoboken, New Jersey.
Published simultaneously in Canada.

Wiley Bicentennial Logo: Richard J. Pacifico

For general information on our other products and services or for technical support, please contact our Customer Care Department within the United States at (800) 762-2974, outside the United States at (317) 572-3993 or fax (317) 572-4002.

Wiley also publishes its books in a variety of electronic formats. Some content that appears in print may not be available in electronic formats. For more information about Wiley products, visit our Web site at www.wiley.com.

Library of Congress Cataloging-in-Publication Data:

Bouroudjian, H. Jack, 1961–
    Secrets of the trading pros : techniques and tips that pros use to beat the market / H. Jack Bouroudjian.
        p.   cm. – (Wiley trading series)
    Includes index.
    ISBN: 978-0-470-05411-6 (cloth)
    1. Futures–United States. 2. Investments–United States.   I. Title.
        HG6024.9.U6B68 2007
        332.640973–dc22

                                                                        2006037553

Printed in the United States of America.

10 9 8 7 6 5 4 3 2 1

To my wonderful wife, Donna, and my beautiful children, Robert and Emily. You have made me wealthier than I could have ever imagined.

Contents

Foreword   ix

About the Author   xi

Acknowledgments   xiii

Introduction   xv

CHAPTER 1   Trading Is an Art, Not a Science   1

CHAPTER 2   Many Are Called, Few Are Chosen   19

CHAPTER 3   Know Thy Market   35

CHAPTER 4   Managed Futures: The Holy Grail   55

CHAPTER 5   Within Every Disappointment, There Is a Gem of Opportunity   71

CHAPTER 6   Technical Analysis   89

CHAPTER 7   Random Walk Theory   105

CHAPTER 8   The Psychology of the Marketplace   119

CHAPTER 9   Demystifying Economic Releases   137

CHAPTER 10   Information Is Gold   155

CHAPTER 11   Risk Management   171

Index   187

Foreword

I n *Secrets of the Trading Pros*, Jack Bouroudjian shares the wisdom of successful traders who served as his mentors, and at the same time reveals his broad knowledge of market structure and the forces that make markets move. He views trading as more of an art than a science and explains why respecting the market at all times is one of the most important lessons any trader can learn.

Bouroudjian brings wide experience to the writing of this book. He is a former president of Commerzbank, where he oversaw the creation and development of equity futures operations, and has been a member of the Chicago Mercantile Exchange (CME) since 1987. He also served on the CME board of directors from 1996 to 2002.

While providing the breadth of a textbook, *Secrets of the Trading Pros* is written in a narrative style that makes readers feel as if Bouroudjian were sitting across the table sharing trading anecdotes and offering insights into market fundamentals. The book discusses the benefits of knowing the market and understanding the various players in different industries. It also explores the qualities that make exceptional traders—from exercising discipline and courage to understanding risk and reward—as well as the strategies that make them successful.

In addition to breaking down the thought processes of great traders, *Secrets of the Trading Pros* also delves into external influences that affect markets and trading. These include:

- Capitalizing on other traders' raging emotions
- Making sense of the trading methodologies that dominate today's marketplace
- Understanding the fundamentals of trading, especially futures trading
- Learning how headlines can affect a market's liquidity
- Observing the effects of economic releases, such as unemployment or housing, on the direction of the market
- Turning disappointment into opportunities

Secrets of the Trading Pros serves as an easy-to-read guide that can help traders weed out the bad trades from the good and become more successful overall. As executive chairman of the largest financial exchange in the world for trading futures and options, I see this book as a valuable resource for those looking to break into the world of futures and options as well as for trading veterans seeking to boost their command of the ever-changing marketplace.

TERRENCE A. DUFFY
Executive Chairman
Chicago Mercantile Exchange
December 2006

About the Author

Hagop Jack Bouroudjian has been senior vice president of Equity Futures for Nikko Securities, the second-largest securities firm in Japan; Credit Agricole Futures, a wholly owned subsidiary of Credit Agricole, the seventeenth-largest bank in the world; and Commerz Futures, a subsidiary of Commerzbank, the fourth-largest bank in Germany. Jack also served as president of Commerz Futures from 1999 to 2002. At each of these firms, Jack oversaw the creation and development of the equity futures operations. Jack has been a member of the Chicago Mercantile Exchange (CME) since 1987, and he is currently a principal at Brewer Investment Group, LLC.

Jack was a member of the board of directors of the CME from 1996 to 2002. During that time he was chairman of the equity indexes committee when the revolutionary e-mini concept was successfully introduced to the CME membership. Jack was also a member of the strategic planning and executive committees, which planned and executed the exchange initial public offering. He was also chairman or cochairman of over a dozen educational, product, and regulatory committees during his term.

Aside from industry experience, Jack has had extensive media experience. He has done over 1,000 international and domestic live TV shots over the last several years, including CNBC, CNN, CNNFN, Bloomberg, PBS, and countless local and regional broadcasts. He has been interviewed by numerous CEOs and CFOs of major corporations. He currently is a Friday regular on the CNBC *Squawk Box* segment. He appears daily on Bloomberg TV at various time slots during the trading session, and hosts a business talk radio broadcast (*The Jack Bouroudjian Show*) from 3 to 4 PM central time for the BizRadio network. Jack is a graduate of Loyola University of Chicago and is happily married with two children.

E-mail Jack at: Jack@BrewerFuturesGroup.com.

Acknowledgments

This book would not have been possible had it not been for the efforts of many people. I would like to begin by thanking the folks at John Wiley & Sons, Kevin Commins, Emilie Herman, and Laura Walsh. It must be a bit frustrating guiding a novice writer from start to finish! Thanks for being patient and constructive with your comments and suggestions. Thanks to everyone at Brewer, including Rita Karpel, Nick Patel, and Victoria Prado, for their assistance in creating this book.

The real heart of the work lies in the stories and experiences that came with the time I spent on the floor. I want to thank Bing Sung, Vince McLaughlin, Dennis DeCore, Brian McDonald, and a host of other customers and traders not mentioned who helped shape my world and opinions over the last 20 years on the floor of the exchange. Along with my experience on the floor came the time I spent in CME politics and my three terms on the CME board of directors. During that time, I learned more about the nature of the business than at any other time in my career. I would like to thank Leo Melamed, perhaps the most innovative personality the futures industry will ever know. Sitting next to you for five years taught me more than you could ever imagine! Thanks to Brian Monieson (my political mentor)—may he rest in peace! A special thanks to Terry Duffy and Craig Donahue for leading the institution I love into the realm of the great global corporations. The CME could not be in better hands!

The staff at the CME, including Anita Liskey, Rob Kosin, and Leslie McKeigue, is the finest in the industry. Not only do they handle dozens of live shots a day from the CME floor, but they have the ability to make a five-foot six-inch balding Armenian man look like Tom Cruise—thank you! My gratitude also goes out to Ted Lee Fisher and Rick Santelli for allowing me to interview them, which added so much to this manuscript. The acknowledgments would not be complete without thanking all the personalities on the floor who were a part of my life everyday: Adrian Byrne, John and Dan Scarnavac, John Fiandaca, George Sereleas, Aaron Reinglass, and Mike Tracy. My heartfelt gratitude to Bobby Gault and family for allowing me to share their miracle. Bobby, that experience changed all our lives!

Thanks to Don Sliter, Steve Helms, and Mark Plantery for showing me how it should be done.

Finally, I would like to thank my friends and family, who have been such a large part of my life. In particular, I want to thank my sisters, Lola and Sara, and all my cousins (there are too many of you to name). A special thanks to Ani Homolka and Flora Barrowman—I love you gals; thanks for being my older sisters! Thanks to Lind Burke for inspiring me to complete this project. Thanks to Raffi Antablian, Greg Hadley, and Pete Feit—I cherish our friendships more than you could ever know! I would be remiss if I didn't extend a special thank-you to Steve Buending and Gary Homolka. Your courage is amazing! Gary, there's a special place in heaven just for you! Last but not least, thanks to my parents, Avedis and Arshalous Bouroudjian; my children, Robert and Emily; and my wife, Donna. In the end, family is what really matters!

H.J.B.

Introduction

I remember the first time I walked onto the floor of the Chicago Mercantile Exchange (CME), as a 20-year-old liberal arts major at Loyola. It seemed like a world away the from the theology and philosophy courses that filled my core curriculum. It's a feeling that is hard to describe—a combination of basic human emotions producing raw energy from every corner of the large room. It was a very intoxicating tour, and I loved everything about what I was experiencing—the way it looked, the way it smelled. If I closed my eyes, I could almost smell the money! The feeling is much the same for those who venture onto one of the few surviving active trading floors in New York or Chicago for the very first time.

If you go to the visitor's center or have the good fortune to walk onto the floor of the CME today, you will still witness a sea of humanity waving their hands frantically as expressions of fear and greed race across their faces. It didn't take long for me to notice that there were two groups of traders—those who made money and those who struggled. I immediately asked myself, "What makes a trader good? Better yet, what makes a trader *great*?" That was over 20 years ago, but that subject is as relevant today as it was the day I first asked the question.

Walking onto the exchange floor today is different than it was back in 1982. The pits are still around, the wall boards are still lit up with flashing red and green lights that change as the price of the market moves, but the incredible energy that once exuded from the floor is now a thing of the past. It hasn't disappeared so much as it's morphed into something that is completely unique. It's now a hybrid market, a combination of open outcry and cyberspace. Simply put, if trading in an open outcry environment is the thesis, the antithesis would be a fully electronic market.

What the CME did was create a synthesis, a blending of the two concepts to create something unique, which the rest of the financial world has taken notice of. I guarantee that any exchange that has demutualized, or is considering such a move, is using the CME model as a template for future growth and consolidation.

In the 20-odd years I've spent in the futures industry, working my way up from floor runner to president of a bank futures commision merchant (FCM), I've encountered a range of individuals whom I considered to be teachers and mentors in trading. All of these people had one thing in common: They were all brilliant in their individual accomplishments, and they all taught me that there are secrets to the market that the professional trader knows but the average trader will never learn. How could that be? How is it possible that millions of traders around the world don't have access to the same information, yet they make trading decisions risking thousands of dollars? It became clear to me at an early age that if I were to succeed in the industry, I needed to pick up the secrets of these pros.

As a student of the markets, I have taken these lessons and incorporated them into my own trading, and I have shared bits and pieces with the public when doing market analysis on TV and when I speak at conferences and seminars. Doing daily appearances on Bloomberg and weekly appearances on CNBC gave me a platform from which to offer viewers a small dose of the fundamentals I believe everyone should know. The hunger for this type of fundamental information became very noticeable when I began to receive e-mail messages from viewers of Bloomberg, CNBC, and ROBTv (Canadian business television) asking me to explain, in greater detail, the points I had discussed in that day's interview. Speaking at industry events gives me an opportunity to see what type of information is available to the trading public. As I walk down the aisles of the conference halls, I notice hundreds of books on technical analysis—everything from Japanese candlestick methods to astrological market timing—but the one thing that I seldom see is anything written about the basic market structure and how to incorporate this type of fundamental information into the process of making trading decisions. There seems to be a lack of basic understanding among the general trading public about what really makes the market move.

It is so easy to look at a chart and make a simple trading decision based on what the support and resistance lines indicate, or put on a position based solely on technicals without looking at the fundamentals of a given trade. Professional traders will tell you that charts confirm what the fundamentals are saying and, in some extreme cases, will argue that the only thing that matters is fundamental analysis of a market. It has become my mission to enlighten the public about the little things that happen daily that professional traders watch when putting on trades rather than applying a thesis that explores after-the-fact analysis of market pricing or market timing.

Traders are a rare breed. It's been said that the life of a moneymaking trader is a charmed life indeed! Anyone who has ever traded anything would have to agree. The incredible high experienced when you are right and have a winning trade on can be matched only by the depth of disappointment you feel when you are covering a position for a loss and know you have been dead wrong. It's the constant swing in emotions that excites traders. We are nothing more than thrill seekers in the most pure form, except that we've substituted the market for roller coasters and skydiving. I have been fortunate enough in my career to be exposed to some of the greatest traders in the world, and some of the worst. It might sound silly, but bad traders—even more, horrible traders—taught me more about trading than anyone else.

I have written this book in narrative form rather than creating a textbook on futures trading, as it's my belief that you can learn much more from the daily grind of the market—in my case, the floor of the Chicago Mercantile Exchange—than anywhere else. Hopefully, the characters and traders who played a role in shaping my career and those who influenced me the most will have the same tutorial effect on you, the reader, as they have had on me throughout the last 20 years of my life. I'll share with you the thoughts of many of the greatest traders as they put trades on—and took them off—for a profit or for a loss.

We'll explore the psychology of trading and examine the panic and euphoria that drive the market to extremes and, more important, how a good trader makes a profit from the price aberrations created by those raging emotions. I've seen so many good trades turn into bad trades because the traders simply didn't understand the underlying emotion that was driving the market. A good example is the recent run-up in tech stocks. Sellers just could not grasp the euphoria that was driving that sector of the market, and many old-timers stood in amazement as the Nasdaq soared past 4000, then 5000, asking themselves with painful looks on their faces, "What is happening?" Those investors who did their homework and made a fortune during the late 1990s understood what was driving the market—a combination of Y2K spending coupled with an Internet revolution, producing a buying panic that laid the groundwork for one of the biggest balloons the stock market has seen in decades.

It is important to understand who trades futures and why. We will ask ourselves who trades options and, even more important, how their trades impact what we do on a daily basis. We will explore and understand the true nature of liquidity and leverage and realize that these are the concepts that determine the success of an exchange-listed contract. In fact, it can be said that what an exchange brings to the end user—any exchange, regardless of whether it's the NYSE or the CME—is simply liquidity and leverage, nothing more. It is imperative to look at the different participants in the marketplace and try to understand the logic that underlies the trades that they initiate.

What most new traders don't recognize is that knowing the players in the game is half the battle! We'll look at different trading and investing method-ologies that make sense in today's marketplace. The Peter Lynch method (Chapter 1) is a wonderful example of a simple strategy and perhaps the biggest secret in the trading community. If you're trading futures, know what you are trading, and if you're buying stocks, know what you are buying. It might sound simple, but it's the lesson most often forgotten by experienced market professionals, not to mention the general trading public. These are the types of mistakes I've witnessed over the years, which, if properly analyzed, can help teach students of the market what we should know—the nuances of daily market price action. The essence of this work is summed up in that very question: What drives the market from day to day, and how can I capitalize on the price action created from the volatility?

It's been said that when it comes to trading in the markets, many are called but few are chosen. We must discover what the qualities of those rare few "chosen" are (Chapter 2). For example, what makes a great scalper a position trader? What are the qualities that make a great options trader? What is it about risk that these players inherently love, which gives them the ability, physically, emotionally, and mentally, to take on the markets on a daily basis?

Often, the commentary we hear on the various business television shows becomes the extent of our market knowledge. We hear the terms *communized trading* or *asset allocations*, whether it's a fixed income, equities, or Forex, but do we really understand what the mechanics of the trade will do to the pricing of the market we're presently trading (Chapter 3)? The impact of these orders can be huge! I've described these orders by saying it's as if someone is trying to turn around an aircraft carrier in a small bay, leaving a big wake, and it's up to the trader to capitalize on that disruption and ride that daily aberration to a greater trade and a better profit.

We'll take a good, hard look at news and corporate events and how a single headline can change the attitude of a given market's liquidity. There are news events and corporate actions that guide traders on a daily basis regardless of earnings, expectations of those earnings, or board actions. We'll look at arbitrage and the different types of arbitrage opportunities that drive the market and have become a large, important liquidity provider in the marketplace daily.

Understanding the various types of arbitrage hitting the market will give us a better feel for direction. Keep in mind that there is index arbitrage, statistical arbitrage, and risk arbitrage, and collectively they create a pool of liquidity the market has found essential. And this book would not be complete without adding the impact that hedge funds have had on market action, especially as they become larger in size and trading activity. A question frequently asked of me when I bring guests to the Chicago Mercantile Exchange is "What are the traders watching?" The next few chapters should give you the ability to step into a trader's shoes and view the market the way that that trader would.

We'll take an in-depth look at managed futures (Chapter 4), about which an entire book could be written. This has become an important part of any lesson on futures trading, because the proliferation of these products has turned managed products into the fastest-growing segment in the alternative investment universe. (I hate using the term *alternative investments* when referring to managed futures; quite frankly, these are investments that should be regarded as mainstream.) We'll discuss modern portfolio theory and unveil another of Wall Street's well-kept secrets, the exclusion of managed funds from the portfolio.

What most investors don't know is that every investment model allocates a portion of assets to commodity-based exposure. But investment advisors are asked to eliminate that from the recommended portfolio. Why? For two reasons: The advisor simply doesn't understand the vehicle (unfortunately, a growing problem in the wealth management industry) or the investor doesn't fit into the qualified investor category. The latter problem has been solved as a result of the proliferation of registered multiadvisor managed funds open to general investors. These have low minimums—in the $10,000 to $25,000 range—and accomplish their main objective, true diversification of the portfolio.

We will examine the creation of the e-mini, the most successful concept the futures industry has seen in decades. As a former member of the Chicago Mercantile Exchange board of directors and chairman of the equity index committee when the concept was introduced to the trading community, I'll share my insights into the introduction, marketing, and growth of the products that have revolutionized trading futures. Looking at the e-mini, we will discover that the role of the market maker on the floor of the exchange has changed considerably. In short, the floor has lost the right of first refusal—in essence, what has taken place is that the trading edge has shifted from being a geographical edge in the pit to being a technological edge off the floor. In an open outcry arena, the market maker or local can change from being a buyer to being a seller in an instant, based on order flow and pit positioning. Locals made the market. But now the pit no longer determines the trade, it is no longer the central price discovery mechanism, and in fact, it can be said that what was previously an open outcry market with a small electronic pool of liquidity attached to it has turned into an enhanced electronic futures market with a small captive pool of floor liquidity attached to it.

The psychology of the marketplace is a very important subject. Many books have been written on the psychology of trading, but most average traders fail to remember that the market is based on two simple human emotions: fear and greed. I've always tried to understand the emotions driving the trade almost as much as the underlying fundamentals of any given market. I'm a true believer in feeling right about any trade, and understanding the market sentiment gives the trader an emotional edge. Why is it that the best professional traders have had their biggest profits in markets that go down? It's because they know that the psychology of a breaking market is much different from that of a rallying market. Euphoria, greed, panic, fear— these are all very real emotions that play a role in every trading decision made.

We will look at random walk theory (Chapter 7), which is a guiding principle for many professors teaching graduate school in many of the business programs around the country. We'll look at the world of technical analysis and ask ourselves if it really does work and, more important, if there is credible evidence that it does, how we can use it in a fundamental way to guide our trading activity. It's almost comical how often a derivative form of an old technical analysis methodology is heralded as the new Holy Grail for trading the markets. I've seen too many traders live and die as dogmatic followers of a trading system rather than using the work as a tool for proper risk management. The best traders use technical analysis in the array of tools at their disposal, but they justify trading decisions based on the fundamentals of the market regardless of where support and resistance have been identified by the charts. I'll look at the economic data that comes from both Washington and private sources and discuss how these periodic releases can impact the market on a daily basis.

Taking the mystery out of those numbers is very important to me. I do this on a daily basis on Bloomberg TV, on CNBC, and on various other business programs. It is vital to weed out the data that might be insignificant or after-the-fact analysis in order to determine the numbers that give you, as a trader, a better feel for the future direction of inflation, unemployment, and consumer sentiment. Collectively, they give you a gut feeling about where the market will go and, more significant, how you can trade and make money from that information on a short-term basis.

Sometimes we need to remind ourselves that what we are doing is not brain surgery or rocket science. New traders seem to get so caught up in the excitement of the trade that they become obsessed with the markets. They eat, drink, sleep, and breathe trading! I regard that as the most destructive behavior for traders because they will eventually burn themselves out and end up hating the very thing that excites them the most. We have to realize that trading the markets is an art, not a science, and some days we're better artists than others. It's an art form that is slowly being lost to computers, but, more important, it's an art form that is very, very hard to master.

The most difficult thing is shedding the yearning for instant gratification. Every new trader wants to make a million dollars right away. That is *not* the way it works! It takes time, and you must realize that you have to *earn* the right to be able to make money, you have to *learn* the pain of the marketplace, and most important, you have to respect the market at all times. When new traders started on the floor years ago, there was a rule of thumb that said if you can survive the first six months, chances are that you'll make it as a local on the floor. It's one of those kernels of wisdom that stick with you—that if you don't fail within the first six months, you will succeed. It's a very important concept to digest, especially when you are a beginning trader because trading, at first, is completely overwhelming. You feel like fresh, bleeding meat in a pool full of hungry sharks; you need to be able to see the light at the end of the tunnel.

My last name is an Armenian name, Bouroudjian, which is unique in that it has survived the ages without being lost. Other Armenian-Americans are not as fortunate, ending up with names that were given to their orphaned grandparents who were lucky enough to live and make it to orphanages. My parents are from the Armenian Quarter of the old city of Jerusalem, raised there by my grandparents who escaped as the only surviving members of their families during the Armenian Genocide at the hands of the Turks. Although it is an Armenian name, Bouroudjian has a Turkish origin; *Bouroudj* means "silkworm" in an ancient Turkish-Armenian dialect. My ancestors are from an area in Anatolia called Dikranagerd, which at one time was a thriving trading metropolis on the old Silk Road.

Based on the Tigris River, Dikranagerd was a city lively with commerce for centuries and had an inherent entrepreneurial spirit that was unmatched in all of Anatolia. It was a city where, for centuries, barges loaded with exotic goods and spices from the East were floated down to Baghdad en route to the West. In my romantic imagination I picture myself as a merchant or a silk trader, haggling with strangers from faraway lands about the prices of everything from silk to pepper. Being of Armenian descent makes me feel as if trading has been a part of my ethnic identity for generations, and having the word *silk* in the etymology of my surname convinces me of that fact. Sometimes I feel as if I was born into the markets—a feeling that's hard to shed and, more notably, a sensation that has been amplified by my experiences in the trenches over the course of the last 20-odd years.

As I take you on a tour of my world and expose some of its best-kept secrets, I hope my deep affection for the market and its players is contagious!

Thank you!

CHAPTER 1

Trading Is an Art, Not a Science

I have an old friend, John Labuszewski, who worked with me at Nikko Securities when I ran the equity futures operation on the Chicago Mercantile Exchange (CME) floor. Labuszewski was the president of Nikko funds and the catalyst for Nikko entering the world of managed futures. He was known throughout Japan because of his past successes with Refco in turning the four major Japanese brokerage houses into Refco's best customers. A wonderful storyteller, John would start all his speaking engagements with a tale based in antiquity.

He would relate how the Romans needed large supplies of wine to fuel the increasingly decadent lifestyle of the age. To get the wine to Rome, it became necessary to create a network for shipping and distribution based on contracts set for future delivery. Much of the finest wine of the day was stored in the best possible vessels for shipping in the entire empire: huge jugs lined with lead, which both made them leak proof and sealed them from the elements. However, the lead in the jugs slowly poisoned the wine, transforming the most expensive commodity into a slow, debilitating death for those who drank it. Labuszewski would thus conclude that futures contracts helped destroy the status quo by poisoning or driving insane the elite citizens and thinkers of the day, ultimately helping to bring down the entire Roman Empire.

I tell that story because most people who trade in the markets don't really understand what futures are all about. Labuszewski would tell that story in order to create a frame of mind that would allow his listeners to change any misconceptions they might have about the subject he was about to discuss—the futures markets. A common perception of someone who trades the futures markets is that of a big risk taker—the last of the true entrepreneurs, embodying capitalism in its pure essence. The reality is that the futures markets and those who trade them collectively serve one ultimate purpose: They create a liquid vehicle for risk management.

WHAT ARE FUTURES?

When the Chicago Board of Trade (CBOT) and the CME were founded over a century ago, futures markets were created to give farmers and speculators a central place for price discovery. On any given day on the grain floor of the CBOT, many of the old-time grain customers can still be seen doing business, using the contracts in much the same way that they've been used for over 100 years.

However, the world of futures changed in 1971, when Leo Melamed, then chairman of the CME, together with Nobel laureate Milton Friedman, created a revolutionary concept called the International Monetary Market (IMM). They called the end product *financial futures*. This advance in futures no longer entailed a physical delivery of the products traded, but, rather, called for a cash settlement for the underlying contract marked at expiration. This innovative evolution opened the door for institutions and arbitrageurs who had never seen the futures markets as a way to create a legitimate return on capital. In short, it created a new and sophisticated customer base for futures, which has grown dramatically since its inception.

As the use of financial futures proliferated, the number of jobs in the industry that both traded and serviced the markets exploded, starting with local clearinghouses based in Chicago and progressing to large money-center banks based in Europe. Prior to the establishment of the IMM, many of these banks had enjoyed a monopolistic interbank market in both currencies and fixed income, which allowed the spreads in the markets to remain wide— the spread, in this case, being the difference between the bid and the offer, or in reality, pure risk less profit potential.

It became apparent to all those trading at the time that these new markets in Chicago were slowly taking the edge away from their country club network and making the underlying markets much more efficient. That's when every bank with a currency trading operation began to view the markets in Chicago, not as a bastard stepchild, but as a necessary part of pricing every transaction.

WHO USES FUTURES AND WHY?

One of the most-asked questions in this industry is: "Who really uses futures and why?" The conventional answer is: farmers and ranchers looking for price discovery for their products, speculators and risk takers who have an opinion about direction, and spreaders who spread both intramarket and intermarkets. These are the obvious players, but this falls short of telling us the crucial role each plays in creating an efficient, liquid futures market. Trading is more than learning to buy low and sell high. The seasoned pro knows when each group of participants is entering the market and can usually identify the impact of those orders.

This understanding of players' actions has nothing to do with transparency; it's a matter of access to the right information, which then develops into a gut feeling. Every market has its own nuances, and those who spend day after day watching a given trade are able to capitalize on the adjustments made by the various market forces. For example, good cattle traders understand that hedgers come into the market at given times in the slaughter cycle and create an aberration in prices. These traders know that if they are positioned properly, the market will inevitably open a window of opportunity that they can turn into trading profits.

OPTIONS

As we begin to study options, it becomes immediately apparent that they are a world unto themselves. In fact, if we think of futures as a game of checkers, we would have to regard options as a game of three-dimensional chess. It takes a completely different type of personality to trade options than it does to trade futures on a daily basis. One might make an argument that the personality of a futures trader is that of a great risk-taker and the personality of an options trader is that of a very cerebral, risk-averse individual. That is no longer the case.

Today we are experiencing a marriage of the two worlds, as trading between futures and options becomes more and more intertwined; however, regardless of the incestuous nature of the trading, the financial world continues to look upon the options trader as more quantitative by nature than the futures trader. One reason for this generalization might be that the options markets, and the models that are used to price those markets, are based on pure mathematics. The Black-Scholes model—the definitive model for pricing options created by Myron Scholes and Fischer Black in 1973—or a derivative of the Black-Scholes model is the mathematical formula used in every options trading group and every institution with options exposure in its portfolio. One thing that new traders often don't understand is that these option trades become so large at times, especially around expiration and at month's end, that they move the market in very strange ways. Later, we'll look at how good traders take advantage of the aberrations created by the large options flow at certain times in the cycle.

Who are the end users of the options markets and, more important, why are they using these contracts? This is a question that many novice traders neglect to ask as they venture into a world that is quite foreign to them. It only makes sense to realize that anyone in the capital markets who has exposure to a certain sector of the marketplace is looking for an affordable way to hedge out that exposure, creating a solid risk-to-reward ratio. Individuals use options to write covered calls, enhancing the yield on a stock, or they look to buy puts as an insurance policy against any downturn in their portfolios.

Of course, there are many sophisticated investors who understand the nature of the options markets and use them with greater intensity, but they are the exception rather than the rule and the order flow created by this small minority does not have much market impact. In the fixed-income world, institutions use options to create caps, floors, or collars for interest rate exposure, thus creating the type of leverage that they need and insulating them from any wild fluctuations in price. It is these options strategies that allow the creative mortgage solutions proliferating in the present-day housing market to be engineered.

Some of the largest trades taking place in the entire financial world are done at the CME in the Eurodollar options pit. As the former president of Commerz Futures, a division of Commerzbank of Germany, I saw firsthand the importance of the products and the role that they played in pricing every transaction involving fixed income by the banks' traders. The situation has matured to the point that every major banking institution from around the globe has found that maintaining a presence and monitoring the action in the Chicago markets is not done out of luxury but has become a necessity.

Institutions with equity exposure use options in many different ways. Aside from using the options markets in the traditional ways, institutions, and in particular hedge funds, use the vehicles for creating extra leverage and giving customers and investors an easier way to increase volatility in their portfolios. Many of the new players in the options world are index funds that have looked to enhance their returns either by selling premium against their core positions or by selling premium against a sector position. This strategy gives them more yield per million under management but increases the risk with the investment.

OPTION PREMIUM AND VOLATILITY

Speculators love options because they can buy a call or a put and know exactly what their risk will be by paying a premium. It becomes an insurance policy of sorts and is a much easier way of protecting a portfolio or playing a direction in the market. Unfortunately, many speculators are not professional traders and don't understand the nuances of the options market, such as time and volatility, which could make the right directional trade into a monetary loser.

One good example of this phenomenon is the market crash of 1987. As a new trader, I was taught that when the market begins to break hard, it is imperative to remain calm and not get caught up in the emotion of the moment—a very difficult thing to do when the world looks like it's coming to an end. I watched as the put market began to trade at price levels that would have taken an Armageddon to enable to break even! Worse yet, I watched in terror as retail customers sent in market orders buying put options at any possible price without understanding the effects of spiking volatility on options premiums. I quickly learned that trading any market without understanding the fundamentals behind the pricing of that market was financial suicide—maybe not an immediate death but one that could lead to a slow, self-inflicted debilitating disease.

Professional options market makers, however, have a whole different mentality and strategy associated with their approach to trading. They are taught to make markets on every strike, and at some exchanges they are obligated to make a two-sided market regardless of their firms' proprietary positions. It's been said that a good options market maker picks up the nickels and dimes in front of the bulldozer. Well, every now and again the bulldozer runs them over, but they've got to be sharp enough to understand how to cover the exposure that enables them to come back tomorrow.

One of the best-kept secrets, which most professionals on the Street don't even know, is that options traders buy premium, both calls and puts, when the market begins to panic. A common misconception is that everyone is selling everything when the market has a huge move down. And why not? Everyone knows that over 80 percent of all options contracts expire worthless. That is definitely not the case with options traders, who are taught to be "gamma long" with the positions that they acquire. Simply put, they are trained to be long premium because volatility will spike higher, pumping up premium levels on all options strikes, regardless of direction.

The best options traders in the world always have themselves hedged out to both the downside and the upside by buying what are generally referred to as *baby puts* and *baby calls* that end up expiring worthless. These are options that are out of the money but are incorporated into a position for a number of reasons, least of which is to allow the risk manager of the firm the comfort of being able to sleep at night.

Myron Scholes, one of the two creators of the Black-Scholes model, was my colleague on the board of directors at the CME for two years. A Nobel laureate and brilliant thinker, Scholes was very fond of saying that there were many options traders over the course of the years who thanked him for creating the formula that allowed them to make their fortunes. It was an honor to have served with him on the board of directors, and the CME is still blessed to have such a distinguished person in its boardroom.

Most of today's options market makers have evolved into what the Street refers to as *delta-neutral traders*. Delta-neutral options trades are tied to futures, which create a market-neutral strategy allowing traders or investors the luxury of trading pure volatility with no slippage as they enter or exit positions. In short, traders try to capitalize on the speed of movement, or the rate of price swings, which simultaneously provide both opportunity and protection.

Seasoned traders understand that there are only three ways you can trade the market: direction, time, and volatility. All three of these variables are factored into the price of every financial transaction that takes place in the capital markets. As simple as that might sound, it's something that most individual investors and traders just don't recognize. Trading volatility is much different than trading time or trading direction, and anyone looking at the markets conceptually must understand that basic fact. Directional trading, the easiest concept to grasp, allows the new trader to explore the short side of the market, usually for the first time.

We look at directional trading every day as we decide whether to buy or sell stocks, bonds, or any listed vehicle. Trading the volatility of a given market allows investors or traders the opportunity to profit on the movement of the market regardless of direction. Anyone who understands options can trade volatility without being a professional, but the question is whether they're willing to do the homework and crunch the numbers that enable them to take advantage of the pricing of these strategies. When a trader decides to trade time, it usually encompasses strategies that sell out of the money premium or credit spreads in the options marketplace and monitor those positions very carefully. A strategy based on time is usually looking for decay of premium levels as the contracts get closer to expiration. This approach disregards direction and volatility in favor of the length of time left until expiration.

LIQUIDITY

Liquidity is a concept that many have studied for years, but only a few have acquired a realistic notion of the theory. In studying liquidity, we must take into account the fact that there are different types of daily liquidity that traders will encounter. There is the liquidity of a market that we can gauge through the open interest of a given futures contract. This is really a barometer of the health of the contract rather than an indication of the size that flows through the market. For example, when we first began trading the S&P Mid-Cap 400 and Russell 2000 contracts, it was imperative for open interest levels to be at a minimum of 5,000 contracts before institutions could trade the product. The major end users called this the *critical mass level* needed for the institution to commit its capital resources.

In some cases, the critical mass issue has been mandated by the charter of the institution, which, in many ways, becomes the vanguard of the capital protecting investors from positions put on in illiquid markets. The daily intraday liquidity of the trade gives us an indication of how large day-trading positions can be without much market impact when entering or exiting the trade. One of the best-kept secrets in the trading pits is that it becomes possible to become bigger than the market. This occurs when a day trader acquires a large intraday position and finds it difficult to manage the risk for various reasons, market impact being the greatest one.

There are times when locals move markets as if they were institutions by virtue of the sheer size of the position they have accumulated. Every now and again, I'm asked to explain liquidity to a visiting group of students or dignitaries in the gallery overlooking the trading floor at the CME. I usually ask them to close their eyes and visualize a pool of water, then imagine small streams and large rivers feeding into and out of that pool. Some are large, gushing rivers (Goldman Sachs, Merrill Lynch, etc.), while others are small streams and tributaries. This analogy usually gives the audience I'm addressing a good idea of what liquidity is really about, or at the least, provides a starting point for their education.

If you think about it, the central price discovery mechanism, the pit, and the electronic platform collectively create that liquid pool of capital. Either way, monitoring the liquidity of a contract allows you to witness the liquid flow of funds as it works its way in and out of the market and, more important, how the liquidity is affected by conditions throughout the daily sessions. One of the most important things that hedge fund managers or portfolio managers do before they trade futures contracts is look at the slippage on execution of those contracts. How easy is it for them to enter and exit trades? How much slippage will occur when the trades are put on? And finally, what is the health of the exchange listing the contract? It becomes a function of smart money management on the part of the traders and compliance officers.

Usually, the tools employed include the open interest or the open positions of a given futures contract. But open interest can also be deceptive because a contract or a market with a large number of contracts open doesn't necessarily give you a clear indication of the daily liquidity that you would need to put on a sizable position. This is most evident in futures contracts that are used as a passive investment vehicle; an example of this is any of the commodity index contracts like the Goldman Sachs Commodity Index (GSCI) or the Commodity Research Bureau (CRB). These contracts have healthy open interest numbers with low daily volume figures, but they also have the market makers and liquidity providers to create huge markets when needed.

Passive positions are put on with a strategic vision and rolled from month to month from quarter to quarter, thus creating a synthetic type of exposure for investors, with huge leverage, rather than a position that they are trying to alter and monitor daily. The GSCI is a contract I traded and brokered during my days on the floor of the CME, but in order to put on a large position it became very important to know when the daily volume would allow such a trade with as little market impact as possible. This was true not only for the contract itself but also for the underlying components that make up the index. But it's got wonderful open interest, and during the rollover of that contract—the physical rolling of positions from the front month to the new front month—we see quite a bit of activity, making that period in the cycle the best time for customers to execute a large order without leaving a big footprint in the marketplace.

Liquidity can make or break a contract. In fact, as new contracts are created by the exchanges, it is the one thing that they will constantly nurture and encourage more than anything else. When the S&P contract was first introduced to the membership at the CME, everyone wore buttons that read "Fifteen minutes please." This was the exchange hierarchy's way of asking all the exchange traders to commit 15 minutes during the day to help support the new contract.

I remember seeing pork belly traders, cattle traders, and currency traders all making markets in a brand-new stock index they had no business trading. Yet there they were, putting on positions fearlessly to help a new exchange concept succeed. Simply put, liquidity and leverage combined are what the exchanges are marketing and selling to the financial services industry. Together, they, the liquidity providers, are the true essence of the CME and every other exchange around the world.

LEVERAGE

Many investors and traders don't fully understand the concept of leverage; therefore, it scares everyone. More and more people tell me that they understand how leverage works—they realize that futures give you the type of leverage that no other financial vehicle gives you—yet these are the same people who will go out and buy an index fund paying 100 percent margin rather than establishing a futures position, which creates synthetic exposure and gives the investor much more leverage and flexibility. That fact proves to me that people talk about leverage but don't really understand how to use it.

Perhaps the best example of institutional use of leverage in the marketplace is found in the world of index arbitrageurs. Index arbitrage is a strategy that takes advantage of the disparity between the futures price and the underlying cash price of a given index. Whether you're doing an S&P arb, a Nasdaq arb, a Russell arb, or a GSCI arb, the actions and mechanics of the trade are identical; it's the execution of the underlying products that differs. All index arbitrage is basically the same in structure. The only difference is when the arb is executed with a commodity-based index rather than using equities as an underlying market. Either way, the trader is taking advantage of the aberrations based on what you would consider to be a fair value between the futures contracts and the underlying index.

Most arbs are successful because they are able to use the 20-to-1 leverage that futures inherently give them. Without the incredible amount of leverage that's available to these trading desks, they would not be able to put on the enormouse multi-billion-dollar positions that drive the market up or down, especially during expiration and at times when the indexes are being rebalanced.

Leverage also gives the hedge funds the ability to enhance the yield on a given product. This is evidenced by the many index funds being marketed at present that use a synthetic futures position to replicate equity exposure and sell covered calls and credit spreads overlaying the core position. Many of these funds give investors what they consider to be a two- or a three-beta fund, which, in layman's terms, gives investors double or triple the amount of leverage they would normally get through a conventional investment. The most critical element in dealing with leverage as a concept is managing the risk created by the trade.

HEDGING

True hedgers are a completely different breed than the other players in the capital markets universe. Old-time hedgers were exactly what you would expect them to be: farmers, a cattle ranchers, people looking to lock in the future price of their underlying crop or herd. But now hedging has evolved into a strategy that is much more sophisticated than ever in the history of commodity trading. At present, the large hedges that we see moving the market are fund managers who are looking to cover exposure in an entire portfolio without having to upset the balance of that portfolio.

It becomes much more effective and efficient for a portfolio manager with a sizable portfolio to sell futures instead of the underlying cash position in the event of expected market weakness. An example is a portfolio manager at Fidelity or Putnam who would use a short position in the stock index contracts to hedge out any downside exposure to the portfolio without having to sell out individual issues of stock. There are swap traders and forward rate agreement (FRA) traders who hedge out every transaction, turning fixed-rate products for variable-rate products or vice versa, by using the eurodollar futures or options, which have turned what was a small, niche fixed-income contract into the world's largest and most liquid.

Those swap trades—specifically, the flow that comes off of the swap desks of the major money center banks and institutions around the world—have created the largest spreaders marketplace in the world. That's not to say that we still don't see the old-time hedgers using futures for their intended purpose in the agricultural markets.

Some of the old-time houses such as Cargill and Archer Daniels Midland (ADM) are still in the marketplace using the contracts the way they've used them for the past 100-plus years. The questions are, at what point does hedging out the risk make sense, and at what point does the cost of the hedge become an obstacle to profitability? A strategy called *dynamic hedging* was employed during the 1987 stock market crash, which was a trade that sold index futures, regardless of fair value, to cover exposure in a breaking market. The hedging technique that was being incorporated became a self-fulfilling prophecy for a market that was already in a weakened state.

Unfortunately, the strategy added incredible amounts of selling pressure, which helped to break the market. There are many reasons why that happened, most of which have been fixed through a strong cooperative agreement among the exchanges in Chicago and the equity exchanges in New York, with the Federal Reserve acting as ultimate vanguard. But the most important lesson learned from this experience is that at times hedging simply doesn't work. It took a stock market crash for institutions that were new to futures to learn what farmers and ranchers have known forever—that hedging is an art form like no other!

KNOW THE MARKET YOU TRADE

One of the biggest problems that I've seen over the course of the years is that people get caught in bad trades in markets they simply don't understand. Nothing is more painful than seeing good S&P futures traders stuck in a horrible hog position, having no logical explanation for why and how they got into the position. It is very important to pay close attention to the market that you're trading, so you pick up on the nuances of the trade. It's clear that knowing the players, knowing the participants, and knowing when this flow is coming in and when they're getting out of trades are what separates good traders from *great* traders.

You learn these things over the course of time, but even more important, you learn them through observation and by doing your homework. One of my first employers was a great trader named Bing Sung. Bing was a boy genius, having graduated from the prestigious Phillips Academy in Andover, Massachusetts, at the age of 16, and from Harvard at the age of 18. By the age of 21, he was an associate professor teaching analytic decision making at Harvard.

I considered Bing a mentor. He had both brain power and a great gambler's instinct, a combination that made him one of the best market thinkers I have ever met. Bing went from being an academic at Harvard to helping run the Harvard Endowment Fund. After he had left the fund, I became his assistant on the floor of the CME, trading futures and options for him throughout the course of the day and engaging in a daily Socratic dialogue that taught me more than any university curriculum ever could.

"I ONLY KNOW HALF THE SCORE!"

Many of the lessons that I learned in trading the markets were learned from Bing during those first formative years. In fact, many of the sayings that I use to this day originated as "Bingisms." I find myself, at times, unconsciously using his colorful language to describe events when I do my daily TV shots on Bloomberg or CNBC, and I'm reminded of my early teacher as I hear myself talk.

Spending hours on the phone with Bing gave me plenty of information to process while attempting to execute my clerking duties without an error. Whenever the market began a significant move up or down, Bing would ask for my opinion. As I described to him the technical levels and the flow moving the market, he would invariably say to me, "Jack, my boy, that's only half of the score. It's as if you're telling me that the baseball score is Cubs 3, White Sox . . . silence?" I remember being confused by the comment the first time he said it. I asked myself if it was Bing's attempt at being difficult, but I eventually learned that he was trying to teach me that there was a large order moving the market—we just didn't see it!

I would explain to him that I would see order flow doing one thing or another, that I would look at the board or check through our network and realize there was an asset allocation, but he would always follow it up with a compliment and then say, "That's still only half of the score." I would respond, "I guess I need to do more homework?" He would usually laugh and in his own colorful way say to me, "Don't worry, sweetie pie, you'll eventually get it!"

Bing was a storehouse of information, showing me how institutional traders think and act and what strategies were driving daily volatility. One of the Bingisms I remember is: "There are over 2,000 rules in the book of trading [an imaginary book he thought up] and over the course of my career, I've only learned 20!" Now that was over 20 years ago. I hope that Bing, as brilliant as he is, would have been able to pick up on at least a thousand of those lessons by now, but I know that if I were to ask him that question today he would say the number is probably no higher than 50. Still, learning those lessons is worthless unless the trader incorporates what has been experienced into the daily routine.

DO YOUR HOMEWORK

Learning a hard-earned lesson in the markets and not using it to become a better trader is a waste of energy and, even worse, a waste of money. But how do you try to find the full score? How do you do your homework in an environment where the market information might not be transparent?

These are questions that all new traders should be asking if they are to regard trading as a serious business rather than a passing hobby. New traders are sometimes so enamored of charts and technical indicators that they neglect to study the real foundation of the price movements. This is where access to a proper information network is vital, and it's likewise vital to keep your eyes and ears open at all times. In fact, I think the best traders are those who hear and see everything around them, then refine and synthesize it into a trade.

In mid-October of 1987, I was on the phone with Bing, and we watched the market start to break hard. For those of us on the floor at that time, it was an experience we'd never forget. Prior to this, Bing and I had participated in markets that went down, and we were successful in making money, but this was a trade that became scary. In fact, when I heard the fear in Bing's voice, I started to become afraid myself. The conversation was no longer centered on whether to buy or sell the market, but rather on how much damage the system could endure. Would the economy seize up? It got to the point where Bing started to be concerned about the entire banking system, which worried me even more. Up until then, as a 26-year-old novice trader, I had thought only about making the right trade.

It had never dawned on me that we might be looking at the potential collapse of the entire financial system as a result of a stock market crash. Fortunately, as we all know, the system didn't collapse. In fact, years later, studies were released proving that futures helped save the system on the way down by being the only place where portfolio managers could limit their risk—they acted as a buffer for a falling market. But what it taught me at the time, and what Bing's concerns taught me, was to never lose respect for the market. It can carry us all through!

That experience also taught me the importance of doing my homework. For months prior to the break, the long end of the interest rate curve was yielding 10 percent, which created a serious competitive risk for the dollars that were being invested in equities. Bing had pointed that out to me time and time again by recognizing an asset allocation order or by noticing volatility in options premiums long before a volatility index (VIX) was created, but it wasn't until we actually witnessed the market reacting to this phenomenon that I began to feel the market as a trader.

THE PETER LYNCH METHOD

Knowing and understanding what you're trading are not new concepts—and this does not just apply to futures. Peter Lynch, who managed Fidelity Magellan, the best-known mutual fund in the 1980s and 1990s, talked about that with regard to stocks. In fact, Lynch's approach to investing is probably the most practical methodology that the average investor could ever adopt. His advice was simple: Don't buy anything that you don't know or understand! I learned from experience that taking a walk through a shopping mall could be just as effective as looking at a company balance sheet, and in many cases, it means much more.

Browsing a mall or a shopping center to see what people are buying will give you an idea of what the trends are, and even more important, it will give you an idea of where future earnings might be. Practical information collected through observation, coupled with due diligence on company management and governance, enables you to form an educated opinion about a stock, its sector, and the economy in general. Better yet, it creates what every trader wants—a high-percentage trade!

I love telling the story about my daughter Emily coming to me with a stock pick—Claire's, a retailer that girls in her age group were frequenting. Emily was 13 years old at the time, and she and her friends spent quite a bit of money at Claire's. Knowing I was a professional trader, she asked questions about what I was doing; as she began to understand the basics of what drives stocks, she quickly developed an opinion. She urged me to buy stock in Claire's because she thought it was a great store.

Although her purchases looked like junk jewelry to me, I realized over the course of a couple months that it really wasn't junk at all—the girls were spending a lot of money on it! In a last-ditch effort to be the Warren Buffett of the seventh grade, Emily pleaded, "Dad, please, I think you should buy Claire's stock because we see a lot of people there and all our friends are spending all their money in the store." I thought to myself, "Okay, Sweetie, what do you know?" I patted her on the head and assured her that I would take her advice and buy the stock. The next day Claire's announced earnings significantly higher than expectations and the stock was up 10 percent within the first 10 minutes of trading.

Having two teenage children is a retail stock picker's dream because of the nature of the spending habits in their demographic. I find myself constantly asking both my son and my daughter what they're buying and what their friends and classmates are talking about. This gives me not only the parental control necessary to successfully raise teenagers today, but also a knowledge base for a simple investment strategy.

WHAT ARE THE FUNDAMENTALS?

Another of the best-kept secrets on the Street is that many people trading in the markets don't really understand what the underlying contract they're trading is all about. They don't understand the composition of the indexes or the size of a cattle futures contract, but that doesn't keep professionals from placing huge positions in markets that might be a mystery. Case in point: Many of the professional liquidity providers trading the S&P futures contract, both in the pit and electronically, don't understand the basics behind the contract; they don't understand how it is composed or rebalanced and what types of strategies are being engaged in the marketplace. The best traders understand the fundamentals that drive a market on a daily basis, regardless of what they might be trading. When I raised this issue of market knowledge with some of the greatest locals Chicago's trading pits have produced, I got a definitive analogy in response: "I watch television, but I don't necessarily know how the machine really works."

Most average investors and most traders assume that everyone on the floor and in the pit is an expert on the capital market structure. Nothing could be further from the truth. I often tell people that their educated opinion is in many cases better and more informed than those of a majority of the professionals on the trading floors. Trading in a pit environment is much more physical than sitting and staring at a screen for a good portion of the session. It's very difficult for traders on the floor to get accurate, timely information because their attention is divided between the action taking place in the pit in front of them and the large information wallboard where they might find a headline that would change the pricing of the market at any given time.

THE LEMMING MENTALITY

Back when I was doing institutional brokering, I encountered two of the finest traders that the index arbitrage world ever produced: Vince McLaughlin and Dennis DeCore. The two met at Merrill Lynch as the concept of stock index futures was being introduced into the capital markets. Index arbitrage takes advantage of the disparity in price between the futures market and the underlying cash market, creating the arbitrage. Pioneers in this game, Vince and Dennis, over time, took the strategy to a new level. Later chapters in this book will explore this strategy in more depth, along with the ancillary effects that are being created as a result of the sheer size of the arb positions in the present-day market.

I consider the years that I spent on the phone with Vince and Dennis to be my version of graduate school. The two gave me a good feel for what was going on in the outside world, what was hitting the futures market, and the aberration in pricing that occurred through various corporate events that drove the index one way or the other. Vince and Dennis opened my eyes to a world that I had never been exposed to before. To that point, I had spent my career in the world of futures, and I had never been around or thoroughly understood the equity markets. The two worlds are so different in terms of both culture and regulatory oversight, and these differences have been institutionalized since the creation of the Commodity Futures Trading Commission.

As I now look back on the days I spent with Vince and Dennis, I find it strange how much of their vocabulary and personality worked their way into my market options and attitudes. Dennis, in particular, had a funny way of describing what he saw as a foolish trade. A contrarian by nature, he loved to watch as traders moved the market, creating a stampede of emotions that extended the moves and brought on aberrations in price. He called this movement the "jumping of the lemmings." Whenever the market started running one way or another, Dennis would invariably say to me, "Jack, the lemmings are at it again."

Let me explain: The lemming is a rodent that has been mythologized as being suicidal—it's possible to witness lemmings jumping off cliffs in Norway en masse into the sea. Thus, the lemming has always been associated with a herd mentality, regardless of whether the final outcome is destructive. Dennis hoped for that herd mentality to drive prices into the inefficient condition that allowed his trading desk to generate profits. He often commented on the silliness of traders putting on positions and having enormous amounts of capital at risk because the trader next to them in the pit was doing the same—yet that's exactly what would happen in the market at any given time of the open outcry trading session.

The best example of the lemming mentality is the Nasdaq bubble experienced in the late 1990s. I had never seen a period in the market when more professionals were baffled by what was happening daily in Nasdaq stocks. I saw the most experienced traders in the world fight the tape consistently for the three or four years of the balloon and get to the point physically, emotionally, and financially where an economic disaster was the only thing that would make them break even, let alone make a profit. These were not novice traders and investors; they were seasoned pros who had been in the game for 20 or more years and thought they had a full grasp of what drove price action.

Many of the big bear funds and their bearish market strategists had their day in the sun a few years later, when we watched valuations on some of these tech stocks break down 90 percent from where they had been during the late 1990s. But it was the lemming mentality that drove the market to unforeseen heights and unattainable valuations, and it was a good trader who could recognize and capitalize on the condition that was created. Perhaps the most difficult thing to do as a trader is to be a contrarian and fight the crowd by fading the collective bullish or bearish mood. When day traders see others putting on trades, they feel as if they're missing the boat if they don't have anything on—it's only natural. Every trader who has had any success in the pits has adopted what I call a trader's ego, which will not allow trading profits to be the exclusive domain of the next trader.

One of the most important lessons the lemming mentality actually taught me is to make my own mistakes without following the herd. Why should I get an opinion from someone sitting in an office a thousand miles away from the action instead of using the tools I have at my disposal through observation and analysis? There are many wonderful technicians and market strategists who have educated opinions on market direction or geopolitical factors, but my opinion, based on their work, is the only one that matters. It's my own opinion that will either garner me a profit or turn my analysis into a losing trade.

MAKE YOUR OWN MISTAKES

Every now and then I'll get a call from somebody soliciting a certain stock or a certain strategy over the phone and I'll ask the person why he or she is making that recommendation. After going through an entire sales pitch, the person admits that the only reason this stock or strategy is being touted is because it was on the recommended list of the person's firm. I usually respond to that type of solicitation by saying, "Thank you, but I can make my own mistakes. I don't need your firm or you to make them for me." It always surprises me that people will take their hard-earned money and put it at risk with information that is so often inept and incomplete.

What's really ironic is that these are the same educated, Internet-savvy people who will do months of research before buying a car or go to great lengths to find the right doctor, but they will make a trading decision based on a whim or a gut feeling. Granted, a trader should not trade without a good gut feeling, but it's an educated gut feeling that's needed. A gut feeling that is not supported by the proper homework or analysis is nothing more than a gambler's hunch.

A client of mine in the mid-1990s was an individual with one of the highest net worths to ever trade futures for his own account. A natural-born gambler, he would refer to me as his "walking casino." He was worth well over nine figures and understood the concepts of risk and reward better than anyone else I had ever met, but he preferred a winning trade based solely on his feeling to one requiring days of painstaking analysis. There was nothing he liked more than making money in the market, but it wasn't the profit of the actual trade that excited him as much as being right about the market.

I realized that somebody who had made that kind of money and had been that successful in life didn't really care about the few hundred thousand dollars shifting from a profit to a loss on a daily basis; rather, it was the trader's ego that was involved with every decision he made. It was the pure satisfaction of knowing when he was right and the disappointment when he realized he was in a bad trade and had to cover the position. Such emotions are incomparable! This man made and lost millions of dollars trading through me, but the one thing he would tell you to this very day is that he enjoyed every minute of it because he made every decision himself.

For those who are successful in other businesses, the lure of the futures markets is magnetic. More important, the ability to make an analogy between their chosen profession or business and futures trading is absolutely necessary in order for them to feel the action. One of the best descriptions of the pit that I've ever heard came from this same wealthy gentleman, who came and watched the markets trade right next to me on the floor of the exchange. He saw the order flow come in and out and watched the pit react to every order. After silently observing the trading for 15 minutes, he turned to me and said, "Oh, well, this is just like the auto parts business." I told him I didn't understand. "Well, Jack" he said, "I would give hub caps away for free until somebody asked me how much hub caps were—then the price went up to $10 apiece."

He had made the analogy between the auto parts business he had built from scratch and the futures market—and it was perfect! He was saying that as demand for hub caps increased with the seasons, the price would go up. As demand dwindled and the way hub caps were used changed, prices would go down. It was no different in the pit. His insight was a revelation of the obvious! But it showed me what had been drowned out by the noise of the pit, offering me a crystal-clear lesson.

CHAPTER 2

Many Are Called, Few Are Chosen

P it etiquette is a custom created by the open outcry environment, which essentially self-polices the trading activity in a given pit. It was common for traders to become "invisible" to the order-filling brokers when they committed an act that was determined to be disrespectful of pit etiquette. One major violation of the practice was when a pit trader, watching another pit trader trying to buy or sell an order, jumped to grab the trade and, even worse, made a market for the stuck trader at a profit.

One of my earliest recollections of being on the trading floor was as a runner being shuffled between the Chicago Board of Trade (CBOT) and the Chicago Mercantile Exchange (CME) in my first weeks of employment. I saw two older veteran grain traders staring each other down. In the middle of an altercation, they were tossing obscenities obliviously, as if they were everyday adjectives. It became apparent that the short, rotund gentleman in his 50s was accusing the other gentleman of stealing a trade. The smaller of the two took a swing and hit the larger trader so hard that it sent him to the floor, with papers, pens, and trading cards flying out of his pocket. It shouldn't have shocked me—I came from what I thought to be a somewhat rough neighborhood on the far north end of Chicago—but I nevertheless felt uncomfortable watching these two grown men, who were older than my father at that time, fighting like schoolboys. The much larger and heavier trader went down like a heavyweight fighter catching a perfect punch on the jaw.

As the exchange's security guard arrived on the scene, I found myself eavesdropping on the conversation and it quickly became apparent from the security guard's tone that the aggressor of the incident would have to pay a monetary fine, which, in this instance, depending on the disciplinary committee's ruling, could be in the neighborhood of $500. These days an incident involving physical aggression can cost a trader as much as $30,000 and a suspension that could last for months. For the very worst offenders, it might mean expulsion from the floor. But the late 1970s were a different day and age for the floor, and a country-club mentality ruled.

As the dialogue turned to the prone body of the unfortunate recipient of the punch, the trader who had hit him pulled out a handful of hundred-dollar bills and threw them at the poor soul. The security guard, seeing that the pile of money far exceeded any fine that would be assessed, asked with a puzzled look, "Why have you thrown down twice the normal amount?" The aggressor responded, "Pick up every bill. When the son of a bitch gets up I'm going to hit him again."

This was my first revelation. At the time, I remember thinking to myself, "Do I have the personality for this business?" In fact, I remember scratching my head, observing the anger coming from this one gentleman, and asking myself, "Is it possible for me to get that angry... at anything?" I realized that it takes a certain type of personality to be in the markets daily and make a successful career out of the organized chaos that I was observing. It was an eye-opener at the time, but I remember discovering that money intensifies emotions more than any factor other than religious fanaticism.

WHAT ARE THE QUALITIES OF A GOOD TRADER?

The markets bring out the best and worst in a trader's personality because the act of trading the markets and putting capital at risk taps into an incredible array of raw emotions. A trader's true personality surfaces when he or she is faced with the difficult decision of covering a losing trade or is finally convinced to establish a position. Traders are a strange breed. Superstitious by nature, some floor traders have been known to wear the same shoes or tie for years because they consider these items good luck charms. Even I find myself falling into this pattern by walking through the same turnstile every day and having a cup of coffee in the same location. My day wouldn't be complete if these little rituals were not followed.

As a creature of habit, before every TV shot—and I do roughly 15 live shots a week—I walk over to the same spot on the floor where I have conducted my business for 15 years. Standing next to John Scarnavac, Adrian Byrne, and the rest of my former floor colleagues, I observe the market from my comfort zone and absorb the day's events. I feel as if I can get a better sense of the market's pulse and, better yet, give TV viewers a solid report by talking to the traders and brokers who are responsible for making the action happen.

SCALPERS

To understand the personae of traders, it's important to understand that the personalities of different types of traders are diverse. The personality of a local who scalps the market during the day is much different from that of a spreader who is taking less risk and trying to lock in profits through the physical act of laying off the risk in one market, or one sector of the market, against another. The personality of a scalper or spreader is much different from that of a true position trader. Each of these distinct types of trader has a certain type of personality that enables the person to do what is necessary day after day. For many in the pits, it's a question of endurance and mental toughness that separates success from failure on the floor, qualities much like those of professional athletes.

One of the interesting phenomena that I've noticed over the course of the last few years, and something that not many people would know, is that athletes seem to make wonderful traders. It only makes sense—an athlete is trained, both mentally and physically, to endure the hardships of training and the pressures involved with the actual game. Athletes recognize that they are considered only as good as the last good season or, in some rare cases, the last play. The world of sports, much like that of trading the capital markets, is not very forgiving.

SPORTS AND TRADING

Thus it should come as no surprise that many former college and professional athletes look to the floor as a way of transferring the energy from their chosen sport into a trading methodology and discipline that they can quickly learn and understand. More specifically, of all athletes, tennis players and hockey players seem to make the best traders. One reason for this is that both tennis players and hockey players are taught from an early age to play both offense and defense simultaneously. They are thinking defensively as they're playing offense; they are thinking offensively as they're playing defense. This becomes an integral part of their approach to the game, and with many traders it becomes a natural part of their approach to the markets.

There are some great examples of tennis pros and semi pros who have become successful traders, many of whom are still on the floor of the exchange today. Likewise, there are hockey players who have demonstrated their ability to succeed in the trading pits just as they did on the ice. Some of the best locals that the S&P pit ever produced can trace their roots to professional sports. The Hughes family—George, Jack, and Jim; Troy Murray; Jack O'Callaghan of Olympic gold medal fame; and Mark Plantery are only a few of the former hockey players who have become successful local traders. Mark Plantery and George Hughes, in particular, stepped into the pit with fearless attitudes and total disregard for the bullying tactics that seemed to dominate the crowd in their era. They came in with a mind-set acquired during their playing days, which is exactly what is needed to supply the courage to trade.

Plantery started trading after playing professional hockey for six years in the National Hockey League and one year in Italy. He played with Winnipeg and became a good defenseman specializing in penalty killing. I sat in awe as he and other former professional hockey players told stories of going up against the best players of the day, including the great Wayne Gretzky. But what separated Plantery from the rest of the crowd, in my mind, was his ability to remain emotionally detached regardless of the market condition. Mark wasn't the biggest trader in the pit, but what he lacked in market size he made up for with pure hard work and determination. That's what made him the definitive athlete turned trader, in my opinion. Looking into his eyes, you wouldn't be able to tell whether he was having a profitable day or whether his position was down thousands of dollars.

It was obvious from his inaugural experience that there was something very different about this individual. On his first day, the trading pit's biggest tormentor raced up to Plantery with a closed fist, appearing ready to swing a punch and yelling profanities. Without flinching, Plantery stared the bully down and with a cold, hard look proclaimed, "Take your best shot... then I get my turn!" A long, uncomfortable silence followed. But the point had been made. It was enough to stop the aggression and, more important, established Plantery as someone not to be messed with in the pit. But it wasn't only the fearlessness that made the man; it was also the discipline of doing the proper homework and preparation before every trading session. Every day I watched Mark study price charts and headlines as if he were watching game films of opponents' offenses.

In contrast, Hughes was pure speed and determination. A Harvard alumnus, Hughes took the natural feel he had developed for hockey and used the speed he showed on the ice to become one of the top local traders in the S&P 500 futures. He would be in and out of trades so quickly that he wasn't able to write up one side of the trade before immediately jumping on a bid or an offer to cover the position.

You might think it would be the same for any athlete—say, a baseball player, a football player, or a basketball player—but not so. Anecdotally, the only advantage larger athletes have on the floor is a function of their sheer size, which makes them more visible to the order fillers in the pit or if they, themselves, are filling customer orders. But for whatever reason, hockey players and tennis players have consistently been able to take that intensity and draw through the emotion of the moment of the trade, thus becoming great locals. Both great hockey players and great tennis players think and act much like great chess players in that they are always thinking two or three steps ahead of the game. Tennis players are taught to automatically envision two or three shots in advance of the one they're playing. The same is true for hockey players, who are trained to play both offense and defense up and down the ice, regardless of their given position.

But athletes aren't the only ones who seem to make natural traders. The success stories encompass everyone from construction workers to electricians to computer salespeople. A seemingly endless list of occupations, both white and blue collar, have been abandoned for the thrill of victory in the futures markets. The pit is one of the few places in the world where an MBA stands next to a former truck driver, who's standing next to a former professional athlete, and they all have roughly the same opportunity to succeed. It's not that former athletes are any more intelligent than the rest of the crowd—they just seem to find the relentless daily physical and mental pressures a lot easier to handle than those from fields that do not routinely require that kind of daily psychological and bodily abuse.

AVERAGING DOWN

The thing that new traders don't understand and what the general public doesn't realize is that not only is the personality of these traders unique but it really becomes part of the methodology used to trade. For example, former athletes usually become scalpers, which requires a very high level of intensity and stamina. Remember, scalpers don't hold a trade for more than seconds. In fact, it's been said that any scalper who holds a trade for more than a minute or two is probably stuck on that trade and will inherit a de facto opinion without qualification or research. One of the biggest mistakes made by new scalpers is that they add on to losing positions, looking to maintain an average price as the market goes against them. More often than not, the traders keep adding to the loser, hoping to break even on the trade by creating an average price that will allow them to scratch the position or trade out of the contracts with a small profit. This is called *averaging down*.

When I first came down to the floor, I met a wise old man named Sam, who took a liking to me. I tried to make Sam laugh by telling a joke every time I saw him. Knowing I was a new member, he would walk by my desk every morning asking about the day's data or economic releases. hoping that I would start looking at the correct indicators. As I began to trade, I noticed that Sam would watch me from his spot in a quiet section of the pit.

After my first full week of trading, during which Sam, my new guru, watched everything I was doing, he took me aside and said, "Jack, you're Armenian, right?" I said, "Yes sir, what about it?" He continued, "Well, my boy, don't ever forget that averaging down killed more Armenian traders than the Turks." He said it with the affection of a loving grandfather, and then quietly walked away. I didn't know what to make of the comment. It shocked me at the time because I had been averaging down my position from the moment I started trading.

He had watched me buy one and then buy another one and then buy another one. I added on to the position four times, all of which were losers, before finally covering the trade and establishing a loss. The logic was that if I kept my average price lower and lower as the market went down, it would be easier to break even on the position. Think of how idiotic trading in that manner really is. Average up . . . to catch up! Even though I was a new trader, I had been around the floor for years prior to becoming a member, so the revelation that I was making what was considered a beginner's mistake was crushing to my fragile trader's ego. But Sam's comment taught me an important lesson about risk and reward. It made no sense to add to losing positions just to even up my exposure. The risk-to-reward ratio was way out of whack! This was not the way to trade the market.

BORN TRADERS

Some of the greatest scalpers I've seen are people who must have been born as pure traders. The best example of the quintessential scalper is Donald Sliter. Growing up in Rogers Park, my old working-class neighborhood on the far north end of Chicago, Sliter was known as one of the local tough guys. But something always stood out about Don that separated him from the crowd. He was always a bit smarter than the rest. When his friends started fights, Sliter tried to break them up. When they drank in bars, he was always the bouncer. And when his friends gambled on sports, Don figured out how to middle the point spread. What Sliter lacked in the way of a formal education, he made up for with a natural gift—an instinctual gut feeling.

If you were to ask Sliter what makes him a good trader, he would have a hard time explaining the qualities that give him an edge. Sliter's philosophy involves the frequency of trades. To watch Don trade is to watch a master; he plays the pit and the order flow as if it were a violin, making sweet music with every profitable scalp. He's been known to say that the rest of the market trades against support and resistance but they fail to realize that there are hundreds of profitable trades hidden between those levels. This is the type of comment that would be expected from a scalper. A position trader can't think like that.

The one quality that every scalper in any market must possess is a total disregard for money. As the profit and loss for the day are calculated, very seldom do you hear scalpers talk in terms of dollars and cents; rather, they describe the equity swings as "ticks" made or lost. Maybe they're entwined; maybe it's ironic, but necessary that anyone trading the huge notional size of a local would completely lack respect for capital. Bing Sung, my old mentor, would say to me that when you're scalping the market you have to leave your brains at home. If you think too much about it, it becomes possible to think yourself out of every trade made as a local.

As a scalper, it is imperative not to think about the notional value of the position or the amount of risk acquired. For the very best, including Sliter, the amount of activity is dictated by the frequency of customer order flow and daily intraday liquidity of a market. All scalpers will tell you that what makes them profitable is the geographical edge associated with making markets in the pit when it's the center of price discovery. It's logical that the only reason a scalper will take down a large trade is because there is a perceived edge in the trade. Many markets, especially in the stock index and fixed-income futures, have experienced the proliferation of electronic trading, which has dwarfed the pit in notional value and rendered useless the geographical edge once associated with the pit.

So what happened to traders who had a geographical edge and watched it slowly evolve into a technological edge on the screen? For many veterans, it became a matter of survival, and they began to reinvent themselves as electronic traders. They morphed scalping into a different art form. Many former floor members left the trading pits and were able to take advantage of the spread between the e-mini contracts of the S&Ps against the large contract, which has had a supplementary effect of creating an amazing amount of liquidity on the screen.

But more important, these traders picked up larger intraday patterns that enabled them to use the same scalping techniques they used in the open outcry pit on a grander scale and with many different markets at their disposal. Their frequency of trade isn't nearly as great in any given market as it was when they were on the floor, but they're trading many different types of markets and it allows them the diversification that enables them to find the higher-percentage trades that were formerly hidden from them.

SPREADING

The world of spreading is completely different from those of other trading methodologies. A spreader is a trader or investor who takes out whatever differential might exist between two different markets and capitalizes on that disparity. Some people trade an intermarket spread, which is one market's calendar month against another calendar month, and others spread intramarket, which is one contract against a completely different market. An example of an intramarket spreader is a trader who makes a market in pork bellies versus live cattle or S&P versus Nasdaq. An example of an intermarket spread is trading the August live cattle versus October or trading the S&P December contract against the S&P March contract.

Trading the intermarket spread enables you to take advantage of the seasonal adjustments of the contract as opposed to the differential and price disparity between the two completely different markets. Spreading really developed into an art form in the 1960s as trading of the livestock products became more and more popular. One of the pioneers in spreading, Joe Segal, came from the agricultural pits in Chicago. Joe was a good market maker who discovered he could take advantage of a differential in prices between the months of any given market as the seasonal adjustments came in that would create aberrations in pricing. Prior to Segal's legitimization of this art, the act of spreading the markets was never looked upon as a viable trading methodology; in fact, many of the traders from that time frowned on the practice, as one of the byproducts of the strategy was that it made their markets more efficient.

The most important ancillary effect of the emergence of spreading was the creation of instant liquidity. It's a difficult academic exercise to gauge and understand where these markets would be without the spreaders, who make huge markets for the commercial houses and other end users of the products. Spreading became more widely accepted as foreign currency contracts emerged, which quickly became a part of mainstream futures trading. As financial futures proliferated throughout the 1970s, currency trading became more and more popular. Most educated players who trade the currency contracts even today overlook the fact that every currency transaction is essentially a spread.

The differentials between the currencies—Swiss franc/Deutschmark, Deutschmark/yen, yen/British pound, the U.S. dollar/everything—became wonderful ways to spread the Forex market with very little effort. Spreading is an art that has worked its way into many different strategies found throughout the trading community; it has helped generate a huge pool of liquidity in every market and has been an intricate part of legitimizing the use of futures among institutional users. One of the secrets of the trading floor is that the act of spreading and the personality of the spreader are unique. Spreaders are very risk-averse individuals.

SPREADERS AND OPTIONS

Spreaders will often tell you that they are not in the market to take risk. This seems like a strange comment coming from people who trade as a profession, but the reality is that most spreaders don't take much risk at all; instead, they are searching for profit, which they lock in immediately. Most options traders are naturally spreaders. Very few market makers will stand in the OEX or SPX pits at the Chicago Board Options Exchange (CBOE) and speculate on puts and calls; if anything, they look for the same type of action that excites futures spreaders. They look for value or for aberrations that will create opportunity and lay off the risk using another market or another strike price.

Perhaps the most important thing about the personality type of spreaders is that they think quickly. Speed in the thought process is the most important quality that an options trader can have. Some of my clients were traders who worked for Cooper Neff (CN), a derivatives company based outside of Philadelphia. With a great pool of intellectual capital and always on the cutting edge of technology, CN turned into one of the best options trading houses on the Street. They had a wonderful way of evaluating potential new employees by administering a grueling exam composed of math and logic. The average person would take approximately an hour to complete the test; Cooper Neff would give the person between 5 and 10 minutes. The function of the test was to discover the personality of potential traders and gauge how well they were able to estimate . . . or guesstimate. The aim of the exam wasn't to test the knowledge of the candidates but to see how fast their minds worked and, even better, how that quick thinking could be migrated to the markets.

It's very important to keep in mind that the type of personality the Cooper Neff brass was searching for incorporates quickness and flexibility. The worst possible thing any spreader can do is to have formed an opinion about market direction. The best spreaders in the world have the worst gut feelings when it comes to picking the direction of the market. Vince and Dennis, my old friends and clients, who have had probably the most successful index arb careers of any traders on Wall Street, used to be fond of telling me that when they walked in every morning, they placed their manhood, figuratively speaking, in a sealed jar in the coat room. (I'm assuming they would reverse the process when they left for the evening!) As silly as it sounded, it was their way of telling me that they were not in the business of taking uncalculated risk.

Another great options trading firm is a group called KC-CO, which had its humble beginnings in the early 1980s. KC-CO is a quantitative shop that specializes in exchange-listed options products. Based in Chicago and founded by Kent Hager, a pioneer of the OEX options pit at the CBOE, the firm grew to include roughly 80 traders before being bought by the British institution S.G. Warburg. The purchase came at a time when global players had arrived at the conclusion that in order to survive they needed the finest systems for risk analysis that were available. During the period from 1987 to 1992, small regional trading house systems evolved into a global institutional methodology. S.G. Warburg merged with Swiss Bancorp, which created regulatory problems and allowed KC-CO to buy itself back from the newly merged institution.

The buyback enabled the original partners to reestablish the cutting-edge technology and regroup the brilliant human capital that once traded around the globe, combining these two factors to become a formidable new player. The quantitatively driven methodology that is used by KC-CO, Cooper Neff, or any other successful derivatives trading group on the exchange floors is exactly the type of technique that is employed to this day by every major money-center bank and financial institution.

The term used on the floor to describe both options traders and many spreaders is *quant jocks*. This term implies that most of the trading decisions are made by taking a formulaic approach rather than from a gut feeling. Some futures traders regard that as an insult; others seem to use the term out of jealousy. I happen to be in the latter category. I look at quant jocks with a certain amount of envy. I love the fact that there are people out there who can look at numbers and figure risk and value instantaneously. Many of us wish our minds would work as fast as a computer!

Writing that the personality of a position trader is unique is an understatement. Position traders are usually investors in addition to the day-trading activity you might see in their trading accounts. Many good traders trade around the core position, thus giving them a better price on the position. For example, a good position trader has a long position as a core but might be in and out of that position many times during the course of the session, always trying to maintain the core long.

Scalpers, spreaders, and arbitrageurs must be temperamentally suited to handle the nuances inherent in their respective type of trading. The high-energy, short-attention-span scalpers possess traits that are best suited for their particular style of trading, but these would be an obstacle to spreaders or arbitrageurs trying to stay focused and methodically searching for mathematical anomalies. Understanding how different these traits truly are and analyzing the personality of a typical position trader are perhaps the most difficult things to do as a student of the markets.

Every person who trades the markets—even someone trading in the same style—is distinct in the way he or she approaches the difficult task of making a decision. It's been said that great local market makers have pure energy flowing through their bodies; if that is the case, then "real" position traders have ice water running through their veins. If I were to gauge who the greatest traders in the business are, I would have to say that position traders are the best. One of the wealthiest men I ever met best explained it to me. When asked how he amassed a fortune well over $300 million, he answered that it was important to find the right horse . . . and keep riding him till he drops! I didn't get it at first, and then it hit me. He was telling me that to find real wealth an investor needed a long-term vision and the courage to put capital at risk to make the vision a reality. If it's the right vision, stick with it and success will follow. Putting on any type of position is a very difficult thing to do.

POSITION TRADERS

The energy level for position traders is almost nonexistent. You put on passive positions, and then you sit and you watch them. Position traders have simple rules that every novice quickly becomes familiar with: Don't add to losers. Only add to winners. Cut your losses short. Let your winners ride! It might sound easy, but every wannabe futures trader has memorized these four rules of the game; however, only a handful of the millions who trade around the globe have the ability to be real players. Many position traders will tell you that it's much more difficult to deal with a winning position than a losing position. It's easy to know where to get out of a losing position by limiting your risk to a certain level, but dealing with a winning trade becomes, at times, harder for the trader to handle because of the element of the unknown.

The best of the position traders will tell you that they will not get into a trade unless they know exactly what they want out of the trade. In other words, they have a target in mind before they even pull the trigger. Disciplined investors understand that placing stops on losses is an important part of smart money management, but when they're winning on a trade and, more important, adding to the position, they're letting it run, which immediately creates new disciplinary guidelines. It's a very difficult thing to digest as a new trader because it's a very easy way to trade—putting on a position and just holding it. But to do it successfully time and time again and consistently come up with high-percentage trades that are profitable is a very, very difficult thing to do.

One of the best position traders to come out of the Chicago markets is a gentleman named Steve Helms. A product of Burlington, North Carolina, and Davidson University, Helms came to Chicago in the hope of learning the world of commodity trading, to which he had been introduced back in North Carolina. He came to Chicago with modest means, but he intuitively picked up on the markets and became one of the finest position traders in the agricultural markets at the CME. Helms moved on to the S&P 500 futures pit, but he always has positions on in many different markets simultaneously. What made Helms a great trader on the floor and what makes him a great trader to this day is his ability to detach emotionally from the trade.

I spent hours talking with Helms, and his eyes never made contact with mine, as he stared constantly at the quote boards or the Quotron headline screen, looking for his next trade. Helms's strength as a trader, aside from being one of the most intelligent market observers known, is that he has the patience of Gandhi coupled with the guts of a riverboat gambler. Once a position is established, traders can no longer be neutral; they have opinions, they have researched those opinions, and, most important, they have put their money at risk based on those opinions.

What makes Helms and other successful position traders different from the rest is their ability to do the homework and put on high-percentage trades but remain as objective to the market condition as humanly possible. This is not only a question of forming a methodology based on a combination of fundamentals and technicals; it's also a matter of having an intuitive feel for the marketplace. Many position traders look at their technical work and form an opinion that the fundamentals might justify, but the gut feeling tells them it's the wrong trade. Most of the time traders faced with a conflicting gut feeling will not make the trade even if their homework tells them it's the right trade to make. All successful traders will tell you that they're better off not making the trade that feels wrong because it would be hazardous to future trading decisions.

As Bing used to say to me, when you're scalping sometimes you have to leave your brains at home. I think that, as a position trader, the opposite is true. Your brains are working all the time when you have these trades on, and if you fall asleep at the wheel, you could crash. In fact, the most successful position traders tell me that they go home and monitor the markets at all times. They watch business television into the wee hours of the morning and play around with positions in overseas markets while the rest of us are sleeping. What they are looking for is something that might change—a news event, a corporate event, anything that gives them an informational edge and might drive the market one way or the other.

A good example is the speech given in the mid-1990s by former Federal Reserve chairman Alan Greenspan in which he referred to "irrational exuberance." At the time he gave the speech, there was a roaring bull market and monetary policy seemed to be well maintained. In short, the market was not ready for it. Chairman Greenspan might have been right about the state of the market in the long run, but he was way too early in his assessment of the situation. We saw the market react immediately to the downside, but it was a very short-term break. Immediately the market turned around and we saw a rally of biblical proportions, which lasted throughout the next four years and took both the S&P 500 and the Nasdaq indexes to record highs. The position trader who monitored the "irrational exuberance" event realized there was something significant that could be read from the action. The fact is that the market did not want to go down. It was a clear warning signal for anyone looking to try the short side of the market that this was no ordinary bull. The best traders got the message loud and clear—when the chairman of the Federal Reserve tells you equities are a little too high and yet the market rallies, all bears must hide! There were many sharp traders who made a fortune being long over the course of the next few years because they realized that, as a result of the Y2K phenomenon, we were entering a period of prolonged earnings growth that would be unparalleled.

OPTIONS TRADERS

Unlike position traders, options traders, aside from being spreaders, can sometimes be very robotic in the way they approach the markets. Watching the options pit trade on a daily basis would reveal countless market makers all staring down at a stack of papers that show value in any given strike price. All the traders are looking at spreadsheets showing how much a certain option is worth with the underlying market trading at various levels. In other words, the spreadsheets price the options as the market moves up and down. In this type of trade, the market direction takes a backseat to a mathematical edge.

What most people don't know is that all of these options trading groups station people in every options pit or electronic market in order to be fully informed about like-traded products. For instance, any firm serious about trading listed equity options will have a presence in the S&P options pit at the CME, the S&P 500 futures, the OEX and SPX options at the CBOE, and also any exchange-traded fund (ETF) that might have an incestuous relationship with the other markets. Options traders and the firms they work with have always been the segment of the industry that has pushed the technological envelope as far as the exchanges will allow. A trading group such as the one I described earlier would most likely have everything electronically synchronized to give every trader firmwide instantaneous changes in positions as they occur.

As the positions are readjusted, the handheld proprietary screens created by the various groups show changes in the firm's market exposure and any concentration of a particular strike. In many cases, these groups conduct morning meetings that allow both managers and traders the ability to conceptualize what they want to do as a group. These meetings are vital to the information dissemination within a group, and more important, they provide the traders with a collective brainstorming session, ensuring that the risk is laid off for any large, major standard deviation move to the upside or the downside. It's important to remember that options traders are robotic in their approach, and every position is quantified. They are looking to lock in profit with a minimum of exposure but, more important, always position the firm to capitalize on any major move.

Options traders are the financial engineers of the present day. Most of today's globally available creative financing and structured products trace their roots to the world of options. In fact, many of the options traders go to the large international institutions and come up with some of these complex over-the-counter products that are huge in notional value and trade privately between two qualified institutions. These products have become so large that they are now an intricate part of the financial services landscape. One of the interesting things about options is that any options trader or market maker will tell you that they make their profits from others' hedges. What I mean by that is that when a customer wants to put on an option position or an institution is looking to incorporate options into its portfolio, usually it's in the form of a hedge position. It is that hedge—the physical act of executing the order—that options market makers feed on. It is their lifeblood.

Without the world of those seeking to hedge exposure, the world of options market making would be a very unprofitable one. Very few of the large institutional orders that come into these markets are speculative positions. In many cases—especially in the CME's Eurodollar (ED) options market, which encompasses the short end of the yield curve—options are being used for caps and collars, which give mortgage and finance companies the ability to extend variable-rate loans with ceilings on interest rates embedded in every contract. A student of the market would have to agree that the use of the ED options by these institutions is the intended purpose of the product. It's why all futures contracts were created—to give end users what they really need: risk management!

THE NATURE OF THE TRADER

The one thing that all of these different types of traders have in common, whether they are scalpers, position traders, spreaders, or options traders, is that those who succeed understand the nature of the trader and the personality required to survive in this realm. Scalpers who trade in an open outcry arena drive the market one way or another through the cooperative effort of the community as a whole. This is still evident in many of the New York markets that have clung to the Luddite mentality and resisted electronic markets and the technology that brings the world into their markets.

If the pit gets too long or short, you could see the market react accordingly. A position trader, however, takes advantage of the aberration created by the concentration of locals on one side of the trade and more than likely uses a contrarian's strategy by selling into a rallying market or buying into a breaking one. Spreaders, in contrast, come in and move one leg or segment of the market, depending on what happens in the secondary leg of the spread.

For example, when the rollover condition takes place four times a year in the S&P contract, large, bulky orders come into the deferred month, which is less liquid, creating what looks to be a feeding frenzy and forcing spreaders into the front month, driving prices out of whack. It's the inefficiency of the moment, which most spreaders will find profitable. This happens every now and then, usually on the open or close of the session, but it's very significant because it's a prime example of one segment of the trading population directly affecting another.

I can't tell you how many rollover conditions in the S&P 500 futures pit I brokered and traded as price anomalies produced opportunities for spreaders to quickly lock in huge profits within seconds. Each one of these groups understands the importance of monitoring and assessing what the various other groups of traders are doing. Some of the best position traders I know will tell you exactly what they see happening in the options markets as a result of the indirect impact any large options order might have on the pricing of the underlying. This can give you a fairly accurate gauge of what side of the market the scalping community has concentrated their efforts on.

Most traders, regardless of the style they have chosen, become victims of the need for instant gratification. This is the common denominator found among all traders on the floor of any exchange. I discovered this addiction to instant gratification firsthand, when as a local I found it very difficult to slow my pace after the closing bell had sounded. After I left the trading floor each day, the world outside the exchange seemed to be moving in slow motion compared to the hectic frenzy of the CME. I found it hard to turn off the energy and go back to being a father and husband in a quiet bedroom community outside of Chicago. Even worse, I knew that every investment I made would be judged by the risk-to-reward ratio that trading had automatically given me, which is a recipe for disaster.

It became much more difficult to invest my assets for a 10- or 20-year horizon when I felt the future was now! Think of how boring a real estate trust or a tiered bond portfolio sounds when you compare it to the possible returns in futures. It became apparent to me that the need for instant gratification was starting to skew my perception of reality, which can be very dangerous when you are dealing with your personal net worth on a daily basis. This is one of the main reasons that scalpers and high-energy floor traders have found it difficult to migrate to the world of the "upstairs" screen trader.

For those who entered the industry at an early age, as I did, the culture and camaraderie found on the exchanges were hard to duplicate when they left the floor during the electronic trading revolution. For floor traders to successfully transform themselves into good screen traders, they must leave the floor behind and be educated afresh as traders. Bing advised me not to get too cerebral about the markets when I was scalping. Electronic day trading requires traders to maintain a pulse on the markets and keep up with any information that might send price action into a volatile condition. The big advantage is that these new electronic traders can now monitor and trade many markets simultaneously, whereas in the past it was impossible to watch more than one or two effectively.

Traders whose entire careers were spent looking up at a wall board with prices and headlines experience culture shock to find themselves upstairs staring at quiet screens with a TV on mute and positions that seem almost emotionless at times. The hardest thing for these new traders to overcome is the feeling of helplessness because they are at the mercy of the aggressor as participants on the electronic platform. Most floor traders had come to regard the right of first refusal as inalienable when they were creating liquidity in the pits. Now, however, the liquidity provider stares at a two-dimensional screen with no hope of monitoring the order flow or gauging the collective position of the pit community. There's a new mantra for floor traders that every veteran of the pits has memorized: Change with the times or perish!

CHAPTER 3

Know Thy Market

S ometime after my inaugural trip to the Chicago Mercantile Exchange (CME), a college friend who wanted to ask his godfather for financial assistance asked me for a ride to the North Shore of Chicago, one of the wealthiest residential areas in the country. As we approached a street lined with the biggest mansions I had ever seen, he instructed me to turn in at an enormous house on the shore of Lake Michigan. I was reluctant as I made the turn, convinced that my friend had pulled a fast one by making me turn there. It quickly became apparent that this was no joke and the house we were about to enter belonged to his godfather, who happened to be Ralph Peters, the chairman of the Chicago Board of Trade (CBOT) at that time.

As a new member of the capital markets/traders fraternity, I was given a quick education on the biggest players in the city and how they acquired their wealth; Peters was my first lesson. Peters was a visionary on the Chicago market scene, having been one of the pioneers in the use of technology in trading. Tall in stature, Peters likewise had a reputation as a large trader, in addition to what many would call his greatest asset: Nerves of steel.

Peters had made his fortune many times over. One story that stands out concerns the original wealth he created in the soybean market during the Cuban missile crisis. He stepped into a soybean market that had been in a limit-up state for days due to the impending situation in which Soviet missiles would be positioned in Cuba; he established a maximum short position.

He had come into a market that had been going straight up for a week, and he sold everything the exchange rules would allow. Being in a limit-up state, the market was very accommodating to Peters, allowing him to sell as many contracts as he wanted—after all, there was a threat of a nuclear conflict over the weekend, and anything could happen. Who wanted to be short in such a situation? Soybean traders gathered around and watched in amazement as he carefully and meticulously carded each trade he made in the pit. When asked why he was putting so much capital at risk under tense market conditions, his reply was classic: "Come Monday, I'll either be dead or the richest trader in the pit!" The rest is history. The Soviets withdrew the ships and the soybean market was limit down for days.

Peters, out of respect for the market that had provided his fortune, bought an estate on part of a key in the Bahamas and named it Soya Beana. Wow! Imagine the guts it takes to do such a thing! The first time I heard this story was as I was driving his godson, my friend, to his house that time. When we entered the house, Peters was sitting at his large desk. Without taking his eyes off his trading screen, he suddenly asked me whether I was going into the markets, as was his godson. I said no, that I was thinking about going into law school and pursuing a career in law or politics. He sprang to his feet, towering over me, and said, "Kid, forget law, go into the markets. It's the most overpaid business in the world! But whatever you do, know your market!"

As I left that house, I remember giving serious consideration to a career in the capital markets for the first time. When a man as successful as Peters tells you one of the secrets to acquiring wealth, it might be a prudent thing to heed his advice. Years later I became acquainted with Ralph's son, who had become a trader in the S&P pit at the CME. We would occasionally have lunch and chat about markets and the characters who made our profession so colorful. During one of our lunches, the subject of the Cuban missile crisis and Peters's soybean trade came up. His son asked me what I had heard about this story.

With a twinkle in my eye, I told the story that I had told countless times at parties and business functions. I could see Peters's son leaning back with a big smile on his face. After I finished the story, he leaned forward and said, "Is that what you heard, Jack? Well, now I'll tell you what really happened." As it turns out, Ralph never made a large trade without doing his homework and gathering all the information, and the classic soybean trade' was no exception. He had a vast network for information that stretched from California's Central Valley to the halls of Congress in Washington, D.C. His contacts in the diplomatic community gave Peters the word that the ships had indeed turned around and the Cuban missile crisis had been averted. *Know your market!* It had been 10 years since Ralph Peters had uttered those words to me, but it was then that I fully understood what he had meant. Information is gold. Or as Bing Sung taught me later, don't make a trade without knowing the whole story, Ralph died a few years ago, but his stories and market exploits have become legendary.

KNOW YOUR MARKET

"Know the market that you trade" is perhaps the best advice I have ever received from anyone. Having the power of information allows the trader to establish positions with confidence and understand the true nature of the risks associated with the trade. To understand the power of this tool, it's important to understand how you acquire knowledge. The biggest secrets among traders lie in the everyday factors that drive daily volatility and the way you work the volatile nature of the market to create high-percentage trades.

ASSET ALLOCATION

When I do my daily market commentary on Bloomberg TV, I often talk about asset allocation models and the effects a shift in the model have on the daily action. Simply put, an asset allocation is the redistribution of assets from one class to another. To make our examples easy, I'll describe a basic asset allocation strategy and the tactical approach that fine-tunes the positions. Many fund managers have models they make known to their investors that show the percentage of assets in stocks versus bonds, the largest portion of the portfolio.

The strategic model of an asset allocation shows the overall percentages of the fund, for example, 50 percent in stocks, 40 percent in bonds, and 10 percent in alternatives. The tactical adjustment would take a percentage of assets from, say, stocks, and transfer them into bonds or alternatives. A 5 percent tactical shift in the asset allocation of the example given would create a portfolio that might end up looking like this: 55 percent stocks, 35 percent bonds, and 10 percent alternatives. But the questions remain, how do you identify when a trade is being done and, more important, how do you profit from the situation?

At times we have witnessed large, strategic institutional asset allocation trades hitting the market. These are huge positions that take days to accumulate and have enormous staying power because of the passive nature of the investment. Working with Nikko, I would occasionally be involved with one of these large strategic trades, which required days of moving huge orders into the market with as little impact as possible. The trades were in the $1 billion to $5 billion range, with most of the activity centered on the equity markets and the fixed-income market. The orders would come in to buy S&P 500 futures and sell the 30-year bond, and the orders would come simultaneously!

It didn't take me long to figure out that there was a pattern developing with every order I received. Not only were we buying in one market, but we were selling just as aggressively for the client in the fixed-income bond futures. Every half hour we would get the order to buy a large quantity of S&Ps, and as I would quietly place my orders into the equity pit, I would notice selling pressure in the bonds. The more I did those asset allocation orders, the more I realized that the opportunity existed for the sharp trader to capitalize on the aberrations created by the size.

The Japanese seemed to do things in tandem; therefore, if Nikko was executing an institutional asset allocation order in that manner, so would Nomura, Diawa, and every other large Japanese brokerage house of the time. As large as the strategic orders would get, it's the tactical application to the overall asset allocation model that drives the market on a more frequent basis. When I report the evidence of an asset allocation in the daily trade, I'm usually referring to a tactical AA that drives the market on a short-term basis. Often I'll notice that the orders stop at approximately the same time that the European fund managers are leaving for the evening. Although they all have operations that run around the clock, a large portion of any such order is completed by the close of the European bourses (exchanges).

It's also important to try to identify the type of maturity that is involved in the trade because it allows the trader to watch as the order creates a market impact. The role of the broker, or brokers, in an asset allocation order centers on the execution of the trade and the slippage and market impact they create when entering or leaving the market. One thing is for sure, not all brokers handle the large asset allocation orders the same way; in fact, traders will tell you that some large brokerage houses tip their hands by using time orders or other easily identifiable tactics. The shrewd trader will quickly realize that there is ample opportunity for profitable trades when the order is handled by the less capable brokers.

Many times the markets involved in the order move in opposite directions at the same time. It becomes obvious to the seasoned veteran of the markets when waves of buying come into the equity markets as selling pressure hits the 10- or 30-year bond futures that an asset allocation is being executed. The only question for the trader is whether the order's origin is domestic or foreign. Identifying the source of the transaction is important because it gives the trader an indication of when the order might be complete. A European or Asian order is usually

75 percent complete by the time Europe closes, around 11 AM Chicago time. A domestic order, however, will continue into the bond close at 2 PM U.S. central time, and at times will continue electronically well past the closing bell.

FOREX-RELATED ASSET ALLOCATION

Equities and fixed income are not the only asset classes used in an allocation model. In some cases, the asset allocation involves the currency market with direct relationships that spill into the commodities markets. As we've witnessed the creation of a new European currency, the need to manage risk between the dollar and the other major currencies of the world—yen, pound sterling, euro, and now the yuan—has never been greater. The global nature of the markets makes the Forex market the most dynamic asset class the investment community has seen in decades. Because of the high level of participation of the major money-center banks of the world, the vast liquidity within the currency market has provided opportunity to traders and investors alike. Many of the orders that involve the Forex market come from foreign sources of capital, which use the dollar as a discounting mechanism when they search for value in U.S. equities.

Simply put, European fund managers will buy U.S. equities as the dollar weakens, hoping for two possible scenarios: a rising stock market with the dollar under control or a stagnant stock market coupled with a rally in the dollar. The logic is that any appreciation in the currency gives the European fund manager a profit even if the market goes sideways because of the Forex exposure, or if the market were to appreciate, they would see an even better return on capital. Fund managers can use this strategy both for a declining dollar and for a rising dollar; in both cases, the volatility created by the global currency markets drives the trade.

The first time I became aware of a Forex-related asset allocation was when I was with the Japanese at Nikko. The huge swings in the dollar-yen market of the late 1980s and early 1990s gave the global institutional managers fodder for trading methodologies that have grown into one of the most influential institutional strategies in use today. At the time I remember thinking how creative it was for these financial engineers to construct trades that had a currency component that created opportunity for profit in so many different ways. Because of the nature of the cash Forex market, much of the volume is done there as opposed to the futures markets.

In the equity-fixed-income AA, the futures markets are the vehicle of choice because of the speed and efficiency involved in the use of the products. Think how difficult it can be for a fund manager who has an AA order to sell every stock in the S&P 500 rather than sell a basket of futures and exchange the position for the stock in the EFP (exchange for physical) market. This EFP market allows the position to be transformed from one in the futures market for the actual stocks that compose the index. This nuance in the market gives the fund manager the speed and efficiency needed when handling vast sums of money.

The larger the amount of capital under management, the more difficult it becomes for the institutional trader to execute the order. The futures markets allow the traders the flexibility to use derivative forms of the underlying markets with the leverage and liquidity they need. As an institutional broker, it became vital to identify the asset allocation as it drove the market in either direction because the natural momentum of the trade created a path of least resistance, which became valuable information. Using the upside or downside pressure created by any type of AA to the clients' advantage separates the good brokers from the bad ones.

When I'm reporting on the various business TV programs during the course of the session, I will point out what I think might be an AA in either the equity-fixed-income world or involving what looks to be a currency play. I tell the viewing public how important it is for traders to let the volatility work in their favor. Let the pressure that is brought on by large orders bring the market to the individual as opposed to chasing a rally or break. It becomes a question of patience.

When Bing first educated me on the concept of asset allocations and their effect on the daily movements of the market, he used a line he had borrowed from a coworker at the Harvard Management. Whenever he identified an AA, he would place orders above and below the market and tell me, "Patience comes to those who wait!" As strange as it sounded at the time, the lesson he taught me was as clear as it could be: Let the market come to you!

INDEX ARBITRAGE

I was introduced to the nuances of index arbitrage by the finest teachers trading the strategy at the time, Vince McLaughlin and Dennis DeCore. Vinny and Denny, as they were known to the pit community, started trading index arbitrage at Merrill Lynch when index futures were born in the early 1980s. Even before I met them, Vinny and Denny were legends in the business, having taken index arbitrage from being a quaint trading strategy to being an art form that many would copy.

Vince is a New York Irishman with an affinity for Celtic music; the story has it that he traveled around Ireland as a youth, singing for his traveling expenses from pub to pub. Always a quick wit, Vince was perhaps the best storyteller I ever came across. I would listen to him for hours at a time when the market was slow, laughing at the insane characters he described in his yarns. What made them all the better was that they were all true—every one of the colorful characters actually existed, and some are still alive today.

Denny was the perfect complement to Vinny. When Vinny would get emotional, Denny would be the epitome of calm and serenity in an otherwise stressful environment. Denny, originally from Trenton, New Jersey, grew up in a working-class Italian neighborhood. He took the lessons learned from the rough streets and coupled them with an innate gift for logic and numbers. If ever a trader combined the cunning instincts of a great riverboat gambler with the opportunity the market provided, it was Dennis DeCore. What Vinny and Denny did for one another was balance the emotional volatility that runs with trading the markets. Whenever Vinny would get excited, Denny would calm him down. Whenever Denny needed to get excited about something, Vinny would work him up.

Index arbitrage is a strategy that takes advantage of the discrepancy between the cash market and the futures market. The action taken by the arbitrageurs is determined by whether the premium—that is, the spread between cash and futures—is cheap or expensive according to their calculations of fair value. Fair value is a dynamic number determined daily by a combination of a several different factors: time till expiration, dividend flow, and the cost of capital that you are charged as an institution. The terms *buy program* and *sell program* were derived from the vocabulary of the arbs, which changed the nature of liquidity in the markets forever.

I began working with Vinny and Denny after they had left Merrill Lynch. Before I started, I was warned by their former clerk not to ask too many questions at first because it might give them cause for concern. At this time in the industry, the kind of proprietary trading knowledge that Vinny and Denny possessed, and had left Merrill with, was more valuable than gold.

I understood that if I was to learn anything about what they were doing, I would have to be slow, cautious, and deliberate in my inquiries. The action of the arb takes concentration on many parts, especially the floor, where identifying the price aberration before it begins allows the arbitrageur to react that much more quickly. As they became more and more comfortable with me, I would spend the entire session on the phone quoting the market and acting as a color man to the players in and out of the pit.

The more time I spent on the phone with either Vinny or Denny, the more I would overhear about what they were doing and, more important, why. After the first couple of years with them, I became confident that

I could ask almost any question and get an honest response. To my surprise, as they became more comfortable with me, they became mentors, teaching me the little things about their end of the business that regularly affect futures.

NUANCES OF INDEX ARBITRAGE

Of the hundreds of lessons that I learned from Vinny and Denny, the three most important things that can be easily understood by individual investors are basis levels, EFP activity, and rebalancing the indexes. To many veterans of the market, it might sound strange that I would pick these three factors above all the rest, but I'll explain the importance of each and how individual inventors can profit from the information. The basis levels in the market show traders the spread between cash and futures. The basis can be a premium, whereby the futures trade above the cash price, and they can also go to a discount, such as we saw in 1987, whereby the futures market actually trades lower than the underlying cash market.

In the morning most business programs report what they consider to be fair value for the day. When the trading session begins, it becomes vital to watch the spread between the cash and futures in order to gauge the affects of the computer-driven buy and sell programs being done by the arbitrage community. By observing the spread, or basis, the skilled trader can tell if pressure is igniting programs or if the price movement in the market is happening without the benefit of the arbs. When the market is breaking, the basis becomes a reliable indicator of the action of the arbs and how the market digests the programs hurled at it. Many day traders watch the programs hit the market and play the wake created by their actions.

Most index arbs first put on the futures position before sending orders to the underlying stock market, but a few put one side of the trade on without the other. This is not true index arbitrage, where the trades are made almost simultaneously. It's called *legging the spread*, but it's really speculating on the outcome. There's an old saying on the floor: When you leg your spreads, it's like spreading your legs—the same thing can happen. Vinny and Denny taught me never to leg the spread unless absolutely necessary. Remember, they were the ones who used to tell me they placed their manhood in a sealed jar in the coatroom when they walked into the office in the mornings.

Paying attention to the basis also gives traders a hint about if and when the market might turn in the opposite direction. In a breaking market, should basis begin to widen out to the point where buy programs would be expected, the index arbs could be responsible for stopping the break. The opposite is also true: In a rallying market, should the basis become cheap, the arbs orders would stop the rally in its tracks.

The second important lesson for any new trader to understand is the EFP activity that takes place in the index arb universe. The EFP market allows the arbitrage community to flip the positions from cash to futures, and vice versa. It's important to note that an index arb needs inventory in order to make money at the strategy. Inventory comes to the trader in one of two ways. The first is that traders must wait until the market gives them an opportunity for acquiring the inventory by trading with a rich basis. That is, the markets are trading with a premium level that allows the index arbitrageur to sell the futures and buy the underlying stock market. This action creates inventory and makes the arbitrage position a de facto index fund.

The other way inventory can be found is in the EFP market, where any institutional account can find a market for the other side of a futures transaction. Why is inventory such an important factor? When arbs are out of inventory they refer to the situation as being "out of bullets." Without the ammunition to trade a breaking market, the arb is left with a cumbersome short-selling technique that is not nearly as efficient or profitable as the normal sell program.

I realized the importance of this information when, while working with Vinny and Denny, I noticed that no one around the marketplace was doing sell programs even with a basis that showed the programs would be profitable. Not only were Vinny and Denny not doing anything, but as I looked around the pit no one was entering orders below the market. Something was wrong! I quickly called the boys and asked them if there was a computer glitch in the New York Stock Exchange (NYSE) system, but the answer was something I did not expect. "The Street is out of inventory," Denny told me. As soon as the words were out of his mouth, I noticed buy programs coming into the market at levels that seemed to break even at best. I realized that the arbitrage community needed to put on the inventory, and that some were willing to lose a little by putting the positions on, hoping to capitalize even more when covering the trades during a breaking market.

REBALANCING THE INDEXES

During the few times a year when we witness a rebalancing of the indexes, the opportunity for a high-percentage trade is never better. Listening to Vinny and Denny during an announcement of a rebalancing was the equivalent of listening to two children who find out that Christmas is arriving early. The act of taking one stock out of the index for some reason—bankruptcy, buyout, whatever—and replacing it with another more profitable company creates a condition in the market that gives those who do their homework a natural high-percentage trade.

The recent addition of Google to the S&P is a perfect example of the way the markets digest information. Upon learning that Google was being added to the S&P 500 index, I advised our brokers to tell their clients that the natural trade was to buy Google Nasdaq 100 or the Russell 2000 and sell the S&P 500. The logic is that the hundreds of billions of dollars that are indexed against the S&P 500 must make the changes so the portfolios under management don't have any tracking errors. Many of the index funds must, by charter, make the changes on the close of business, as the rebalancing is complete. I immediately told the listening audience on Bloomberg that this was the trade of the month, if not the year.

Many of those who took my advice made a tidy profit, as the market did exactly what one would expect: Google went up for days along with the Russell and Nasdaq, and the S&P 500 stayed flat. I first became aware of the play when, during the amazing run in the tech market in the late 1990s, JDSU was added to the S&P. This was at a time when technology was king and any large addition to the index would create a giant wake from the index funds. Following the announcement that JDSU was being placed into the index, I could hear Vinny and Denny buying the stock quietly and selling what appeared to be the SPDR ETF against it. In short, they were buying the JDSU and selling the rest of the S&P 500 against it. Finally, after listening to them for hours talking about the situation among themselves, I asked what was happening and why. That's when I learned about the best trade the market can ever give a trader.

CORPORATE EVENTS

Ever since that fateful day, I have played the addition to the index the same way that Vinny and Denny did and have found that the profit potential in that situation is greater than that from any other single phenomenon in the market. The opposite can be true also. Microsoft found itself on the other end of the trade when it announced a large one-time dividend of $30 billion that was to be paid out to shareholders. I cohosted *Squawk Box* with Mark Haines the morning of the Microsoft dividend payment and told the world that we would witness a rally at the end of the session because of the need for the index funds to reinvest the dividend that was being paid out. Sure enough, the day ended with a late surge that led the S&P up more than 10 full points as Microsoft ended unchanged minus the $3 paid. There are small additions and deletions to the indexes a few times a year, and Vinny and Denny taught me that the shrewd trader can capitalize on the situation.

It's the corporate events such as the Microsoft dividend, or any stock that goes ex-dividend, that launches the equity funds and those holding index arb positions into action. This is especially prevalent when a merger or a buyout is announced that affects the underlying components of the positions they carry, creating what is commonly referred to as *tracking error.* The trader will identify a company in play and find another company that is in a related industry and spread the two against each other. This is a crude example of what is called *risk arbitrage.*

Many of the risk arb desks on Wall Street follow the mergers and acquisitions (M&A) activity with a microscope, hoping to find the next diamond in the rough. Vinny and Denny taught me to play off the risk arbs in the market. Using options, Vince had been the original options trader for Merrill Lynch when the concept was introduced to the financial community. Vinny and Denny showed me the leverage and how to identify the trends taking hold of the market. Searching for the next opportunity turned many of us into addicted tape watchers. It became almost second nature to stare at the headlines that raced across the walls of the exchange, hoping to catch an informational edge and create an opportunity for a high-percentage trade.

STATISTICAL ARBITRAGE

Another form of arbitrage activity that has become very popular in the last decade is statistical arbitrage. Stat arb, as it's called, is based on the science of statistics and is used in different methods by the hundreds of global institutions that employ the strategy. There are different types of stat arb, but the most proficient traders using this technique were those at Cooper Neff (CN). CN originated as an options trading company based out of the Philadelphia area and had made a reputation for being a good currency options trading house. In fact, prior to its acquisition by Bank National Paris (BNP), the firm had been an important part of an Asian institution that had used CN's systems and knowledge to hedge out the bank's inherent global risk.

A simple form of stat arb consists of finding two stocks, completely unrelated sectorwise, but which track one another dollar for dollar. Stat arbs have been found that spread auto stocks against cosmetics companies, for example, or technology against cement. This market-neutral strategy involves being both long and short the market at the same time, but finding statistical anomalies that yield the desirable high-percentage trade. A more complex derivative of stat arb is the strategy that most new traders ignore, even though it makes up 10 to 20 percent of the daily volume on any given day. Statistical index arb, which became an art form at Cooper Neff, incorporates the math behind basic stat arb and morphs it into a form of index arb.

The best trader using this strategy that I've ever come across is Scott Weisblum, a brilliant young Wharton grad who was hired by CN. I first met Weisblum when I was chairman of the CME's equity index committee and we decided to launch the S&P MidCap 400 and the Russell 2000 futures contracts. Knowing that the new contracts were in desperate need of instant liquidity, I contacted the index arbitrage community, starting with Vinny and Denny to muster the critical mass necessary to ensure the success of the new contracts. I was told by many that index arbitrage with the new indexes would be difficult because of the number of stocks and the illiquid condition of most of the composition.

When I came across the group at CN, I quickly realized that they were doing something completely different from what I had seen from any other institutional arb traders. Weisblum came on as both the mid-cap and Russell markets began to heat up and found an audience with the global fund managers. It was very important to get both contracts to the point that the passive funds, those that used a futures position as a synthetic equity holding, to participate in the daily session. Weisblum and CN found a statistical anomaly that they were able to capture at various times during the course of the session. It was a combination of cutting-edge technology and creative mathematical thinking that led Weisblum and the traders at CN to incredible levels of success for themselves and for BNP.

During the late 1990s, the geographical nature of the pit environment made it critical that my operation be able to handle all the different markets in which the arb was being done. I found myself in the highest-priced real estate on the exchange floor, right between the S&P 500 futures and the smaller, newer indexes that had just been started. From the time the contracts were created until late 1999, Weisblum was the largest user of both the Russell and midcap futures contracts, taking what were little niche markets and transforming them into the dynamic trade we see today.

Much of the success we are witnessing in the Russell and midcap futures are a direct result of the liquidity provided in the early days by Weisblum and a few others. Aside from being a crucial part of the liquidity, CN always found itself on the cutting edge of technology, constantly asking the exchange to push the envelope when it came to tech. As a member of CME's board of directors, I was in a constant dialogue with the group at CN about a number of subjects, including the use of certain types of connectivity that had previously been banned. Some of the biggest arguments I found myself in concerned bringing technology into the pit, which many floor traders saw as an infringement on their franchise. I can still see the faces of pit traders yelling at me, insisting that my actions, and those of my fellow board members, were detrimental to the market!

In hindsight, nothing could have been further from the truth, and I'm proud of the decisions we made during those critical early days. It was only through the efforts of customers such as CN and Vinny and Denny that the board of directors acquired the credibility to drag the exchange membership, kicking and screaming, into the twenty-first century.

EARNINGS

When looking for factors that drive volatility during a session, earnings season has no match. During the four times a year when corporate earnings are announced to the waiting financial world, the opportunity for traders to find profitable trades can be numerous. Not only does the earnings release of a company directly affect the price movement of the stock, but many traders fail to realize that most of these large-cap stocks are also an important part of the composition of the various indexes. As small as it may seem, a move in one or two large-cap stocks can be enough to skew the entire index one way or another. There will be sessions when most of the broader indexes are lower, yet we look at the Dow Jones 30 and find it positive on the day. This aberration is usually the result of a single stock, after an announcement, changing the entire complexion of that index.

The effect is much greater in a narrow-based index such as the Dow than in a broader index like the S&P 500, but with some of the leviathans of the NYSE even the broadly based indexes are at times vulnerable. As usual, Vinny and Denny were the ones to point out the importance of following corporate headlines as they were being made. By watching the newswire, it became possible to find companies buying back their own stock or headlines warning of a miss on earnings or a change in the company's expectations.

Aside from the world of arbitrage, there are other factors that drive the market on a daily basis. Hedge fund activity can dominate the price action on a given day when positions become larger than the market can handle at certain times in the session. Many funds have based their trading on pattern recognition and the probabilities that are derived from the analysis. The higher the probability for a winning trade, the larger the position becomes for the fund. This is a problem for many managers, as assets under management become so large that it is difficult to create the same type of return on equity that a similar strategy would generate with less money at risk. The effect of hedge fund activity is nowhere greater than in the different agricultural futures markets found at the CBOT and the CME.

As funds look for more opportunities, they have begun to explore the once forbidden world of agricultural futures and options. At first, many of the institutional fund managers shied away from the old-time ag markets, leaving them for the commercial houses and the natural hedgers that needed the products for price discovery. But as the amount of money under management in the industry began to grow, so did the need to find other markets that could foster the opportunities necessary for the fund to find a profitable trade. It's not uncommon to find funds that trade everything under the sun from cotton and sugar to Malaysian palm oil. Most of the funds have been forced to become global in their approach and have 24-hour operations to take advantage of the Asian and European time zones.

When I first started in the industry in the early 1980s, the concept of a hedge fund was foreign, not only to the general public but to those of us in the business. It wasn't until the successes of legendary managers such as Paul Tudor Jones and George Soros that the financial community woke up and began to realize what many of the endowments had already discovered: that investment in the proper hedge fund is crucial to the overall stability of the portfolio. What started as a trickle in the early days turned into a massive wave as the creation of hedge funds became the sweet spot for every major trading house. The proliferation of these funds has become a double-edged sword for the industry, as the sheer number of funds has shed more light on it. To the horror of many, Congress has decided that the growth in activity requires its expert oversight.

What many off the trading floor don't understand is that the size of the funds could cause huge price swings in the market and traders who can identify the wave can ride the wake created by the aberration, taking a nice profit. Some traders will trade only when the funds trade, the logic being that they are doing the homework with hundreds of hours in research and capital; therefore, any position taken by a large hedge fund is a calculated bet. When reporting on television, I refer to fund activity constantly because I want people off the floor to understand the impact that the fund is having on the daily volatility. The analogy I use is that a fund establishing or liquidating a position is much like an aircraft carrier turning around in a small bay. The analogy is a good one because it helps listeners grasp how cumbersome it can be for many of these fund managers to minimize their market impact when they are active.

Smart traders recognize the impact the fund is having, not only on the market that the order hits, but on the ancillary markets that might be affected by the primary. The growth in the industry has also created a problem in that many of the funds that have sprung up over the last few years have considered themselves alternatives, yet they have a strong correlation to the stock of the bond market. This has made the term *hedge fund* a more generic way of describing assets under management. In fact, many refer to a hedge fund as a mutual fund that is allowed by charter to be short the market. Remember, a true hedge fund will have a low or no correlation with the rest of the portfolio, and any investment that is not structured to capture that part of the investment universe cannot be called a true alternative investment.

Another of the best-kept secrets on the floor is the impact that the closing orders have on a session. More and more of the funds have started to mark the daily activity on the closing bell of the stock market, which closes 15 minutes before the futures markets close. The creation of the synthetic funds has been a blessing for traders who can identify the trade and follow its impact as stocks close. Very often, traders will come back into the markets at 2:30 PM Chicago time so that they can find the closing order and capitalize on the aberration it might create. These funds give investors exposure to the equity markets through an investment in a fund that finds a futures position as its largest holding. This synthetic market exposure allows investors to garner more leverage and liquidity and gives market timers a powerful new tool.

Most of these funds mark the buy and sell orders against the close of the stock market, which creates a large trade at 3 PM Chicago time, the cash close. The orders are executed in the market the same way every day, with some managers asking brokers to work the orders a little early in order to beat the race to the door on the bell. It's the three o'clock order that makes some traders the most money day after day. The impact of these closing orders has become larger and larger as the products they represent have become an important part of the investment world. Smart traders will time the orders and ride the price aberrations that are created by them. It's almost as if the seasoned trader can sense a cash close order coming, especially on days when there are huge moves in the market.

CAPITAL FLOWS

The popularity of these types of funds have made it almost impossible to move a large order on the close of the stock market without leaving a big footprint on the pricing taking place. Another problem for the funds is that positions seem to become concentrated, which breeds an even more volatile condition when the orders hit the market. The end of the month also creates some excitement, as the traditional futures brokerage community, which gets paid commissions monthly, inevitably covers customer positions, only to reestablish them the following month.

Another end-of-the-month anomaly is the settlement of the stock index futures markets to fair value. This is done primarily for the synthetic fund managers, who get marked on their performance on the monthly settlement. The exchange employed the practice because, too often, the action between 3 PM and 3:15 PM Chicago time skewed the fair value due to the lack of an underlying cash market to keep it in line. The only other time during the day when it becomes critical to watch the clock is when the European bourses close. At roughly 11 AM Chicago time, we witness the last of the European fund managers' activity as they close up shop or pass their global book on to New York for the evening. This is why there always seems to be a flurry of activity around that time of the day, as the markets feel the effects of bourse closes in a quiet afternoon condition.

Another major factor in the daily price movement of the futures markets is sector rotation. It used to be that equity traders would talk about sector rotation in the traditional way—that is, moving from one sector of the stock market to another. The concept of rotating assets has taken on a new dimension as we have witnessed the futures industry being viewed as a legitimate asset class. We still can see the effects of sector rotation in the stock market by watching the price action in the large-cap stocks as it relates to the other indexes. Many times I will report what looks to be a sector rotation that is done by watching the relationships in the intermarket spreads between the different stock indexes.

When the S&P 500 is strong and the Russell 2000 is weak on any given day, it is a sign that there could be a rotation out of small-cap stocks into the large-cap companies. When funds fine-tune their equity exposure, the easiest way to execute the order, if they are tracking against any index, is to use the futures markets and the efficiency they bring. But sector rotation has taken on a new meaning as managers have looked to commodity exposure as a necessary part of the portfolio. This has created an almost incestuous relationship between the world of basic commodities and the equity markets. Much of the recent run the world has seen in commodity prices has been attributed to cheap money and the rise in demand for the growth experienced globally.

ETFs

A byproduct of this tremendous growth has been the invention of the exchange-traded fund, which takes a basic raw material such as gold or crude oil and transforms it into a listed equity. As managers allocate assets accordingly, they have begun to use the ETF market much more effectively. This growing audience for the commodities represented by the ETFs has created a new customer base for the old-time futures exchanges—the small retail stock traders who have never traded futures before. Most every ETF on the market today would find it impossible to exist without a futures component that allowed the market maker of the product to hedge out the risk. That's why the first ETFs that came into existence were created off the backs of the open interest and liquidity provided by the futures markets representing the underlying cash market. The SPDR and the QQQ are perfect examples of products that experienced success in some way because of the risk management provided by the markets in Chicago.

Too often, the market experiences movement that can be directly related to the cash flows that are invested on a monthly basis. It used to be that a good trader would know that on the first and fifteenth of every month, institutions put capital flows to work so that they can be true to their investment strategy. The first and fifteenth represent the pay periods in which retirement money and investment dollars are available for exposure in a given asset class. This has been a consistent theory for those who trade equity futures, but that hasn't been the case for those in the traditional physical commodity markets. The large sums of retirement money have always seemed destined for the stock or the bond market, but the recent acceptance of the ETF market has changed the nature of the trade. Investment dollars are sent into many of the ETFs, which have, as their underlying component, exposure in a given commodity.

The recent run-ups in the gold and crude oil markets can, in some way, find their genesis in the speculation brought on by the ease of buying the representative ETF. These days, smart traders watch the fundamentals of a given commodity and the cash flows in and out of the ETF they represent in order to take advantage of the twice-a-month trading opportunity. Many in the investment community are starting to become very concerned about the proliferation of the ETF concept among the trading public.

One of the main concerns involves the lack of education on the part of the investors sending in retail orders in order to get commodity exposure, something most investors want. But few ETF investors realize that if they were to either do their homework or find a good broker who understands the futures markets, it would be much more cost effective to put on a synthetic futures position that has huge leverage rather than tie up capital in an equity position that has none. It becomes a question of smart money management and where the capital is better used.

Monthly timing is smart, but even more important is to know at what time of the intraday session to find an opportunity. Back when I was working with the index arbs, Vinny and Denny taught me that at 2:40 PM Chicago time, some 20 minutes before the close of the stock market, stock imbalances are shown to the world in order to find an orderly way to correct the imbalance rather than have a surprise ending to the session. This is precisely why the market has one final move at the end of the day. I find it odd that so many traders who put large sums of capital at risk daily have no concept of the order imbalances at the end of the day or the effect they could have on the closing price action. It's funny how no matter what they were doing, both Vinny and Denny would get on the phone together, using me to do the arb in various markets simultaneously, as the imbalances were released.

I found that there was a great trade if the imbalances were large enough, and more important, they would give me an idea of what stocks were in play. I came to understand that the larger the capitalization of an indexed equity, the greater the effect of the imbalance on the closing price action. Another variable to the 2:40 PM trade is that many of the market makers on the floor of the NYSE and other equity exchanges are asked to cover some of their short position by the firms that clear their daily trades. On a day when the price action is one-sided, this late-day phenomenon gives experienced traders two different opportunities for a high-percentage trade: They can play the reversal in the price action by being contrarians to the daily trend or they can wait until the imbalance effect is finished and reestablish the original trade.

The question most often asked of me is what the professionals are watching during the course of the session that might give them an insight into the next trend. If you were to ask 10 different traders what they watch on a consistent basis to give them the needed confidence to establish a position in the market, chances are you'd get 10 different responses. The market has become very dynamic and the things that seem important today might seem irrelevant tomorrow.

A good example is the way the stock market used to treat the release of the money supply figures during the week. The Federal Reserve issued the figures at 3 PM, 15 minutes before the futures markets closed. Many traders today got their start by being clerks during the infancy of the S&P 500 pit, relaying the money supply figures to their customer desks as they were released. The stock market, sensitive to the inflation-fighting Fed of Paul Volcker, had many violent reactions to the release of the figures. Today's traders have very little need for money supply but will find a fundamental direction in the market by watching what they think the Federal Reserve is watching.

WATCHING THE RUSSELL INDEX

Another well-kept secret in the investment world is the impact of the small-cap stocks as measured by the Russell 2000 and the leadership they've shown through the last few years. Many experienced equity traders have come to realize that the market has a difficult time moving in either direction if the Russell doesn't comply.

　　To get a better understanding of why the small-cap universe has become such an important factor in the movement of the daily price action, you must go back to the catalyst—the 2004 Jobs Creation Act passed by Congress, which was looking to free corporate capital held in oversees subsidiaries of multinationals. This act imposed on the companies in question a one-time flat tax of 5 percent on all capital repatriated to the United States. Over the course of 2005, the dollar seemed to defy logic by staying strong, while all the experts looked for a complete implosion of the currency.

　　The act was very specific in its intent: to expand the research and development teams of the corporations and help create jobs. It was not intended to be used to buy back company stock or issue large dividends to shareholders, but it did free up capital expenditure dollars that were budgeted for R&D, which were redirected to internal use.

　　There were two important ancillary effects the Jobs Creation Act had on the way the market moves. First, the dollar had natural support around the globe, as the swap market for any currency into dollars was the most active it had been since the creation of the euro. As companies repatriated capital from the foreign subsidiaries into the U.S.-based headquarters, the demand for U.S. dollars skewed the entire Forex market, creating a difficult situation for the traders not following legislative activity in the U.S. Congress. At a time when the dollar was under tremendous pressure, moving some 30 percent lower against the other major global currencies, it was Congress, of all things, that came unknowingly to its aid.

　　The second and more important effect of the act on the stock market was the way it fed into the supply chain. The small-cap universe is represented by many of the companies that are directly in the supply chain of the corporations that repatriated capital back to the States. These smaller companies became the direct beneficiaries of much of the freed-up capital that came back home.

　　This is one of the main reasons that professionals have started to watch the Russell index regularly and, taking it one step further, have realized the importance of having the small-caps participate when the market moves. I have come to believe that the Russell index is the best indicator of the overall health of the stock market. Many might look at the S&P 500 or the Dow for a clue about how the economy feels, but those who understand the changing market structure have begun to watch the Russell very closely.

　　The Russell stocks represent the suppliers, and the suppliers to the suppliers—this incestuous relationship with the larger-capitalized companies has drawn much more attention to the small-cap universe than ever before. It has become a leader for the entire market on the way up and on the way down. It has also become a place where the larger-capitalized stocks have a difficult time moving higher if, in fact, the smaller-cap stocks, as measured by the Russell 2000, move lower.

Know your market. Those words are as true today as they were when Ralph Peters said them to me over 25 years ago. But one of the most important things to keep in mind is that the market does not remain in a static condition; on the contrary, it is very dynamic. By nature, the condition of the market changes with the technology and the participants who make up the daily liquidity. Many remain in the dark about the various types of arbitrage or the timing of certain daily events but still find it necessary to risk thousands of hard-earned dollars on positions that are totally speculative at best.

It's only by becoming a student of the markets that you can acquire the knowledge needed to be a good trader. The best in the world have the ability to shut out the noise of a session and tune in to the market with full focus and attention. As Bing said to me, there are 2,000 different lessons to be learned about trading. However, I have found that the daily observation of the price action and the factors that drive the action teach more lessons than any single act. There are no books that teach the role of the different types of arbitrage and the market-maker activity that drive volatility. In fact, it was the lack of material about the fundamentals of the daily price action that led me to believe that the most important thing I could contribute with this book would be to give the average investor an insight into the nuances that are an important part of the market structure.

I have never read anything that might offer me a clue about how to pick up an asset allocation or a series of buy or sell orders hitting the market; it's only through watching the trade day in and day out that the unwritten rules of the market become obvious. For a trader, understanding the changing nature of the market is a necessary survival mechanism. The latest and most recent test for the floor trading community is the revolution of electronically traded futures and options and the migration of liquidity away from the open outcry session. This dynamic event has forced many of the old faithful floor traders to evolve into a hybrid of sorts, remaining in the pit but trading most of their positions electronically.

This concept of creating an electronically traded futures contract based on the open interest and liquidity provided by the larger, more established contract has revolutionized the game and contributed more to the industry than any single event since the design of financial futures in the early 1970s. We are in the infancy of a financial revolution that will change the face of futures trading forever.

CHAPTER 4

Managed Futures: The Holy Grail

T he year 1989 was very tough for someone trying to make a living trading anything equity-related on the floor of any exchange around the country, but it was especially difficult for those of us in the S&P 500 futures pit at the Chicago Mercantile Exchange (CME). The New York regulators, not understanding the nuances of the derivatives markets, had come to blame the 1987 stock market crash on stock index futures, which had begun trading as a new concept in the early 1980s. As it turns out, the studies exonerated the products and showed that futures not only didn't bring down the stock market but acted as a buffer for all the selling pressure that a deteriorating fundamental condition brought forth. It was the only market left open for a world rife with panic and fear.

Many—myself included—are convinced that the futures market helped save the entire financial system. The effects of the crash, regardless of the ultimate result years later, created an environment that made order flow in the equity futures pits scarce and institutional use of the products a rare thing. Battles among the various government regulators in Washington brought about an era of tension and alarm not seen in the industry before or since. The regulatory uncertainty that surrounded the product made selling or brokering the market so difficult that many who had created a nice business for themselves soliciting and servicing S&P day traders went on to other, more familiar markets such as the Eurodollar futures at the CME or the fixed-income pits of the Chicago Board of Trade (CBOT).

As a trader, I found that the prosperity of the pre-1987 market was slow to return. When United Airlines (UAL) announced disappointing earnings in the fall of 1989, I was caught long the S&Ps and watched as stocks broke down in a huge percentage move, unable and, even worse, unwilling to change my opinion. As the market broke, I continued buying the dips, hoping for a bounce and a chance to make back the small fortune that I had just lost. In hindsight, trying to buy the market when it starts to break with the emotion and intensity of a panic sell-off is like trying to catch a falling knife without sustaining a cut. The term for losing everything in the account is *blowing out*. It had just dawned on me that I was one of many in the history of trading who was on the verge of blowing out my account.

I remember spending the entire next day trying to analyze the small portfolio that my new wife and I had built over the first few years of our marriage and realizing that I had put all my eggs in one basket, my trading account. I was never a big fan of diversification in the portfolio because, watching market makers risk their entire net worth every day, I felt that if I had an opinion on the market, I should have the courage to back it up with capital at risk. Luckily, I still remembered some of what Bing had taught me and managed to maintain a small sum in my account, hoping to, as Bing would say, have some ammunition left for the next day. By taking a large loss in the account but holding on to enough money to return the following day, I was able to survive that character-building experience and use the knowledge to improve as a trader and broker.

MODERN PORTFOLIO THEORY

One of the first things I remember doing, after the near-blowout experience, was creating an investment strategy that allowed for a diversified approach to the market conditions. Bing Sung had taught me the concept of allocating assets according to modern portfolio theory. When he was a manager of the Harvard Endowment Fund, he insisted on trading derivatives to enhance the return on the university's positions, and he was known as a pioneer by his peers. As I looked at the possible investment vehicles at my disposal, I quickly realized that as a small investor I was not allowed to allocate assets to managers in the alternative asset class. Simply put, modern portfolio theory teaches that to achieve true diversification in the portfolio, the investments should be divided among different asset classes such as equities and bonds, but that a small percentage—10 to 15 percent—should be allocated to investments that have no correlation to the rest.

It came to my attention that if I wanted to incorporate an alternative investment vehicle in my portfolio, I would have to do it myself through trading futures. As the concept of alternative investing proliferated among institutional users, the use of futures as the alternative became much more acceptable as a practice and slowly became an important segment of any intuitive search to find investments that had no correlation to the stock or bond markets. Over the last decade, we in the financial services industry have witnessed an explosion in the creation of hedge funds and the hedge fund style of investment.

Many who invest in these products do so hoping to gain the sought-after diversification that they've been promised, but what has happened is that 90 percent of the thousands of funds that have sprung up have morphed into nothing more than high-priced risk takers. It has also become quite clear that these funds don't create a true diversified investment, but, rather, further study indicates that their performance is directly linked with the other asset classes. That's why many managers have turned to managed futures and use them, consciously or not, as an alternative investment. Many university endowments and corporate planning sponsors have allocated a percentage of assets to managed futures programs in order to create real returns and flatten out the volatility curve for the capital at risk. One of the problems of the day was that the best-managed futures funds, which had consistently shown positive returns in periods of stock and bond market declines, had minimum investments in the neighborhood of $500,000 and higher, making any participation on my part very unlikely. The closed-door environment of the legitimate alternative investment universe has since changed, and with that comes a revolution for the average investor.

If ever there was a secret that all traders share no matter what they trade, it is that the public order flow is the best flow to trade against. Since the beginning of trading, professional traders have made a wonderful living trading off the uneducated customer base, which turns over rapidly. As the president of Commerz Futures, a futures commission merchant (FCM) in Chicago and a division of Commerzbank AG of Germany, I witnessed firsthand the pattern of customers opening accounts from abroad only to close them a few weeks and thousands of dollars later.

It was a troubling period, as we tried in vain to make sure the customers, trading from Europe, had the proper information and product education before putting on their initial positions. At that time we insisted that the bank authorize a program that would allow the creation of structured products such as managed futures that Commerz Futures could market to the growing retail customer base. Unfortunately, the vision for the future of the derivatives industry was not shared with the board of directors from Frankfurt, leaving the division with no genuine managed futures products to market and, even worse in my opinion, neglecting to give our retail clients something they desperately needed—a vehicle for creating true diversification in their portfolios.

ALTERNATIVE INVESTMENTS AND THE EFFICIENT FRONTIER

One of the interesting facts I came across when doing my due diligence for the bank on the concept of managed futures is that most retail customers last six months before finding the process either too time consuming or too costly. The customer who is placed in a managed futures program, however, is likely to last for years. In order to fully grasp the entire concept behind these products and the power they wield in the financial universe, it's important to step back and understand the basics, which have never fully been exposed to the average investor who was new to this world, as opposed to the qualified investor who had had access to these types of investments for years.

Anyone familiar with the concept of managed futures has heard of the efficient frontier, but very few understand the nature of the concept. Salespeople, hoping to land a large allocation for the fund that they're peddling, throw around buzzwords such as *efficient frontier* but have a vague understanding at best of the topic they're discussing.

Producing maximum risk-adjusted returns is the objective of all capital management. The object is to give the investor a true alternative vehicle with zero correlation to the rest of the asset classes in the portfolio, with risk and reward dynamically managed to a point along an efficient frontier that reflects the investor's appetite for each.

Dr. Harry Markowitz, in laying the foundations for modern portfolio theory, described this efficient frontier and the effects it can have on the overall returns of an investment portfolio. Markowitz wrote that given a choice, an investor would look for a similar portfolio with the same return as the one he or she has, but would search for less risk.

Alternatively, the same investor would want a higher return than that of the existing portfolio, but with the same risk. It only makes sense—if you can make the same return and expose less capital to risk, then the risk-to-reward ratio shifts to their favor. Taking it one step further, for a given level of risk, there is an optimal portfolio with the highest return. Likewise, for a given return, there is an optimal portfolio for the lowest risk. Portfolios whose yield can no longer be increased without increasing the risk and whose risk cannot be lowered without lowering the yield lie along this efficient frontier.

John Lintner took the Markowitz model and extended it to include managed futures specifically as a diversifying vehicle for the traditional portfolio managers of equities and bonds. In both Markowitz's and Lintner's work, risk is measured by variance and standard deviation around an average return. A student of the markets can find many pertinent lessons on the use of alternative investments during periods of market turmoil. When I was at

Commerz Futures in 2000, I noticed that the amount of new money flowing into hedge fund investments went from under $10 billion to roughly $25 billion in one year.

While the S&P 500 index was down almost 13 percent in 2001, hedge fund investments, as measured by the Hennesee Hedge Fund Index, showed a positive return of 2.5 percent for the same period. I realized that for the bank's FCM to compete, it must find a way to involve itself in this exploding segment of the industry. As I did my due diligence on the use of hedge funds, it became clear that the protection that investors were searching for in their alternative investments was misleading in that many of the strategies employed by the funds were not diversified at all. It took the effects of the long-term credit management debacle to show the investment community that almost every type of strategy used by the hedge fund community from the long-only strategies to market-neutral trading showed negative returns. The only group of managers who consistently performed well throughout that period of price dysfunction was the commodity trading advisors (CTAs)—managed futures!

One of the things I quickly noticed is that most of the managers were shocked, as were the investors, when the countless hedge fund strategies created concentrated positions in many of the markets and ended up taking a loss together. How could this have happened when so many different traders are managing funds in so many different styles? The answer lies in the fact that during the late 1990s a long bias seemed to unconsciously work its way into every strategy used, with the exception of traditional bear funds. What was even more fascinating is that this long bias was working its way not only into strategies that were equity related but also into those that were designed to be neutral. The problem was that they were making profits from the same conditions that drove the stock market to nosebleed levels.

As soon as the market conditions turned for the worse, many of these hedge funds found liquidity scarce and that their performance was closer to that of an index fund than a true alternative investment. It was very misleading to see the performance of a given fund while the market was advancing; the test of the fund's true nature is when the market turns down. Most investors experienced negative returns because the hedge fund universe had become correlated with the stock market instead of using strategies that would give them protection during downturns.

However, the CTA universe, which was managing an estimated $35 billion—a fraction of the $500 billion run by the hedge fund community taking long or short positions in the futures markets—delivered stellar results during the same period. One important difference between the two worlds is that back in 2001, a large percentage of the assets allocated to the CTA community were divided among 30 large traders. This has since changed, and qualified CTAs now number in the hundreds, a figure that is growing every day.

A large problem that had to be overcome was the high level of fees attached to the managed futures products. It's the dilemma of high fees that caused the industry to miss the explosive growth that was experienced by other segments of the financial services world. But with the recent proliferation of these funds, we have seen a move to dramatically reduce the fees and make the products more desirable as they become more competitive with one another. With the drop in fees comes an overall drop in the volatility of the given advisors. The trading has become much more quantitative in nature, and along with that, the ideals of capital preservation have overtaken triple-digit returns. This also demonstrates the law of diminishing returns, as Bing taught me. When a fund gets too large, with more capital to manage, it becomes much more difficult to deliver results at the same percentage. Many of the best advisors have become conservative in their approach because investors have asked for real noncorrelated returns with limited drawdowns.

Bing showed me that there were many different strategies used by managers running money in the various markets. The most common CTA strategy is a long-term trend-following system in which the trader captures the extended price movements in any accessible futures market. It used to be that we would find the large CTA flow only in the equity or fixed-income pits of the exchanges, but it's now common for large futures funds to trade everything from Malaysian palm oil to pork bellies as long as open interest and other critical-mass elements exist for the trade.

I remember that as the stock market stalled in the middle of 2000, it was this strategy of following trends in other U.S. and European markets that contributed to record returns while equity prices began to crumble. It wasn't only the ability to short the stock market via index futures as it went down—as a matter of fact, many advisors simply ignored the equity markets during the downturn—but, rather, having access to other global futures markets that yielded high-percentage trades and created opportunities for substantial returns. Through having access to the various markets around the globe, advisors can take advantage of deflationary periods in commodity prices as we witnessed in 1998 or a sharp rise in base materials as we've seen in recent months.

Another strategy used by the CTAs is *momentum trading*. There are short-term and long-term momentum trades. Simply put, momentum traders follow the trend as it's breaking out of a given technical formation and hope for instant gratification. Most of these trades are put on with a limited time horizon in mind. For some momentum traders, holding a position for more than a day or two is absolutely torture. The momentum trade is meant to be put on in accordance with the direction of large and fast movements in the price of a market that might last hours or maybe a day. A short-term trader is looking for a move in a matter of hours, while the long-term momentum trader might sit with a position for a few days. Another strategy used by many of the advisors today is contrarian thinking. A contrarian is one who typically will fade the general direction of the market and fight the prevailing trend. Most contrarians make money in an atmosphere charged with emotion, as in times when stocks drop or commodity prices experience parabolic moves up or down.

Most CTAs offer managed accounts to their clients, allowing full disclosure of positions and trades. These accounts usually offer daily redemptions and additions, though some may have lockup periods that could last up to a month. The leverage used by these funds ranges from zero to two times their equity, which has been closely monitored after a string of highly leveraged funds almost destroyed the system—reports had Long Term Capital Management's leverage ratio at an amazing 50:1! The best CTAs have track records that date back 10 to 20 years, which gives the investor a sense of security in the fact that the chosen advisor has managed funds in bull and bear markets with consistent positive returns.

The last few months have reminded us that at times commodities have outperformed the stock market. As we've experienced the explosion in commodity prices, the stock market, as measured by the S&P 500, has not fared nearly as well. But this is not a new phenomenon. It came to my attention in the fall of 1987 that during the last few months of the year, commodities outperformed the stock market. This was primarily because of the loss of value of the equity markets, but it was also a measure of the importance of diversified asset classes in a portfolio.

REAL PORTFOLIO DIVERSIFICATION

The year 1987 taught me many lessons in money management, but the most critical part of my education came as I began to learn about the power of diversifying a portfolio properly. During the months before and after the crash, the stock market lost 30 percent of its value, while commodities gained 10 percent. I quickly realized the power of this alternative type of exposure and began to formulate a method by which I could acquire the same type of coverage as the institutions create in order to give them a proper diversified model. Doing my due diligence, I learned that there had been other, more drastic disparities between the performance of equities and that of raw materials.

During the oil embargo days of the early 1970s, well before I started my career, commodity prices rose a staggering 114 percent while the stock market dropped nearly 40 percent in the same period. But it wasn't only commodity exposure that I was looking for; instead, I was searching for the elusive noncorrelated vehicle that would give my portfolio protection, even if commodity and equity prices began to slip simultaneously. That was the true nature of the alternative investment. In order to create the type of model needed to take advantage of the volatility in price action, it was necessary to trade various markets using different styles. This was done in order to give a multi advisor, multistrategy approach to the methodology.

The logic behind the approach is very simple. Have many different styles of traders trading different markets in various forms to create a diversified investment strategy that doesn't correlate to the any other asset class. This was the way the large institutions allocated their assets, but it became very clear from the start of my academic exercise that it would be nearly impossible for me to re-create the same model alone. For an individual back in 1987 to create a multistrategy, mutliadvisor model using the best fund managers of the day and produce the wanted results, it would have cost over $3 million in minimum investment with the various managers.

As the hedge fund world began to see the power and proliferation of futures managers, not to mention higher fees, it quickly shifted into high gear and allowed smaller qualified investors into the funds with minimums in the range of $250,000 to $500,000. These high-net-worth individuals saw firsthand the importance of these investments when, during the first Gulf war, equity markets lost nearly 15 percent as managed futures yielded positive returns in the range of 20 percent. It was one of the first times in the history of managed futures that the individual investor was able to benefit from a structured investment creating a noncorrelated asset class.

These same investors found a safe haven in managed futures during the worst period for the stock market in recent history. During the third quarter of 1998, when the averages on the NYSE and Nasdaq fell almost 50 percent from the 52-week highs, Managed Accounts Report, the industry watchdog, showed a positive return in the Trading Advisor Qualified Universe Index composed of the top fund managers of the day. There were many on Wall Street who didn't like the idea that markets out of their control in Chicago became the engine for these structured products that seemed to fit into every portfolio's needs. The New York crowd had been the masters of the universe in the financial services world from the beginning and now felt a threat from the Second City. The entire industry received a big boost when in August 1999 the result of a five-year study was published in the *Wall Street Journal* concerning the best of the big brokerage firms and their respective asset allocation performances.

The study included all the big names of the day, including Merrill Lynch, Goldman Sachs, Salomon, Morgan, and Dean Witter. The findings showed that Goldman had the best record for assets under management because it was the only firm that included futures in its asset allocation. Having many friends who went through the training programs of the largest and best houses on Wall Street, I found out that most were told to drop futures from the model they present to customers. This was done for a number of reasons, the two biggest being regulatory uncertainty and a lack of education on the part of registered representatives. But what began to draw serious attention was when Morningstar reported that in a single month, November 2000, the fully diversified average technology fund lost an average of 15 to 25 percent, while Managed Accounts Report showed the Trading Advisor Qualified Universe Index with a positive gain of a little over 5 percent.

MANAGED FUNDS AS AN ASSET CLASS

In 1983, a few years before I began to work with Bing, one of his colleagues at Harvard, John K. Lintner, wrote a revolutionary paper entitled "The Potential Role of Managed Commodity-Financial Futures Accounts in Portfolios of Stocks and Bonds," which took a historical and academic perspective on the industry. The Lintner study was exactly what the institutional investors needed to give the asset class the credibility necessary for the board of directors of the various funds to authorize the use of the products in their portfolios. Lintner wrote:

> ... [T]he improvements from holding an efficiently selected portfolio of managed accounts or funds are so large ... and the correlation between returns on the futures portfolios and those on the stock and bond portfolio are so surprisingly low (sometimes even negative) ... that the return/risk tradeoffs provided by augmented portfolios ... clearly dominate the tradeoffs available from a portfolio of stocks alone or from portfolios of stocks and bonds.

This was the ammunition that many in the institutional trading community were looking for so that they could begin to employ the strategies that had become so very profitable for others. Using the composite of the 15 largest trading advisors of the day and studying the periods between 1979 and 1982, Lintner showed that the risk-to-reward ratio of a portfolio of CTAs is higher than that of a well-diversified stock and bond portfolio alone. Taking it one step further, he found that there was very low correlation between the returns of the advisors and those of a combined stock and bond portfolio.

The concept of having noncorrelated asset classes became the center-piece of any argument to include futures in an asset allocation model. Why should we expect low or zero correlation between a portfolio of managed futures and equity, fixed-income portfolios, or foreign exchange risk? There are many explanations for why this might be the case. Many in the industry have known for years that markets react differently to the various forces driving prices up and down; that's why it is critical to understand why certain asset classes have no correlation to others in the financial world.

To a student of the markets, it becomes painfully obvious that certain conditions not favorable to the cash markets in equities, fixed income, and currencies are usually favorable to managed futures. The very things that drive the price of stocks and bonds down—inflation, deflation, and economic uncertainty—often cause major price movements in commodity markets around the world. It's this disruption in price action that many managers find as the panacea for a portfolio in desperate need of real positive returns. Just recently, as we've witnessed a skyrocketing commodities market, the financial services industry has come to the conclusion that the investment in commodities alone is not sufficient to capture the price volatility of a marketplace.

Most investors who seek commodity exposure make the mistake of thinking they're buying a noncorrelated asset when in reality they're purchasing exposure that makes them strictly long the underlying commodities as opposed to a genuine alternative investment that takes advantage of price swings up and down. Another of the reasons for noncorrelation of assets is that the global and market sector diversity of available futures contracts contributes to the diversified performance between managed futures stocks, fixed-income securities, and foreign exchange. Most individual investors fail to understand that an investment in the proper foreign exchange futures fund creates a de facto hedge of the currency risk that comes with a volatile dollar.

Lately, as we've experienced an increase in currency volatility, Forex products have become the hottest vehicle in the investment industry. Unlike stocks or bonds, investment in the currency markets is very easy for the nonprofessional to understand; it usually becomes the first foray into futures for new traders. One thing to always keep in mind when making an investment into an alternative asset class is that there is no long bias in the futures markets, as there is in the traditional investment markets. When a futures position is taken, it can as easily be a long position as a short position. Unlike traditional investing, where buy and hold is often the strategy, managed futures can easily capitalize on bidirectional profit opportunities and low transaction costs. The most important feature of noncorrelation is that any good managed futures program itself internally uses risk management controls that seek to limit correlation among the various managers in the program. This has the effect of further diversifying the correlation with the investor's portfolio.

VARIOUS MANAGED FUTURES STRUCTURES

There are four basic ways an investor might utilize managed futures in an overall return/risk enhancement program. The first is a simple overlay that offers maximum transparency, with the advantage of being off balance sheet. An account is opened in the investor's name at the broker of his or her choice. A limited power of attorney allows the pool manager to manage the account. The entire amount of the overlay is not funded. Otherwise unpledged U.S. Treasury securities may be used in the account for initial margin and sometimes maintenance margin requirements.

The investor may sweep the account as frequently as he or she deems optimal. Minimal funding is therefore required. Duplicate trade confirmations are sent to the investors daily. Further account information is available intraday from a secured Web site maintained by the pool manager. As attractive as this transparency may appear to the investor, care must be taken in the risk management procedures. It would be a mistake to incorporate individual managed futures positions into the positioning.

The pool manager and the investor can agree on risk tolerances and volatility parameters that are then monitored daily. The managed futures overlay is not a bona fide hedge as defined by FASB 133. As such, everything must be marketed-to-market. The second is the overlay/contingent immunization method, which combines the structure and the benefits of an overlay with contingent immunization techniques. Immunization techniques, in general, refer to strategies used by portfolio managers to shield either their current net worth or future income requirements from exposure to interest rate fluctuations.

Suppose a portfolio manager has decided to pursue a reward/risk enhancement overlay strategy with a sample pool's managed futures on his $100 million fixed-income portfolio. Assume interest rates are presently 7 percent and that the manager can lock in, via conventional immunization techniques, a future portfolio value of $141 million after five years. However, the manager is willing to risk losses from the pool overlay portion only to the extent that the terminal value of the overall portfolio will not drop lower than $136 million.

In an example such as this one, only $98 million is required to achieve this minimum acceptable terminal value. Therefore, since the portfolio is currently worth $100 million, the manager can afford to risk some losses at the outset and might start off with an active overlay/contingent immunization strategy rather than immediately locking in or immunizing the portfolio. This value becomes the initial trigger point, which functions much like a barrier option. If and when the actual portfolio value dips to the trigger point, the managed futures overlay will cease. Contingent upon reaching the trigger, an immunization strategy is initiated instead, guaranteeing that the minimum acceptable performance can be realized. The trigger point needs to be periodically assessed as interest rates and time to the effective horizon change.

The third method of investing in a program is direct allocation. This involves investing in a managed futures fund or pool directly using the due diligence required to allocate to various managers trading differing product lines. There are increased funding requirements under this structure. Account sweeping and the investment of excess funds are handled by the pool manager. There is some loss in transparency as well. Individual positions would not be disclosed as completely as with the overlay structure.

The fourth method, and my personal favorite, is the structured product approach. This method can offer both a guaranteed principal feature and an underlying managed futures portfolio component placed within the framework of a conventional security (e.g., note, bond, certificate of deposit). An example might be a variable-coupon, five-year note with a par put at maturity. The limited liability feature comes at the price of reduced fund performance. Depending on how the product is designed, this may reduce the return/risk enhancement benefits to the overall portfolio. As with a direct allocation, there are increased funding requirements as opposed to the overlay method, and transparency is also usually more complete with an overlay strategy.

Because of the intricacies involved in selecting the various fund managers, an investor should consider outsourcing this valuable function to an outside firm.

The biggest reason to seek expertise in the fund industry is the additional layer of specialized research, technological infrastructure, risk management, and oversight, which becomes an effective extension of the portfolio manager's staff without adding fixed cost.

Most pool operators have an extensive commodity trading advisor database and the staff to perform in-depth due diligence, both quantitatively and qualitatively. In addition, a pool manager's extensive network of industry contacts provides information about traders that would be difficult for those not in the industry to obtain.

At the same time, this addition to the manager's staff has valuable autonomy. Subsequent psychological factors as senior management's opinion at macro and micro levels are discounted by professionalism and objectivity. Subsequent trader biases can easily build correlations that can destroy the entire enhancement process.

KEEPING THE CUSTOMER ALIVE

Many people might ask why I have devoted an entire chapter of this book to a single segment of the industry. This is a good question. It's because, in my humble opinion, the concept of a multistrategy, multiadvisor managed futures fund is the only Holy Grail in the trading universe. The answer lies in the fact that over the course of the last decade I have watched legions of new customers open accounts with a hope and a prayer. The first rule that I think everyone should learn is that there is no hoping, wishing, or praying allowed when putting on or taking off a position.

If a trader wishes that the market would go a certain way, then chances are that the trade was destined to be a loser from the outset. All new traders hope to find that Holy Grail methodology of trading futures. That is, they're searching for the foolproof method that will give them incredible returns on their capital at risk and allow the market to give them consistent high-percentage trades. I have watched at conferences and seminars as countless technicians sell their trading methodologies as if they were in a fast-food restaurant selling hamburgers. Most of the techniques that are taught at these places are variations on the same old technical analysis with slight twists to give them different bells and whistles.

It becomes almost comical when I'm asked to sit on panels with so-called experts on market conditions and find out, as I talk with them, that they haven't traded even a single contract. Imagine someone writing a book an the technical analysis of the market and never having put capital at risk. I always ask the authors of books on the markets whether they trade and, if so, what they trade. It gives me a good understanding of what type of risk profile to attribute to the person. As I sit on these panels, it becomes quite clear to me that if I were to really speak my mind, I would end up calling the rest of the panel a bunch of phonies who rarely understand the true nature of the marketplace. Not only do they not fully comprehend market structure, but others look to these people for guidance and advice when making critical investment decisions. The numbers of times I've heard the term *Holy Grail* associated with a trading technique are as frequent as there are systems.

When I was the executive vice president of Nikko Securities in the early 1990s, it became apparent that the Japanese retail public needed to find investment vehicles that gave them real returns on capital at a time when the Japanese stock market was in a steep decline. They realized that futures funds created in the Chicago subsidiary of Nikko International would be able to create a structure that protected the principle of the investment with a chance to see huge returns on the fund. It became known as a *guaranteed fund*, which essentially would tie up the investor for a three- to five-year minimum and buy zero coupon bonds to guarantee the capital and trade the interest on the note. This would create a structured product of sorts, at a time when the concept was relatively new.

Many of the large brokerage houses began to structure products in much the same way for the Asian investors, which served a dual purpose; it kept the customers happy at a time when no other investment seemed to be profitable, and it did something I found very interesting—it kept the customer in the *game*! Until that point, the average retail-based customer from Japan who was trading futures in the United States had a life expectancy of three to six months per account. These managed futures products kept the customer around for the life of the vehicle, three to five years, which allowed the person to invest in other Nikko products with confidence. This was a revelation. Watching the reaction to these funds in Japan made me realize that the future for the industry lay in the hands of the fund managers trading futures. Not only did Nikko find an investment that gave customers the protection of capital that they desperately needed, they also received a noncorrelated asset into their portfolio that gave them true diversification without even trying.

I went on to become president of Commerzbank Futures in Chicago, a division of Commerzbank AG of Germany, then the seventeenth-largest bank in the world. I quickly rallied the troops in the hope of talking Frankfurt into granting the permission needed for the futures subsidiary to get into the managed funds business. As German institutions go, Commerzbank was always trying to play catch-up with its much larger rivals, who had already found profit centers in structuring the proper products. The meetings in Frankfurt lasted two whole weeks, as we met with board members of the bank hoping to explain the growth we were about to experience and how the bank could capitalize on the opportunity at hand.

The Germans are notoriously slow when it comes to decision making, mostly because of an indentured middle management that finds it difficult to streamline anything. Commerzbank was no different, having a chain of command that was pure German in its enforcement and policy decisions. A lack of timely decision making left the bank FCM at the mercy of the institutional customer base that pressed commissions lower and lower as the markets became more efficient. No funds were ever created in Chicago, and the bank folded the operation a few years later under the auspices of the investment banking team.

What the experiences at both Nikko and Commerz taught me was that it's very important to create products that fill a real need and serve a purpose in your customer base. It also gave me the motivation to find a way to give the average investor a chance at the same diversified and well-balanced portfolio that would be expected from any money manager. The need to create product for the average investor stems from the serious losses incurred by so many small investors during the recent stock market decline. Many of these investors were sold the idea that equity markets never correct or get inflated. It was the new paradigm!

When the market began to go down, it didn't discriminate between well-run companies and the ones that were said to be highfliers. Of course, many of the high-flying tech companies had tremendous declines, in the range of 90 percent, but even the great names in the Dow Jones were not immune to the selling pressure. Many of these great names were thought to be a hedge against the crazy rally being experienced in the Nasdaq, but what happened was a revaluation in equity prices that hasn't been experienced, in some cases, since the Depression era of the late 1920s and early 1930s that took the entire market down regardless of pedigree or market capitalization. If there was ever a case study that extolled the virtues of having managed futures in your portfolio, the last decade would be a perfect time to analyze it. Not only did managed futures programs do well during periods of market strength—albeit not the double-digit returns turned in by the equity markets—but they showed positive returns during the course of the stock market bubble deflation.

The time has finally arrived for the small investor to be able to participate in the market the way the professionals participate. Many of the new funds that are being produced are being created with registrations that allow the average investor to allocate a portion of assets into a proper alternative. For many of the investment advisors I speak with, the idea of selling a registered fund to their clients becomes a portfolio sale as long as the advisor is educated about the vehicle. This revolutionary concept of allowing the general public to create a noncorrelated asset class they can incorporate into their portfolios has not only energized the brokerage community, but had the ancillary effect of creating huge pools of liquidity into what would otherwise be smaller agricultural contracts such as lean hogs or milk. The proliferation of the managed funds industry has sparked a revolution among hedge fund managers, who have discovered that they were all in a position to grow their businesses geometrically with the products being created for the noninstitutional clients. It's only the beginning. This industry is in its infancy, but everyone who is serious about investing should know about it!

CHAPTER 5

Within Every Disappointment, There Is a Gem of Opportunity

In the spring of 1997, I took a page out of Leo Melamed's book. I broke down the largest traders in the pit into groups and worked on them directly in order to garner support for a major change that the board was considering: splitting the S&P futures contract. Leo, as I would learn, was a master of breaking down the different floor constituencies in order to find support for tough board actions. Brian Monieson, a former Chicago Mercantile Exchange (CME) chairman and my self-appointed mentor, had suggested the act because he knew the difficulties I was about to face.

Brian was an old friend of Leo Melamed's and was at his side for many of the critical decisions that shaped the future of the CME. It was Brian's counsel that led me to hold Melamed-style meetings with the major liquidity providers in the S&Ps to gain their respect and confidence. I had talked to five of the largest traders in the pit, which included one whose family had a dark history in the city of Chicago. As a native Chicagoan, I was aware of the relationship, but I also knew that you can't choose your family as you can your friends. I had many childhood friends whose fathers and uncles had shady backgrounds but took painstaking steps to make sure their children opted for a different career path.

As an elected official of the CME's board of directors, it was my job to balance the needs and the interests of the membership I was representing with the day-to-day supervision that my floor brokerage business required. Every day new traders would come with what seemed to them to be a life-or-death situations that needed my immediate attention and actions. I found myself right in the crosshairs of every political argument that pitted the floor community against board decisions. Every small board decision was a major issue for somebody!

On a Monday morning, as I was standing at my desk with my entire crew, waiting for the opening of the equity markets, an incident occurred that would give me a clue about the intensity of the board position for which I was elected. From my elevated perch between the S&P and Nikkei pits, I watched traders walk directly in front of me as they entered the arena to begin trading. Before the opening bell and after my morning briefing with the locals, the trader with the nefarious family history stopped directly in front of me on his way into the pit. With my entire crew standing behind me and my colleagues from various other futures commission merchants (FCMs) next to me, he said, "Jack, this better work. If it doesn't, I'll have to join the family business, and if that happens I might have to come look for you." I could see that he was smiling when he said it, but nonetheless I felt that it was important to respond. Without missing a beat, I stole a line from G. Gordon Liddy, of Watergate fame, and said, "Tell me what corner to stand on so my wife and kids don't get hurt!" I winked as I said it, but those behind me didn't see the wink or the smile on the face of the trader as he made what appeared to them to be a threat!

As I spun around, I could see the surprised look and nervous smile on the faces of those around me because of the comments sent my way and, as I found out later, my response in the dialogue. I put a big smile on my face to defuse the tension and said, "It's all part of the job. What did you guys think I should have said?" The incident was never brought up again, but I know that it showed all around that I was serious about addressing the needs of the membership and the exchange.

THE CBOT LANDS THE DOW JONES FUTURES CONTRACT

For a number of reasons, 1997 was an especially difficult year for those of us who were elected to the CME's board of directors. We had decided to split the S&P 500 contract that had advanced and grown far beyond anyone's imagination in notional value and had driven performance bond margins to the limit. As the chairman of the equity index committee, it was my responsibility to be the liaison between the membership providing the liquidity to the products and the policy makers in the board room. The subject of splitting the S&P 500 futures contract from a 50-0 multiplier to a 250 multiplier pitted the brokerage community against the market makers.

Those trading the product did not want to see the value of the contract cut because it would force them to trade more to acquire the same exposure.

The brokerage community, headed by the largest retail brokers of the day, realized that the contract would be undesirable for salespeople unless the value of the contract made it economically feasible for them to push the product. The heated debate, which took months, was interrupted by an announcement in midyear that the Chicago Board of Trade (CBOT), the CME's longtime rival across town, had landed a much-sought-after deal, with the Dow Jones company allowing the CBOT to launch the Dow Jones futures contract on their floor.

As an active member of the floor community, I had the task of handling the impact of this announcement, which sent shock waves throughout the exchange. Many on the floor saw the CBOT's landing of the Dow contract as a direct assault on what they perceived to be their franchise—namely, the stock index futures market. We quickly called an equity index meeting in which the concerns of both the brokers and the market makers became one. The word was sent to the board that the membership expected a response to the announcement, and the fact that Leo Melamed was back on the board created a sense of excitement that something big was about to happen.

Leo Melamed, chairman emeritus of the CME, is regarded as the father of financial futures and, in my humble opinion, the greatest visionary I've ever met. He could be the subject of a variety of books: There's Leo the holocaust survivor, Leo the father of financial futures, Leo the visionary who created Globex (the first electronically traded futures platform), and now Leo the coinventor of the e-mini. The e-mini concept and the proliferation of other electronically traded products are as revolutionary in the world of capital markets as was the creation of the International Monetary Market (IMM) in the early 1970s.

Melamed is a larger-than-life character who lives up to the expectations about him. A trained lawyer, he has always had a way of rousing the troops and generating the kind of allegiance given to other charismatic figures in corporate culture. As a young novice trader, I watched as Leo and the rest of the exchange power brokers escorted senators and representatives, attempting to convey to them their vision for the futures industry and the importance of maintaining a free and open marketplace.

It amazed me to see awe on the faces of these important visitors as they observed the number of transactions and attached a notional value to the particular trade they were witnessing. Leo's tours of the trading floor remain popular among visitors from Washington, who frequently remark upon them in other contexts. Leo's contributions to the futures industry are too numerous to mention here; however, as a first-hand observer of the actions of the board after his return from semiretirement, I can say, with all due respect to the countless other distinguished board members with whom I've served, that Leo was undoubtedly the greatest thinker I've ever had the pleasure of meeting.

ELECTRONIC FUTURES TRADING

Prior to Leo Melamed's return from semiretirement, the CME had found itself in what I call "the dark ages of the exchange." The innovative CME, creator of new products and services, had begun to lose a certain amount of momentum to the Chicago Board of Trade (the rival exchange across town) and were finding it very difficult politically to introduce new technology to the floor. After a sharp fall in lease seat prices (the price paid to lease a seat on the exchange in order to trade in the pits) a grassroots organization called the Equity Owners Association (EOA) was formed to protect the interests of the seat owners and exert some political pressure on the board of directors.

It was in this climate that I was elected to the board of directors for the first of my three terms. My agenda was clear. Although I wasn't a seat owner personally (I was an officer of Credit Agricole Futures, having taken a job with an affiliate of the French bank in order to build an equity futures operation), I was representing the community of futures commission merchants, who are required by the exchanges to own a certain number of seats in order to be clearing members. Running my own operation on the floor, it became very clear to me, and others on the board such as David Silverman, that technology was needed to counteract the problems of inefficiency caused by the open outcry system. Until this time in exchange history, the only real change in the way business was conducted on the floor had been the introduction of hand signals to speed the process of transmitting orders from the brokers on the phone with customers to the filling brokers in the pit.

Silverman, a fine currency trader and board member, thought it would be advantageous for the floor if we, as a board, were to allow the use of headsets to relay the order flow. Prior to this request, the use of any kind of communications technology in the pit had been strictly forbidden. This created two distinct problems. The first was simple: Regulatory concerns surrounded the use of technology that could not be monitored the way the order flow coming from the traditional order desks was monitored. This forced the compliance department to think creatively and permit some of the floor to try using headsets.

The second problem was much more difficult. The political repercussions of allowing the headset technology into the trading arena brought up serious arguments and created divisions among the floor community. Those who traded in the pit were highly sensitive to any type of listening equipment being used there, especially because an FBI sting had netted a couple of traders at both the CME and the CBOT a few years earlier. With Leo Melamed's leadership, both issues were resolved and a new era of technology was introduced to the CME membership.

TECHNOLOGY LEADS THE WAY

As word that the Board of Trade had landed the Dow Jones futures contract spread across the exchange floor, the concern quickly shifted from the use of headset technology to survival. Many members were convinced that the CBOT was about to steal the equity futures franchise by luring the open interest to the new Dow contract. It became necessary to address two different situations: the perceived threat and the actual threat. The perceived threat was that the CME would lose a contract—much like what had happened to the gold contract earlier in the exchange's history. The CME had lost the open interest to the New York traders, resulting in bitter and paranoid feelings anytime a similar contact was introduced by a rival exchange. The actual threat was much different. As chairman of the equity index committee, I was aware that the Dow Jones index is not the index of choice for portfolio managers. When the CBOT landed the Dow contract, there was very little capital using the index as a benchmark. When asked in a *Chicago Tribune* interview what I thought of the Dow contract, I responded, "My parents ask about the Dow; portfolio managers ask about the S&P 500." The events that followed were a combination of timing, inspiration, and sheer genius.

A meeting of the strategic planning committee was immediately called to address the situation. I was asked to serve on both the executive committee and the strategic planning committee, which constituted, in essence, the board within the board. It was the responsibility of the strategic planning committee to come up with ideas and solutions that would allow the board to take action without getting caught in the minutiae of an issue. The executive committee was responsible for setting the board agenda for any given meeting. Leo Melamed, who had recently been asked to come out of retirement, along with Bill Shepard, perhaps the most influential board member of the day, had an idea they wanted to discuss.

The concept, to counter the threat brought on by the CBOT's landing of the Dow contract, was to give traders a smaller version of the S&P 500 futures contract. It was to be an electronic form of the much larger pit-traded contract, but it would give users lower dollar volatility per trade. In short, the product allowed retail investors to participate in the futures market without the huge margins that the advancing S&P contract created. By 1997 the S&P had advanced beyond anyone's imagining, creating a contract that, at 500 times the index, became more difficult to trade and broker. The sheer size of the contract had taken the performance bond margins from roughly $2,500 per contract to over $25,000 as the index moved from under 200 to 1000!

This resulted in two fundamental problems. First, the brokerage community was finding much less profit in equity trading because of the tremendous volatility and exposure a handful of contracts give the user.

The second problem was that competition for customer flow was becoming much more intense with the introduction of ETFs, which acted like futures but in the form of securities. This was the atmosphere in which Melamed and Shepard came to unveil and discuss the new concept of trading a smaller version of a proven product side by side with the pit-traded open outcry product. This had never been done before—cannibalizing your own proven market with a smaller electronic product.

HISTORY IN THE MAKING

As Leo began to speak, I sensed the anticipation and excitement in the room, as if the board members and staff realized the historic nature of this new direction. His first words were memorable: "Behind every disappointment lies a gem of opportunity." An incredible orator, Leo had the room in the palm of his hand with this first sentence, but it was Bill Shepard, behind the scenes, who gave him the needed political capital to make history.

Shepard is the quiet genius on the CME board, but his credibility at the board level came from his days on the floor as a trader. A large man with a beard, Shepard walked into the currency pits and put on enormous positions, usually spreading one against the other. In fact, he would walk in and out of the pits with such confidence that my friends and I called him "the Rooster." Not only was Shepard the most gifted trader of his day, but, as few people in or out of the industry know, many traders got their start with his assistance. Stories of successful locals who got their start with Bill's financial backing are common.

With Shepard legitimizing the idea, Leo had everything he needed to accomplish his goal—which was to create the greatest electronic futures marketplace the world has ever seen. Several years earlier, in his book *Escape to the Futures*, Melamed had written about his vision for an electronic exchange. As one of the creators of Globex, the CME's electronic platform, he realized the power of the electronic platform and what it would mean for the thousands of members who would own equity in a demutualized CME. We had arrived at the point where much of that dream was turning into a reality.

The weeks that followed the announcement of the e-mini were filled with debate about such things as contract size and position limits per transaction. For the product to proliferate as expected, we believed we would need participation from the local floor community, who would make markets tapping into the larger contract's pool of liquidity. By creating a two-sided liquid electronic market, it was thought—and rightfully so—that the public would decide which platform it preferred. This was a bold and daring move—a market-driven solution made by an institution that prided itself on creating fair and open markets. It could turn out to be one of the CME's proudest moments.

One of the driving factors behind such a monumental decision on the part of the CME was the then recent assault on the London International Financial Futures Exchange (LIFFE) Bund futures contract by the German futures exchange Eurex. Aside from issues relating to national pride on the part of the Germans, it was the existence of their electronic trading system that gave them the needed technological edge to overtake the established London market. This act of "stealing liquidity" sent shock waves into the boardroom of every exchange in the world. If it was possible for the German Eurex exchange to steal the Bund contract from London's LIFFE market, then it was feasible that the CME's lucrative equity and interest rate complex would be in the crosshairs of any predator.

A REVOLUTION IN FUTURES TRADING

As the membership became more and more comfortable with the idea of having an electronic market trade side by side with the larger open outcry counterpart, the world began to understand the value of the new, smaller contract and growth took off at an alarming rate. The question was no longer whether the concept would work but rather were we as an exchange prepared for the phenomenal growth that many of us saw ahead. The board of directors, composed of traders, brokers, and salespeople, became de facto technology experts who would lead the exchange into the next century. We all became obsessed with the speed and efficiency of the new, growing market, monitoring the transactions per second (TPS) as closely as a technology officer.

One of the ancillary effects of migrating the trade to the electronic platform was the disintermediation of the floor. Once liquidity went to the screen, the floor would slowly become obsolete. What makes the evolutionary process in the futures markets somewhat different is that the geometric growth in the number of end users has, anecdotally, created two jobs off the floor for every one job lost on the floor. Throughout the entire process, Leo and Shepherd led the charge in the boardroom. Decisions became more difficult as the concept spread to other sectors of the equity markets and eventually into the other product lines of the exchange. The success of the S&P e-mini led to a launch of an e-mini version of the Nasdaq, the S&P MidCap 400, and the Russell 2000, all of which have been success stories in themselves.

The board of directors at the time of the creation of the e-mini was an intellectual powerhouse. Aside from Leo and Shepherd, who led the charge, many influential directors worked tirelessly to make sure the floor understood the need for the concept to thrive. Jack Sandner, former chairman, and Terry Duffy, present chairman, were instrumental in garnering the support of the floor broker community, who, as a collective, had enormous influence in pre- and post-IPO exchange politics.

Duffy, in particular, exhibited the diplomacy of a seasoned political veteran as he explained to the older floor members the value of the electronic platform and the endless possibilities it created for the CME. Duffy, one of the greatest chairmen in the CME's history aside from Leo, has given the exchange the fresh blood it needs to survive through the next chapter of its history. As chairman, Duffy, with the support of skilled strategists like Melamed and Shepherd, has taken an old, established Chicago institution and turned it into the global powerhouse it is today. I left the board just as Duffy became chairman, but as his former board colleague I can say, with all honesty, that the CME has never been in better hands.

The growing volume in the e-mini product lines made the use of the products more popular among the various proprietary traders in the end-user community. A proprietary trader is one who takes positions for the firm using the firm's capital and risk profile. Proprietary trading houses, or "prop shops" as they are called on the Street, have been responsible for the majority of the explosive growth found on the trading screen. Every index arbitrageur and statistical arbitrageur has automated its system in order to participate at a much higher rate of trade than is possible in a traditional open outcry environment.

It becomes much easier for a trader to write a code that automates the entire arbitrage process, thus allowing the trader to take positions in many different markets simultaneously. Prior to the maturation of the e-mini, it wasn't feasible for a single trader to handle more than one or two markets at the same time. Now, it's not uncommon to walk into a prop shop with two people and find that they are trading 20 different markets electronically and each strategy is fully automated. As the electronic trading system became even more reliable and efficient, two major events happened: The customer base of the electronically traded products began to grow at an alarming rate and the liquidity in the pit moved to the screen.

The first effect was a welcome change for the FCM community, which had found it difficult to make the same profit per trade they had experienced years earlier. Many of the major FCMs are either subsidiaries of larger institutions or are designed to handle in-house proprietary trading. These larger institutions looked upon the futures division as a bastard child. As the president of Commerz Futures, I witnessed firsthand the contempt that the established banking community had for the entire derivatives industry. It always seemed ironic to me that one part of the bank looked down on the industry, while a completely different part of the bank depended on the price discovery provided by the markets in Chicago.

The retail houses had fallen on hard times, as a contraction in commissions had left the smaller FCMs in a difficult position. During this time, consolidation among the smaller houses became a necessity to survive. The only revenue stream that seemed to remain intact was the interest income that sat in customer accounts. Another of the best-kept secrets in the industry is that interest income from customer accounts is a major source of revenue to the bottom line. The world was about to change for the FCMs, and the e-mini was the catalyst for that change.

THE E-MINI CONCEPT GROWS

The growing success of the S&P 500 e-mini led to the creation of the Nasdaq e-mini contract in June 1999. The proliferation of the concept had propelled the Chicago markets into the global limelight. Prior to this, the CME had been a global player with the establishment of Forex and Eurodollar futures, but taking the industry into an entirely new direction turned the exchange into the globally dominant player that it is today. My responsibility as the chairman of the equity index committee was to work through the political problems created by the new concept among the floor traders and brokers.

One of the problems seemed to center around the fact that the FCM community wanted a quick proliferation of the e-mini products. The floor felt as if there had been an attack on the open outcry system and resisted some of the changes being presented to the membership. Retail brokers and salespeople became excited about the prospect of electronically traded products across the equity sectors. The need to quickly roll out products in the other sectors of the stock market became clear as the world watched the Nasdaq market pass 2000, then 3000. The higher the index went, the more unmanageable the contract became. The daily standard deviation (the daily movement of the market) made margins outrageous and left many of the executing brokers on the floor in a position where the risk of executing a customer order became cost prohibitive.

The growing volume of the electronic market took the arbitrage world by storm. In the beginning, the statistical arbitrageurs were able to automate their models so that they could participate in numerous markets. I realized the growing power of the technology on my visit to the Cooper Neff/BNP traders, who had been my largest customers in the smaller equity contracts. Prior to the birth of the e-mini, Scott Weisblum had taken the Cooper Neff/BNP proprietary trading desk to being the largest user of the Nasdaq, Russell, and midcap contracts.

Upon entering the new trading room built for Weisblum in New York City, I was struck by the fact that the fully automated system allowed traders the freedom to do so many other things. During our lunch, the system traded more contracts electronically than I had ever seen Weisblum trade in a full day in an open outcry environment. This was a revelation! If they could trade with that kind of frequency while the concept was still in its infancy, imagine what they would be capable of doing if the concept ever reached maturation. I remember returning to Chicago with an entirely new vision of what the proliferation of the electronic market really meant. For the first time, I fully understood what Leo Melamed had said in one of the earlier meetings about the e-mini: Let technology lead! It was the technology geniuses of the proprietary trading firms who embraced the concept of automation in order to create a true electronic edge for their traders.

What had started as a way to compete with the CBOT in its landing of the Dow Jones contract turned into a revolution for the entire industry. In my reports to the brass at Commerzbank (the parent of Commerz Futures), the electronic volume was the most important statistic requested. The bank had come to the conclusion—as had most European institutions—that the open outcry system was becoming obsolete and must be abandoned so the markets could grow.

THE GREAT EQUALIZER

In early 2001, I was invited to an award dinner at the Conrad Hilton and Towers in Chicago, at which Leo Melamed would be honored by the Anti-Defamation League of Chicago. The guest speaker was the former senator from Illinois Paul Simon, who was also a sitting member of the CME board of directors. The senator had become a close friend during the few years we spent on the board together. In fact, after the first meeting he attended he took me aside and, insisting that I call him Paul, asked, "Jack, are you by any chance Armenian?" As I said yes, I saw the smile appear on his face. He had had an Armenian roommate during his college days and had always kept his love for the Armenian people and culture.

He had been to Yerevan, the capital of Armenia, many times and was knowledgeable about the country's politics and problems with neighboring Azerbaijan. For years after our first meeting, Paul would send me articles about Armenia or come across a picture of me in a local paper, which he would send to me with a note asking if I had paid for the publicity. During one of our pre–board meeting talks, I told him that, being a Republican, I had never voted for him. But after getting to know him, I regret, with all my heart, not supporting him. I will always cherish the relationship I had with Senator Simon and miss him very much since he passed away a couple of years ago.

Knowing that Leo Melamed is a wonderful orator, I was expecting something special as he took the podium to accept the award, and I wasn't disappointed. After thanking those responsible for the evening, he turned to his favorite subject—the market. His speech was filled with great insights about the industry, but the one line that galvanized the audience was when he referred to the markets as "the great equalizer."

His words were a revelation! I had always struggled to find the right words to describe the market experience, but it was Leo's speech that put it all into perspective. In essence, what he was trying to convey in the speech is that the market doesn't discriminate; if you're right the market, then you're a good trader. It doesn't matter what religion or nationality you might be, the only thing that matters in trading is the ability to take the information at hand and turn it into a profitable trade. That is how the market measures success. The speech was prophetic in that it was a glimpse of the market condition that was about to be changed by the growing volume and penetration of the e-mini.

WHAT HAPPENED TO THE EDGE?

The world was about to change, and the CME was at the forefront of the revolution. But as the electronically traded products became more and more popular, the floor community began to see a significant shift in the volume traded in the open outcry session. The noticeable change in activity sent many of the old-time members into a panic, as the dynamic nature of the new market forced them to change their trading style. No longer would they be in the pit looking for the edge that came to them naturally through the geography of the open outcry session. The edge had become as dynamic as the rest of the market.

What followed in the electronically traded products was a migration of the edge to the screen. What was at one time a geographical edge had morphed into a technological edge. Traders were no longer talking about their spot in the pit but, rather, how to make their electronic trading systems milliseconds faster. The general public does not realize the displacement that occurs every time a pit-traded product is migrated to the screen. The thousands of jobs on the floor have been replaced by thousands of jobs off the floor, but not every floor employee or trader can flourish in an office environment.

Even today, with most of the notional value of the S&P 500 futures contract traded electronically through the e-mini, traders are seen in the open outcry pit trading in what has become a secondary market to the screen. The fact that the larger contract trades in smaller increments of

10 points per tick as opposed to the e-mini, which trades in 25-point increments, gives those still trading on the floor a small chance to create an arbitrage opportunity between the two contracts.

Although the spread between the two contracts has narrowed considerably since the inception of the e-mini, there is enough customer order flow coming into the pit for a few traders to prosper. It became apparent to many members that their way of doing business was quickly coming to an end. Leo's words prophesied the change. The market had become the great equalizer—it was, and continues to be, the finest example of economic Darwinism in our time. Only the strong—or in this case, the best—will survive the changing landscape.

But as the CME was going through a metamorphosis, so was the business I was trying to run at Commerz Futures. During the infancy of the e-mini concept, the board made a very important change to the clearinghouse rules. The rule change created a limited liability on the part of the collective clearing members as opposed to a "good to the last drop" policy, which was the custom. "Good to the last drop" implied that if there was a default, then the clearing members would collectively make up the balance needed in order to maintain the market and exchange. This required every large institution to create a subsidiary that would act as a buffer in the event of a major calamity. The reality is that if the CME called and asked for $100 million because Morgan was in default, my first call as the president of Commerz Futures would be to the bank's lawyer, not the treasurer!

The limited liability allowed the FCM community two very important efficiencies: First, it created the necessary financial buffer in a way that made sense to the financial institutions facing the fiduciary responsibility of investors. Second, it allowed the firms such as Commerz Futures the luxury of repatriating the capital that was put up for the sub and bringing it back to a more efficient use by the parent institution. Because of the change in the clearing structure and the growing electronic markets in Chicago, I was called to Frankfurt to give a presentation to the bank's board of directors.

I arrived in Frankfurt on May 1, 2001. Being in a state of sleep deprivation caused by jet lag, I didn't notice the security forces lining the streets as the taxi took me to my hotel. I was booked at the Frankfurter House, directly across the street from the Commerzbank tower in the heart of Frankfurt. After unpacking and taking a light hour-long nap, I ventured outside to experience what I thought to be European Labor Day. But rather than a day of picnics with hot dogs and coleslaw, as we would see in the United States, May Day in European countries is often a day of demonstrations by the working class that are attended by the police. My first day in Germany was witness to a bloody riot between Turkish workers and German security forces. I stood in shock, trying in vain to understand the reason, as I watched the two groups beat each other bloody with sticks and clubs.

The following day was the presentation to board members who would be responsible for the capital needs of the subsidiary of which I was the president. The bank's boardroom is a grand, open space with magnificent floor-to-ceiling windows showcasing the city of Frankfurt from every view. As I began my presentation, I quickly realized that the board members had short attention spans and it was imperative that I work quickly. I went over a PowerPoint that showed the rule change and the fact that capital could be repatriated to Frankfurt. After I had spoken for 15 minutes, a vote was taken. No objections were raised, and the measure was passed. One of the board members, an older gentleman from Austria, said, "Very good, Jack. You're Armenian, right? You know what we say about Armenians in Austria? There's nothing worse than an Armenian Jew! Oh, but this is because of your negotiating power, of course." Confused, I didn't know whether to tell him I wasn't Jewish or throw my pen at his head. Back home, where I have a great number of Jewish friends, being called an Armenian Jew would usually be complimentary. But hearing it said with such disdain by this Austrian gentleman who had survived the Second World War put things into perspective. As strange as it sounds, all I can remember as I went to my hotel room that evening is thinking about my grandparents and their stories of surviving the Turkish atrocities.

The other reason I was in Germany was to spread the word about the new electronic markets in Chicago. As part owner of Eurex, the Commerzbank community was very familiar with the concept of electronic trading. In fact, it was the Bund traders at Commerz who were partially responsible for the forced migration of liquidity from the LIFFE to Eurex for the Bund contract. But everyone seemed to be excited about trading the stock indexes electronically. It didn't take long to realize that the S&P 500, along with the other stock indexes traded on Globex, are the most thrilling action online. A needed rule change by the German regulators allowed the retail public to open accounts without the regulatory ambiguity that had surrounded the procedure previously.

The number of new accounts began with a trickle but soon started to come in waves. Introducing brokers in Munich and Hamburg started to find huge success with traders in remote regions of the German countryside who had never been exposed to the capital markets before but found an exciting hobby in electronic trading. I met with many members of the bank's technology department, who listened intently as I explained the upgrades to the trading systems in the CME's matching engine.

It was the techies who really understood the true power of the electronic marketplace. They grasped that automating trading strategies would allow the trader to multitask and become more efficient. The bottom line was that the introduction of electronic platforms gave the bank two very important things: It gave the bank the ability to monitor traders in a way never before imagined, which was a necessity after the Barings debacle, and it gave the bank a much more efficient use of its capital. Simply put, electronic markets allow the institution to get the most out of its traders rather than having them concentrate on a single market.

WHAT HAPPENED TO THE PIT?

Returning to Chicago, it was clear that the status quo in the pit was changing as the liquidity became divided between the open outcry and the electronic platforms. As the open interest in the S&P and Nasdaq futures contracts began to grow in the e-mini products, the daily sessions were beginning to suffer. The prized real estate of the pit was becoming an open space with room to roam. Only five years earlier, heated debates had raged about the space in the pit, especially when locations and brokerage businesses were sold between members. Merton Miller, a former board member and Nobel laureate, was fond of saying that the exchange should auction off the locations in the pit as they would seats on the exchange. It seemed crazy to most of the other board members, but, in hindsight, it would probably have been the smartest way to handle the situation.

Mert was a wonderful man and a marvelous academic. He had degrees from Harvard and Johns Hopkins and was a professor at the University of Chicago Graduate School of Business, where he received the Nobel prize in economics. Mert always took the time to talk to me when he saw me at the opera or a social event around the city, introducing me as his colleague on the CME board. There are very few things in this world that have made me prouder than hearing Merton Miller call me his colleague. Merton died in the summer of 2000, and we all miss him greatly.

I had become friendly with Mert when he asked me to help stop what he referred to as the "abomination which is rule 80-A." Rule 80-A cut off the index arbitrageurs when the Dow Jones Industrial Average went up or down 50 points. As the stock market raced higher and higher, the 50-point collar became an obstacle to futures growth. At its inception, Mert had called the rule "anti-futures"—and he was absolutely correct.

This rule stopped the natural order flow coming from the arbs, and the absence of their liquidity began to affect the market condition. As chairman of the equity index committee, I called upon my friends at Cooper Neff, who had expressed a desire to help, along with Vinny and Denny to assist me in coming up with the proper arguments to present to the NYSE. It was no secret that the NYSE specialists had no love for the arbs, which they considered parasitic. In fact, upon meeting NYSE chairman Dick Grasso in the CME elevator, I asked him if they were going to do something about the 50-point collar. He snapped back, "Yeah, we're going to change it to 25!" Fortunately, policy makers came to their senses and realized that eliminating the arbs from the trade has the opposite effect of the rule's intended purpose.

As Mert had prophesied years earlier, the collar eliminates a necessary portion of the liquidity equation, leading to increased volatility. Instead of acting as a circuit breaker, the collar was making the market even less liquid and thus more susceptible to panic selling.

MARKET TRANSPARENCY

What was happening to the pit? That was the question most asked by traders as I walked the exchange floor. Even though there seemed to be order flow in the open outcry session, the orders were larger and chunkier than before. In other words, the smaller orders that fed the local community began to work their way onto the screen, leaving the larger institutional orders for the traders to live on. It was obvious that we were in the midst of an evolutionary state. I was watching the market morph before my very eyes. What had been an open outcry market was quickly turning into an electronic market with an open outcry pit of liquidity.

The real secret is that the edge has left the pit. In fact, the lack of information on the floor puts the local at a severe disadvantage to the trader off the floor. This has put the traditional local in a state of flux, forcing many longtime members to do some serious soul-searching as to whether they're traders or are lucky enough to have a great spot to scalp in the pit. For those who feel they are true traders, the transition is relatively smooth, with a short learning curve. It's the traditional scalper who finds the transition difficult. The energy needed to be a good scalper has no place in the world of electronic trading. The mantra for the membership became "Change your approach and embrace the electronic platform—or cease to be a market participant!"

The membership wasn't the only group that was forced to change. The FCM community was in the middle of the evolutionary trend, leaving many in the industry wondering if there was a future in futures. It was during this period that many of the old-time brokerage houses began to lay off floor personal and consolidate their operations out of the New York offices. The president of the CME at the time, Jim McNulty, had proposed a plan that would essentially close down the floor within a five-year period. Many on the board, including myself, thought that a forced migration would not be as effective as a market-driven solution. As an officer of Commerz Futures, I had to try to give my customers the most liquid products available, but it was at a steep cost. The FCMs were forced to offer two different platforms to their customers.

The traditional open outcry platform involved order desks, brokers, and processing, and the new electronic platform had inherent risk controls built into the technology and could be easily distributed to the masses. I quickly began to change the business plan for Commerz Futures, which put a greater emphasis on selling electronically traded products as opposed to the old-style pit-traded markets. It became apparent to me that certain segments of the end-user community, the institutions, did not want to use the smaller version of the S&P 500 but that the retail customer was in love with the concept.

For years, as the stock market moved to new highs, the margins on the stock index futures contracts grew to unmanageable levels. Margins, or performance bonds, are calculated by the volatile condition of the market. The higher the volatility, the higher the margin; the lower the volatility, the lower the margin. This is why an S&P contract worth $250,000 can have a margin 10 times that of a Eurodollar futures contract, which has a $1 million face value. The stock market is much more volatile than the fixed-income market; therefore, a larger financial buffer is needed between the customers and the clearinghouse. As these performance bonds grew larger and larger, retail customers began to shy away from the products. It wasn't only the large haircut involved (a *haircut* is the amount of capital needed to hold a position), but the retail brokers realized they were better off putting clients into positions that were not so capital intensive. The e-mini changed all that. The market was becoming a two-tiered marketplace with the large institutional orders still coming into the open outcry arena and the small retail orders flowing through the electronic platforms. This was a hidden blessing for the FCMs, which had been struggling for years, fighting regulators and contracting commissions. The economies of scale now allowed the FCMs to distribute the products and services with risk management controls built right into the functionality. It was now possible for a futures company to open and monitor 10 times the number of accounts with the same number of brokers and employees.

A LEVEL PLAYING FIELD

But what was a gold mine for a certain segment of the exchange population—the FCMs—was a disaster for others. Locals who had made a living standing in front of brokers whose orders included the small retail customer base began to disappear. The same traders who were taking down 100 contracts at a time now found that their skills as market makers were no longer necessary. It was easy to understand; the smaller order flow that is directed by the brokerage community was taken to the electronic platform because of the increased profit margin on commissions and the added risk management controls.

Prior to the adoption of the electronic platforms, futures brokers had to carefully monitor every retail account so that they did not cause a debit. In the futures industry, the registered broker is the first line of defense in the event a customer goes debit. The FCM is the second line of defense, and the exchange is the final guarantor of all trades that take place within the CME's universe. As the number of retail account openings accelerated, the number of small orders coming into the pit grew smaller and smaller. The pit community began to dwindle. During the years from 2000 to 2004 over half of the market makers left. These were the same traders who populated the S&P pit right from its inception at the old CME at 444 W. Jackson back in 1982, and they now had been forced out by the computer.

As we look back on the past few years, the rapid growth and the appetite for electronically traded products seems amazing. But as much as we would like to think that Chicago is the center of the universe, we quickly realize that the growth of our markets is part of the growing global landscape of trading and investing. When I was in Germany during the early part of 2001 I could see that the average European investor was underweighted in equities. This was done purposely because of the nationalized pensions and an entrenched middle management bureaucracy.

Once the rules governing the pensions changed, capital began to flow from all corners of the Euro zone, which coincided with a weaker dollar, making U.S. equities an even greater value. But as large as I felt the European customer base would be, it's nothing compared to the possibilities that can come from Asia. The order flow from Asia, and in particular China, will, in 5 to 10 years, dwarf what is coming out of any other time zone.

Who could have known that the fact that the CBOT landed the Dow Jones futures contract would be the catalyst for one of the greatest changes the futures industry has ever experienced. Recall Leo Melamed's words: "Behind every disappointment lies a gem of opportunity." He gave us his vision of the futures industry years ahead of time in the last chapter of his book *Escape to the Futures* in 1996. His dreams became our reality. Leo has been a statesman, a great market philosopher, a successful trader, the greatest innovator in CME history—and now he can be called the Prophet of Wacker Drive.

CHAPTER 6

Technical Analysis

The Tools of the Trade

In the mid-1990s, when I was building up my floor brokerage business around the equity pits of the Chicago Mercantile Exchange (CME), I used to maintain my own charts on the markets. I would constantly take the daily high, low, and settlement of the market, desperately searching for a recognizable pattern that would generate a high-percentage trading opportunity. I felt that the technical analysis would be a value-added service to my clients. The art of charting the markets has had a long history. There is a multitude of ways to chart the price action of the market, and the variations on the methods are as numerous as the books found in the business section of any bookstore.

As a trader, I felt that it was important for me to know the support and resistance levels that the rest of the participants had so that I could keep up with the crowd. Support and resistance levels become important for various reasons, the most important being that the rest of the trading community is looking at the exact same chart, which gives a majority of chartists the same levels.

One day as I was updating my technical work at my home office, my seven-year-old son came into the room to observe the work I was doing. He was aware of my profession in the markets and had come down to view the action in the visitor's gallery of the CME with his mother and sister many times. He had grasped the concept of being short the market at an early age. He understood that it was possible to sell something without owning it first. As he stood watching me, he asked questions about what I was doing and the charts I was updating. I told him that I was looking at the Nasdaq futures market, an index made up of the tech companies such as the one that makes the computer we were looking at.

I explained to him that I was looking for resistance so that I could sell the market and establish a short position. I told him that I was to sell the market if it reached a certain level; if that didn't work I would buy it back and try selling it at another level higher. After a few seconds of silence he looked at me and looked at the chart in front of both of us and said, "Dad, why are you selling it? That's stupid. The market is going up!" I immediately laughed and thought how cute it was for my little boy to have an opinion of the market. As he left the room I found myself staring at the Nasdaq chart and then it hit me—like a brick in the forehead—that my son was absolutely right! Why would I want to sell the market when the path of least resistance is up? It suddenly dawned on me that I might have the right information, but I wasn't using it properly.

DOES TECHNICAL ANALYSIS REALLY WORK?

One of the biggest problems that new traders face is the avalanche of material on technical analysis that they feel compelled to read and understand. The average trader finds one or two technical disciplines that they feel give them the best read on the market. There are many different ways to chart the market. There are the Gann methodology, the Elliott Wave Theory, and countless other proven strategies. Every one of these technical forms has had books written and rewritten about the credibility of the discipline. You can create a point-and-figure chart that takes only price action into account. There are time charts that give the observer an idea of the movement of the market at various times in the trading session. You can look at the relative strength of the market by finding moving averages that guide traders along the path of least resistance. Finding the proper form of technical analysis as a trader is much like finding the right pair of shoes—what looks good to you might not be right for everyone.

Often when I sit on a panel discussing technical analysis, I am amazed by the lack of depth on the part of the participants. One memorable day, I found myself between an "expert" on Japanese candlestick charting methods and a new astrological technician who called the market by the placement of the stars. I thought it rather ironic considering that I couldn't care less about astrology and have always considered the candlestick method of charting to be more artistic than practical. After hearing the two experienced speakers talk about their respective strategies, it was my turn to tell the 200 audience members the truth they so desperately came to hear.

I began my talk by asking the audience to forget everything they had just heard. A stunned crowd looked at me as if they couldn't believe what I had just said. As I looked around me, I could see that my fellow panelists were also a bit perturbed at the comment. I thought it was important for someone to give the audience a sense of the fundamental aspect of the markets. I asked if anyone in the crowd had ever done any fundamental research on the markets they were presently trading. To my surprise, only a handful of those in attendance claimed that they did any type of fundamental analysis on the markets before making a trading or an investment decision.

The main point of my presentation was to give technical traders a feel for the fundamental side of the market. In fact, many seasoned veterans will confess that they look at both sides of market analysis before making a decision. One good example is my old friend and customer Vince McLaughlin. Vinny would talk about the fundamentals of the market and his expertise, and avoid any discussion on the technical levels of the day. Whenever I brought up an area of support or resistance, Vinny would respond, "Don't talk to me about voodoo!" He would laugh and call it hocus-pocus—until he found himself stuck on an arb.

As an arbitrageur, it was up to Vinny to make sure there was no exposure when putting on the trade—after all, the concept of arbitrage is to buy and sell a like product, simultaneously making a small profit on the discrepancy and inefficiency created in the market. As soon as he was stuck, Vinny would become a technical trader, asking me where the support or resistance was in the day's session.

One of the first jobs I had in the futures industry was as a runner for a small, local grain company called Chicago Grain. Still a student at Loyola University, I used the analytical training that was instilled in me by the Jesuits and became a sponge for information. I asked every question imaginable, looking for those I felt knew the market structure well enough that they could explain it to me in simple terms. One of the first people who caught my attention was an eclectic individual named Ted Lee Fisher, whom we would affectionately refer to as "Doc."

Doc was a product of the 1960s, taking the lessons learned by his generation and incorporated them into the daily routine of work and life. As a clerk servicing his accounts, Doc would come into contact with me only if there was a problem with a customer or if I had a question regarding the positions acquired. What really stood out about Doc was that he was sincere in teaching those who asked anything that he knew about markets and trading. I became fascinated with the way Doc approached the market. He had a way of incorporating the technical world with the fundamentals around him. For a novice in the markets such as me, being able to make sense of the chaos that exists in the marketplace is important. Looking at the fundamentals of the market doesn't necessarily show traders and investors the true nature of the market condition unless they can look at the price action and time factors that guide them.

Doc was the biggest producer at Chicago Grain when I was a runner. In fact, the first business dinner I was ever invited to came at his expense, when he treated the floor crew for helping him generate a record month in commissions. At that dinner I realized that if I were to ask him the right questions, the knowledge base that I could tap into was enormous. During the drive to and from dinner I must have asked over 20 questions, ranging from his background to his methodology for trading.

I came to understand that he was an original rebel, having taken a year off from school at Ann Arbor to ride his motorcycle across the country. He was a real Easy Rider! Not only was he a wealth of information when it came to futures trading, but it seemed that he had an educated opinion about many of the world's thorniest issues. Much of the technical analysis that guides his trading has roots in the observations he made as a youth in the turbulent decade of the 1960s.

I have met thousands of so-called technicians who claim that their work on the markets is the definitive work when it comes to technical analysis. Out of the thousands, there is only a handful that merits any attention whatsoever. Out of the handful, Doc is the only one I would consider unique in his approach. For decades, he has refused interview requests and has avoided market reporters, until now. For the first time, Doc has agreed to share his ideas and insights into market structure and trading.

INTERVIEW WITH TED FISHER

Bouroudjian: Ted, you're unique in the way you look at technical analysis and your approach to the markets. Many have looked at you for years as the most unique technician in the markets today.

Much of what you are today is because of where you came from and the experiences in your life. Tell us a little bit about your background, where you came from, and how you got into the market.

Fisher: The short story is I went to the University of Michigan in 1966; it was either that or Vietnam. I went to a lecture by a Harvard professor that winter on extraterrestrial travel. That professor's name was Timothy Leary. I also went to a concert by a New York rock band with an artist who had a slide show. That rock band happened to be Velvet Underground and the artist was Andy Warhol. And that more or less set the tone for my undergraduate career. Then I went on to learn. After receiving a bachelor's degree in economics, I studied for a master's degree in philosophy, and I was invited into a social science research-integrated program in which I had to be literate in four disciplines.

The four disciplines were anthropology, philosophy, history, and sociology. My first year in graduate school, my professors recommended me for a Racom Prize—three people at the University of Michigan receive this prize every year; I was one of them. It was an incredible prize at the time.

It was a cash stipend of $7,500, which was well in excess of the cost of a new Corvette, which I wanted to buy. Plus, I was given a teaching position in which I was responsible for my own curriculum, and paid as a teacher. Most important at the time, all my expenses were paid.

When I was coming out of the University of Michigan, funds had been more or less cut off by the Nixon administration for the kind of research that I was interested in, which was, more or less, as punishment for our efforts to end the war. Along with that, I had a personal crisis in which my mother had breast cancer. I was able to talk my mother into seeking therapy, and she recovered and actually, thirty-five years later she has been totally free of cancer. But at the same time, it was somewhat of a personal crisis and I decided, what the heck, I would go into the corporate world, because there was no real opportunity in the academic world.

I had interviewed, of all places, through a family connection at Sperry Rand. They were very excited to meet me. They decided to create a position within their Washington office to do lobbying. As it turns out, they have plants in various states, and the idea was, I would go in and represent Sperry's views that we have substantial votes in their district, and we would appreciate their help. They said, "We have to have approval from New York. Go back to Ann Arbor, relax for a few weeks, we'll call you." So I'm sitting in Ann Arbor one day, and a man walks in. And I'm watching a basketball game; he says, "What are you doing? I never met you before." And I give him the story, and he says, "What? Are you out of your mind? For $17,500 a year, you're going to do *that*? You have to come down to my office tomorrow morning." So it turns out he's a commodity broker. And it's August in 1976 and gold had just been approved for trade in the United States and the Europeans ran it up to $200 an ounce, and as soon as it was legal to trade in the United States, they pushed the price down to $100 per troy ounce.

So I'm sitting in this office the first day and I'm watching it trade $101.50, hitting at $101.50 three or four times, and I buy some contracts with the residual funds that I had from my savings from graduate school. And from that day, gold never really down-ticked, until it got to $270 an ounce. And he and I became partners in a brokerage firm, and built a successful commodities business. After that, we went to Chicago and set up a business with Fred Brosowski at Chicago Grain and Co., and the rest is history.

Bouroudjian: Your approach to technical analysis is much different than other technicians. You have a way of incorporating the world around you with the charts you follow. How did you develop your concepts?

Give us an idea of how it's different in your mind, and what factors drive your work.

Fisher: Well, first of all, I came into the futures industry as an economist, with the understanding that the things that the Nixon administration had done in terms of floating the dollar along with other economic policies, based on certain economic history, would lead to volatile market phenomena. Full disclosure, early in my career, even though I was totally right the direction of the market, I got slapped a couple of times—that means losing 90 percent of my equity (laughs).

I went from being an economist/trader to an economist/technician/trader, and I brought to technical analysis the discipline that I acquired at the University of Michigan. The first thing I did was consume the entire body of technical analysis that was available in print form. This included everything available from the nineteenth and twentieth century. And of course, as I consumed it and processed it, I was always risking my own capital with the ideas that I came to know and understand through technical analysis. And so it was a refining process and a hardening process by risking my own money and applying the ideas that I synthesized through technical analysis.

Bouroudjian: Tell us a little bit about your ideas that you synthesized. What types of work influenced you the most and how did you create your own derivative approach.

Fisher: Well, the root of my understanding of the market's truth came from a book that I highly recommend for everybody to read, *Reminiscences of a Stock Operator* by Edwin Lefèvre. It's really the biography of Jesse Livermore, a legendary market speculator. It's not really about technical analysis, but it is an anecdotal history of every way in which he was right the market, and ultimately got blown out of his positions by hook and by crook.

Initially, that was really the operative tool I had before I became a technician. After reading *Reminiscences*' I read all of Gann's work. I paid substantial sums of money to buy esoteric documents that Gann had produced only for his students, for which they had to pay $30,000 or $40,000 in the 1930s and 1940s to get. Then I read Ralph Distan, Wyckoff, and Elliott. And I have to say that Elliott, and the Elliott Wave Theory, had a big impact on me. But one has to be careful with Elliott, because it's an application and if you subscribe to a newsletter by someone who represents themselves to be an Elliott theorist, even if they were very close to Elliott, you may find that they're more interested in maintaining their track record to sell books, rather than maintaining a track record that will make you wealthy. So the technical analysis, or the methodology, that I have used for years in my trading is a synthesis of what I call structural analysis.

Structural analysis is looking at price and time basically—that would be price charts. I brought with me, from my academic studies at the University of Michigan, an understanding of business cycles because that was one of my pet studies. Long before I knew I was going to be a trader, I heard a lot of people talk about trading markets, using the sun and the moon, and various things, but what I look at is multigenerational cycles that basically relate to the life and death of capital itself. The underlying hypothesis of this is that capital is organic, and by being organic, has the natural life and death cycle. And the second assumption that is embedded in this is that the son will never learn from the mistakes of the father. And if you put those two things together and go back and look at history, it becomes a valuable tool.

I have a chart of 10-year yields that goes back to 1812, and when I put that chart in front of people, even a neophyte can see the amplitude of time. They can instantly notice the cyclic pattern over time. Unfortunately, most people are shortsighted in their approach to trading; a cycle that runs from 1942 to 1981 is irrelevant or not particularly useful for them. Whereas for me it can have a tremendous impact on my work. I'm really trying to catch the long-term trend of any particular market that I'm engaged in, not just a day-trade or a short-term fling, but, rather, a position that could last weeks. So an amplitude of that magnitude is right up my alley. And then using my structural analysis, and momentum studies, I try to enhance my participation in the trend, but maintain my position in the trend.

Bouroudjian: Your concept of structural analysis is unique. Your understanding of the market structure makes your work different in that your foundations are rooted in the fundamental analysis of the capital market's condition.

Would you consider yourself a technician who looks for confirmation through the fundamentals of the economy, or vice versa?

Fisher: Oh, I really believe that the market predicts events, and events do not predict the market, and that if you want to know the future you really need to look at the structure of the market. The work may not be able to forecast what the event is, but you can prepare yourself and participate in the trend that the event will generate. And 9/11 is one of the most classic examples of this. Although, throughout my career, I could give you any number of them.

In June of 2001 I wrote a very brief thesis and gave it to my clients, which happened to be institutional clients, such as funding desks in New York money banks, investments banks, et cetera, et cetera. The Fed funds rate was roughly 6 percent at the time, and everybody around me, all my peers and colleagues, were expecting the Fed to raise rates. I wrote a brief that forecast deposit rates to decline to one and a quarter percent—and that was June of 2001. I took a very substantial position, long Eurodollars, the first 12 contracts, short S&Ps, long gold, long Swiss francs. And the position was paying me all of July and all of August. Then September 11th came along, with a big impact to the market. And not one of those trends was interrupted.

With all that was happening, it was the most difficult time for me to accept the success of my trading. But because of the tragedy that surrounded 9/11, every position that I had was profitable. The position was paying me before 9/11 and it paid huge after 9/11. Those trends remained intact for anything from 6 to 18 months after 9/11. And ironically, deposit rates declined to 1.25 percent. I got 1.25 percent, not out of a hat, but on a mathematical calculation based upon the capital markets structure that I saw at the time.

Bouroudjian: There's been an explosion of electronic trading. The global futures exchanges have witnessed phenomenal growth over the last few years with the creation of the e-mini concept. There has been a migration of open interest into the electronic platforms. We've seen a proliferation of electronic products and services all across the globe.

What impact, if any, does it have on technical analysis, or your work specifically?

Fisher: Well, first of all the larger the volume and open interest of a market, the more valuable technical analysis becomes. If you take a very small market with very thin participation, it becomes easy to push the market around and distort price movements. Overall, you can't ultimately disguise the pattern, but you can distort things. So the larger the volume and the larger the participation in a market, the better it is for a technician. But, in fact, this brings you to one of the most important understandings, whether you're a technician or whatever, about the market. It's what we always call the edge.

When you're standing in the pit, and the market is a four bid at five if you can buy the bid side of the market, when everybody around you is still bid, then you have what we call the edge. Because now you are long at four, with the opportunity to sell the market at five or scratch the trade if fours begin to go. So the edge is the dream for someone who's looking to trade as a scalper. The part of the edge that most people don't understand, and it's integral in my style of trading, involves giving up the perceived edge because I don't normally buy the bid, or sell the offer.

What I normally am doing is, if the market is making new highs, I'm buying the offer, and if the market is making new lows, I'm selling the bid. In other words, I buy strength and sell weakness. It drives most traders crazy to even think of doing something like that, because they want to buy the market cheap and sell the market when it's expensive. But the edge, when you really understand it, is buying or selling the market as it's turning. There's a magical moment when that five offer is turning five bid after you just bought it! That's where the edge really becomes useful to an aggressive trader, who's trying to catch the market when most are oblivious.

In the old days in the pit, I would be standing there, and the market would trade to a new high. Well, now, it's well offered at that price, guess what? I'm buying it. And guess what? Everybody's happy to sell it to me. But then, I'm buying fives, fives are trading—all of a sudden it's five bid! The traders who didn't lay it off to another local just spread out the position using another contract, but now they're short at five, and it's five bid. They no longer have the edge. That's the biggest secret about understanding the market and about understanding trading and about what the edge is. Perception and reality can be confusing—what you think is the edge and what is the real edge are two different things. And until you recognize that the edge is fluid, not absolute, and are willing to flow with the edge, then you're going to find trading very difficult.

Bouroudjian: I'll give you one more question. As a former teacher, aside from the lecture on the edge, which is a wonderful bit of information, what else would you tell somebody who is just starting to trade? What have you noticed throughout your career that can guide new traders? What can they do to become better traders?

Fisher: Initially any new trader must understand risk. And again, most people think of risk in fairly absolute terms. Risk, to some people, means that if I expose my money, then I could lose it. And so they live in fear of investment losses. What they don't understand is that if they don't expose their capital, they can lose it. That is risk!

For me, through my life, I've seen periods in which the world was made for speculation. And if you wanted to compound your money, you could risk a little bit. If you were to take a little bit of risk, and if you were right, the compounding and return would be huge and enormous, and you could create enormous amounts of wealth by doing that. There have been other periods in my life, in a generational sense, in which the time to take risk was over, and the time to maintain purchasing power parity was clearly needed. Purchasing power parity is, in other words, if it costs $100 to buy a diamond in today's market, you don't care what your money is worth. Whether you have $100 in the future or $1,000 in the future, you want to buy that same diamond, something real, something measurable, et cetera, et cetera.

One of the examples I always use is that in 1932 soybeans were $0.44 a bushel and in 1952 they were $4.50 a bushel. And for sure, there was no genetic modification of soybeans from 1932 to 1952. Soybeans still had the same protein count, oil count, et cetera, et cetera, in 1932 that they had in 1952. But we had a government that took away the gold, inflated ourselves out of a depression, and inflated ourselves through a war, World War II. By 1952 it took 10 times, virtually 10 times the amount of U.S. dollars to buy a bushel of soybeans, so from 1932 to 1952, using this example, it's obvious that it wasn't a time to speculate; it was a time to preserve your purchasing power parity.

It becomes a part of financial survival to find vehicles and ways to maintain purchasing power parity. If a trader or investor can understand these concepts, then they have a much better grasp of what risk really is, and how it works. Remember, in the shorter-term concept, markets always trade from fear to greed and greed to fear and you need to find ways to separate yourself from the emotions and to participate in the trend. Whether you do it through fundamental analysis, or you do it through technical analysis, for traders to be successful they must fully understand these concepts.

My one great weakness, and one which I'm still researching, trying to find an answer for, is the exit strategy. Most people spend all their homework and all their research on initiating a trade and they spend no time whatsoever on how to get out. My thesis is that if you catch a trend, it doesn't matter whether you catch it from a fundamental idea or a technical idea or whatever, when the trend is ending, and the move is terminating, you need to have a way to identify that, and a way to take you out of the market before the market takes back what it's given to you.

Listening to Doc speak about his work is exciting for me as a student of the markets and a longtime fan of his work. Most traders don't understand that the true talents in the field of technical analysis are individuals whom the average person has never heard of. A genius such as Doc has always run from any exposure because of what he might call "bad karma." It's also the common denominator among the best analysts in the industry. The less exposure, the better it is. If you find a successful strategy, keep it to yourself or a select group of clients. As a devout Buddhist, Doc has incorporated many Eastern philosophical precepts into his everyday routine. What makes his work so different from that of other technicians is two very important variables: his ability to be correct on the direction and reaction of the marketplace during major price swings and the natural ability to use the fundamentals of the market to justify the work he does.

In early September 2001, I stopped by Doc's desk on the upper trading floor of the CME, as I did every Friday before reporting on the unemployment release on CNBC. During this time I would ask different traders and brokers about their thoughts on the market and if there was any action in Europe that would work its way into our session. On this particular day it was difficult for me to get Doc's attention. I was not greeted with his customary smile and peace sign; rather, he had a concerned, intense look on his face. Talking with him, I realized that he was expecting something very big to happen based on the structural analysis that is an important component of his work. He looked me in the eye and said, "Jack, I don't know what's going to happen, but it's going to be very big!"

He was talking about a major move in the market because his work showed that the entire capital marketplace was about to experience some type of large volatile move. I've always thought that Doc was a bit eccentric, but I had never known him to show this noticeable degree of concern. I remember that the unemployment number was somewhat subdued, with a slightly larger increase in nonfarm payrolls, which made stocks rally and the fixed-income market break a couple of ticks. Later in the afternoon, my thoughts still on the conversation I had had with Doc in the morning, I asked him if we could speak for a bit.

He told me that he had seen certain anomalies in the marketplace over the course of his 30-some years in the business and knew, from his research, that the markets were positioned for a major dysfunction. I have never believed in soothsayers of any kind, whether fortune tellers or horoscopes, but the conversation I had with Doc was as close as I'll ever get. That day was Friday, September 7, 2001. Four days later, on September 11, the United States would be attacked by Islamic terrorists and the capital markets would be sent into shock and turmoil.

The technical analysts in the business fall into two major categories: those who have never traded and want to teach the world what they have never been able to fully grasp, and traders who feel it's important to teach others the niche they have found in the market. Usually it is a derivative of a proven discipline such as the Gann or Elliot Wave method. The first group encompasses the charlatans of the industry. At trading conferences, I laugh at the books I see for sale. Occasionally, I come across a bizarre methodology like *Nature and Trading* and I ask myself, "Who would buy a book such as this?" Invariably, someone walks up to the booth and spends hard-earned money on what is, in my humble opinion, trash. The second group is a little bit more credible, having felt the pain of a position before trying to teach the world to do the same. But ask yourself, "Why is the methodology being shared with the masses?" The finest traders believe it's important to keep a strategy as concealed as possible in order to maintain its effectiveness. Only after a strategy is no longer producing high-percentage trades do you share it with the rest of the world.

Mike Norman hosts a radio show called *Economic Contrarian* on Biz Radio, a Texas-based radio network with large national distribution. Norman is a lively personality whose experience on the various trading floors makes him the perfect person to host a show about the markets. Too often I find myself listening to or watching people who have no clue about market structure and trading. Norman is a refreshing change because of his depth of knowledge and insightful opinions about the markets.

One morning, Norman was booked to interview a gentleman who had based his trading methodology on pure math. T.H. Murrey, of Murrey Math, is a tall southern gentleman from Tennessee who seems an unlikely candidate to be sitting in front of a computer screen trading stocks and options. Murrey has a devoted following of traders who find his approach to the markets an easy discipline to follow but very unorthodox for experienced traders.

The work is based on the power of a single number, which, according to Murrey, is the secret to trading success. At first Norman let Murrey talk about his strategy and his approach to the markets. But as the interview progressed, Norman became incensed at Murrey's statement that he had discovered the Holy Grail of trading. A heated exchange ensued between the two, in which Norman maintained that there is no Holy Grail' in trading, calling the work "garbage" and Murrey "a quack."

While Norman was chastising him, Murrey shouted back that he had won the "Holy Grail award" in trading the previous year. The exchange went on for several minutes until Norman ended the show by saying he could no longer expose his listening audience to something he considered rubbish. It was a fascinating show in which both parties demonstrated the age-old debate between true fundamental skeptics, represented by Norman, and eclectic technical analysts, embodied in Murrey.

EVERYONE IS LOOKING AT THE SAME CHART

If there is any one fault that most technical analysts share, it's the inability to get rid of the charts when necessary. Another Bingism comes to mind: "You have to know when to throw the charts away." The ability to do this is one of the things that made Bing Sung such a good trader. An important part of any trader's character is the ability to incorporate the work he or she uses with natural gut instinct. Too many people become married to a strategy for whatever reason. Perhaps new traders and investors need the simplicity of a discipline that allows them to make what they feel are qualified investment decisions based on a given methodology.

This approach gives part-time traders a tool by which they can map the price action of a market and make sensible trades with the handicap of time and lack of homework. Most people don'trecognize that becoming married to one particular strategy can be disastrous. This is the primary reason that over 90 percent of the retail public who open futures trading accounts lose their money within three months of starting. How can that be? How can so many people consistently lose? When new traders and investors start thinking they can compete with seasoned veterans on an equal playing field, tthey are destined to fail.

New traders cannot compete with the veterans of the markets and expect the same level of success unless they have the right combination of discipline, time, and a proven gut feel for trading. New traders usually find a strategy they understand and then become enamored with it. Most of these traders end up finding out what the old-timers have known for years: If you live by the sword, then you'll die by the sword. In other words, if you find yourself married to a certain methodology, then that methodology might one day bring you down.

Imagine a trader who based his or her entire strategy on the relative strength indicators of the market. This trader would have been selling the stock market all through the late 1990s because the relative strength index (RSI) was so high. With hindsight, it's clear that this trader would have been horribly wrong to stick to this disciplined approach.

There's a big difference between calling yourself a technical trader and understanding the market structure, along with the charts and price action. Aaron Reinglass, an old friend of mine, is a perfect example of the seasoned technician who incorporates fundamentals into his analysis. Aaron is always fond of saying that if a person doesn't know how or why he or she made a profit in the market, then there's a good chance he or she will eventually lose it.

Reinglass is the son of Auschwitz survivors, who had a big influence on his worldview. A skeptic by nature, he's an excellent technician with an uncanny way of finding the hidden news story that could make a large market impact. He occasionally comes to me with an article or story from a major publication or the Internet supporting or opposing an opinion we discussed the previous day. The most memorable thing he ever said to me was at the beginning of the move down in stocks during late 2000 and early 2001: "Remember, Jack, drinking doesn't cause hangovers—stopping drinking causes the hangover!" What he was trying to say was that the charts were confirming what we had suspected all along: that the market was in serious trouble. I've borrowed that line from him and used it, with his blessing, on many occasions.

The real question that all students of the markets should ask is whether charting the markets gives them a true edge in trading or not. As I talk to audiences around the country, one question that seems to come up again and again is whether I use technical analysis and, if so, what disciplines I follow. It seems fairly obvious that the market observer will notice certain patterns that develop over the course of a trading session. You might argue that the market will do whatever it wants (the random walk theory, which we'll discuss in Chapter 7) and that charting the price action is after-the-fact analysis. There are moving averages that can range from intraday to yearly, which give traders an idea of moving value by setting an average price.

Charting price action is a little different in that traders are looking for certain patterns to reemerge so that they can be proactive in placing what they consider to be high-percentage trades. These charts can be generated from a tick-by-tick account of the action to a time frame of any choosing. This type of analysis is the most commonly used by beginners and has its own flaws. Certain types of market study such as point-and-figure analysis and pivot point methodology are destined to fail because of their popularity. Being the easiest way to begin a trading career, these simplistic approaches become self-fulfilling prophecies for professionals that feed off of the retail accounts.

It's only logical: If the entire retail world is looking at the same chart and deducing the same analysis from the price action, then they're bound to do the same thing collectively. Another of the best-kept secrets on the Street is that the professional trader makes a great living off the uneducated retail investor who uses simple support and resistance levels to get in and out of positions. This is almost the same as telling the world what you're doing and thinking as a trader.

EDUCATION IS KEY

I have always made it my personal goal to educate our customers in the nuances of technical analysis. I find it ironic that educated people will open accounts with brokers who offer the most simplistic type of work. Pivot point analysis is the first thing that a runner learns when starting on the floor of any exchange. It takes the high, low, and close from the previous day and comes up with a pivot for the following day's session. It sounds great except for the fact that the entire world is looking at the exact same points. That's my biggest complaint with most of the work available to the general public—if the work is held by the masses, then it's destined to fail because, as we know, 90 percent of the trading public loses money. I tell brokers and customers to try not to do what the rest of the world does.

Being a contrarian doesn't only mean having a contrary opinion on the market condition; it also means knowing when to use the self-fulfilling prophecy that much of this work becomes. In other words, the chart and pivot points become magnets for the professionals who can gauge when the retail public puts on positions and how much pain they can tolerate from a losing trade. In my opinion, the most important thing any new traders can do is find a discipline they can understand and watch the way price action treats the levels brought on by the work. Understand that it's vital to observe the work over a prolonged period of time rather than a short time frame. This is necessary because any one methodology can be profitable for a given period; it's the ones that are consistent that make the best trading tools.

As for me, I think I have been exposed to too many traders who would consider themselves from the school of the random walk theory. Bing often said that the charts sometimes needed to be thrown away, and I found that he was absolutely correct. I've noticed that sometimes technical analysis is a handicap rather than a tool. Vinny and Denny referred to chart points as voodoo, but both of them, along with Bing, realized that at times it's important to look at what might be considered a road map of where the market has been. That's the difference between the greatest traders in the world and the wannabes—the ability to look upon a chart as the past rather than trying to predict the future by prognosticating.

Most gifted traders have this ability to react to the market condition instead of trying to predict the future by using a mathematical equation. It's almost counterintuitive that to be a proactive trader it's important to be reactive. Identifying a pattern, or the lack of a pattern, gives good traders an understanding of how they should react in order to position themselves for the next major price move. I have come across many talented technicians, such as Aaron Reinglass, in my day, but the work of Doc has always attracted me. His work on structural analysis of the market incorporates my fundamental views. The difference between our respective ways of interpreting the same work is that Doc sees the work as a precursor to market fundamentals, whereas I see his work as a justification for my fundamental view. But how can I argue with someone who has predicted some of the biggest moves in market history?

So does technical analysis help you become a successful trader? Sometimes. At other times, the best work available won't help you make a single profitable trade. Those who have survived years in the market will say that in order to succeed, a trader must know how to incorporate a solid understanding of the fundamentals of the market with the available technical information. The truth is that all traders must develop their own style based on their individual personality and tolerance for risk, which varies from trader to trader. When someone asks what trading style would be best for them, I'm reminded of Bing's advice to me when I was starting out: "Do your own homework and above all make your own mistakes. It's the only way you'll learn!" This was true in 1986, and it's still true today.

CHAPTER 7

Random Walk Theory

The Market Is Nothing More Than Organized Chaos

The first Wednesday of every month was when the Chicago Mercantile Exchange (CME) board of directors would meet. This was preceded by a strategic planning committee meeting on Monday and an executive committee meeting on Tuesday. Leo Melamed, chairman of the strategic planning committee, asked me to sit on his committee and Scott Gordon, then chairman of the CME, asked me to be a member of the executive committee. The strategic planning and executive committees constituted the board within the board, the group that set the policy and the agenda for the upcoming board of directors meeting. Every facet of the policy-making process was of great interest, but the highlight of the month was when I would get a chance to sit and talk with some of the greatest minds in the world.

Before the board meetings, lunch would be served in the executive meeting room just down the hall from the boardroom. During those lunches I was able to meet and have dialogues with Senator Paul Simon and Professor Merton Miller. During one of our lunches, the subject of the rallying stock market became the topic of discussion. Everyone had an opinion on why the tremendous movement in tech stocks was happening. One of the more informed opinions came from Ward Parkinson, who had founded Micron Technologies but had since left the day-to-day activities for a semiretired life in the western United States. Parkinson observed that the world was going through a technological revolution that could make the industrial revolution look small in comparison—a very insightful comment from a man who was an integral part of the deployment of technology to the mass market.

As the discussion turned to Dr. Miller and his thoughts on the market, I noticed an interesting change in his appearance from the relaxed posture he normally assumed to one that was upright and serious. I had a feeling he was about to say something of significance. (Either that, or he was simply tired of sitting in the same position.) Fortunately, he *was* serious, and he talked for the next 20 minutes about the movement of equities and the random walk theory. I sat in awe, listening to what many have paid thousands of dollars to hear—Merton Miller's Nobel Prize–winning thoughts on the markets and the economy.

Coming from the University of Chicago business school, Merton was a classic random walk theorist. In fact, it was largely his work that was used as the basis for what we consider today to be the random walk theory. During this particular speech, he made many cogent observations about the euphoric condition the market was then experiencing, but the one consistent theme was that the market will do whatever it wants and that the market is organized chaos. He told me that the first serious work on random walk theory was done by Paul Samuelson in 1965, explained in an article entitled "Proof That Properly Anticipated Prices Fluctuate Randomly" and the other academic works that followed.

As we left the lunchroom for the boardroom that day, I walked with Merton and asked him whether he considered himself a random walker. His response was pure Merton: "Jack, my boy, every theory and invention evolves over time. Who remembers today that steam engines were originally invented to pump water out of coal mines?"

A Random Walk Down Wall Street was written by Burton Malkiel in 1973 and put into print the fundamental premise that it is impossible to outperform the market on a consistent basis. In other words, all the technical work in the world will not help in the grand scheme of things because in the end, investors are better off buying and holding rather than trying to time the market—it is too efficient. Malkiel's work, which was adopted by a majority of the academics at the time, questions the validity of both technical analysis and fundamental analysis.

To the trader who spends hour upon hour staring at charts looking for a chance to identify a pattern, the thought of randomness in price action is tantamount to heresy. The random walk theory also suggests that any success in timing the market is nothing more than sheer luck. The law of averages would also suggest that if enough people are trading the market, some will make money—but in the long term, these individuals still can't outperform the market.

Listening to Merton talk about random walk theory was very insightful. It gave me an idea of what is being taught at the major business schools and, better yet, how they are being taught the theory. I don't think that Merton subscribed to the idea that all price action is random. He found that most technical analysis was a waste of time because price movements on a daily, intraday basis are random. Prices have no memory—they have no past or present—that's why they can't be used in analysis to predict where the market will be in the future. He went on to say that any movement in prices is due to information that hits the market at that moment. As soon as the information becomes available, the prices are adjusted accordingly. The only difference is that the speed at which information is disseminated today gives the entire trading universe access to much the same information, creating a more level playing field. Merton asked me, "How many mutual funds have outperformed the S&P 500 index consistently over the last 20 years?" He had a point—fund managers were having a difficult time matching the averages, let alone outperforming them. In the long run, indexing the market would prove to be the most profitable.

One of the first things that hits someone who ventures to any of the futures exchanges that still use the open outcry method is the chaotic condition that prevails during the trading session. When I first began to trade, it was virtually impossible to detach myself from the noise and emotion that were all around me. I wondered if there was any reason for the price action, or was the movement in the market simply a product of the order impact hitting the market at any given time?

The concept of the random walk is one that many traders have a difficult time digesting. The problem lies in the fact that pattern recognition is the basis for every type of analysis, whether it is technical or fundamental. It seems fairly clear that a fundamental approach to the market relies on the past to understand the present and, hopefully, result in a profitable future. A technical trader looks for the same pattern to repeat itself, thus finding a high-percentage trade from the available information.

WHAT DO MBAs LEARN ABOUT PRICE FLUCTUATIONS?

But what is it that MBA candidates are taught about market analysis? Having encountered a vast number of individuals with MBAs from a variety of business schools across the nation, I have come to understand the nature of what they are taught in this approach to the market. The two big schools in the Chicago area are the University of Chicago Graduate School of Business and the Kellogg School of Management, which is part of Northwestern University. Both have sound reputations and are consistently ranked among the world's best. The one thing that hits you immediately when talking to a graduate from either school is the different attitudes toward the market that are the foundation for the respective market approach and understanding.

Graduates from the University of Chicago reveal Merton's influence when they speak.

Much of what these MBA students are taught about price action centers around random walk theory. Kellogg graduates look at the market using a synthesis of theories that include some randomness sprinkled with long-range pattern recognition. When I interviewed perspective employees, I could quickly identify which ones were Kellogg graduates and which ones came from the U of C business school. Candidates from both schools found different paths to the same place. They explained price movement from two different perspectives, but their results were the same. They became what I called *randomentalists*.

A randomentalist is a student of the market who blends random walk theory with a fundamental approach to market analysis. When I ask any of these so-called random walkers what they think about market action, the conversation inevitably turns to the fundamentals driving market pricing. But this is inherently anti–random walk. How could the observation of news and events, the backbone of fundamental analysis, be of any help when everything, including news and events, is random? This question brings up an even more important point: Has the market evolved to the same stage to which random walk theory has evolved? Could it be that the theory was changing with the marketplace?

When random walk theory dominated the academic and institutional landscape, individual traders and investors were at a tremendous disadvantage compared to the larger broker-dealer community. Small traders had access to information through one source: their brokerage house. Over the last 25 years, not only has the flow of information changed the world of trading, but it has altered random walk theory itself.

Random walkers held the view that news and information were priced into the market so quickly that the individual trader had no chance at timing the market—it was too fast and efficient. What the theory never accounted for was the technological revolution that allows the power to shift from the institutions to the smaller trader. Both brokerage costs and speed of information give the individual trader the same advantage as the pros. The fact that this is coupled with instantaneous execution capability has made even the most diehard random walker do some serious soul-searching.

Why has some of the randomness been taken out of random walk theory? Is the theory no longer credible, or has it, as Merton suggested, evolved, much like the steam engine did? Most individuals don't understand that 30 years ago, when the theory was popular, the market was completely different. Both transaction costs and speed of execution created a bifurcated market in which the institutions preyed on the smaller trader. When price aberrations were created, it was nearly impossible for the individual to compete with the larger institutional trading desk.

RANDOM WALK THEORY AND TECHNOLOGY

With the proliferation of electronic trading and competitive brokerage rates, the trading universe changed, undergoing a very dynamic evolutionary process. It is interesting to note that the brokerage community hates random walk theory. They're in the business of selling analysis and ideas, yet year after year over 50 percent of the listed mutual funds underperform the market (the number was closer to 90 percent when random walk theory was introduced in 1973). There are so many different products today, such as exchange-traded funds (ETFs), that give investors true indexed investments and make it that much more difficult for portfolio managers to find strategies that outperform the benchmarks. But does that also suggest that there remains no randomness in price action?

In January 1986 I was on the phone with Bing when word hit the wire that the space shuttle *Challenger* had blown up at its launch in Florida. Immediately the market began to sink, with selling coming into the S&Ps from all corners of the pit. Both Bing and I were short the market, but we noticed something very strange about the sell-off. It was not following the normal pattern of support and resistance that other breaks in the market had taken. What should have been a panic- and fear-driven break was a confusing volatile trade with staccato-like movements in the market that changed directions abruptly, seemingly for no particular reason.

Any textbook advice about trading would say that in times of disaster, sell first and ask questions later. Those who sold on the shuttle disaster news quickly found that the market does not always do what it's supposed to do. On the contrary, the market does whatever it can to hurt the most people possible. That's what the average person never really understands. The market finds a way of disappointing the day trader because of the randomness of intraday price aberrations.

When it comes to returns on the capital at risk, there are two different form: risk-adjusted returns and absolute returns. A random walker would look to incorporate a buy-and-hold strategy, believing that it's impossible to time the market effectively. History has taught us that this strategy has outperformed the market on an absolute basis, but the problem is that it does nothing to compensate for the risk associated with investing. The buy-and-hold method takes all the guessing out of the market but does nothing about the risk.

Portfolio managers who incorporate market timing into their money management strategy find that it's possible to move capital in and out of equities, creating exposure during rallying markets and putting money into U.S. Treasuries during market pullbacks, and thus adjusting for risk. That is an example of a risk-adjusted return. Today, products ranging from ETFs to futures allow market timing in an efficient manner.

As an earlier chapter mentioned, there is a correlation between risk and reward. The higher the assumed risk, the greater the potential reward. The concept of risk/reward is best played out between the true random walkers and those who believe market timing takes much of the risk out of the position. Many proponents of the Dow theory have proven through extensive research that using market-timing techniques increases the performance of a portfolio while reducing the risk associated with the exposure. Stephen Brown of New York University, William Goetzman of Yale, and Alok Kumar of the University of Notre Dame published a study in the *Journal of Finance* in the fall of 1998 showing the results of a study in which the Dow theory was tested against the buy-and-hold (random walk) theory from 1929 to 1998. It showed that the use of a market-timing approach such as Dow theory outperformed buy and hold by almost 2 percent over that time frame. The strategy allowed the investor to be shielded from risk associated with market exposure during downdrafts. Although the last few years have seen the Dow theorists underperforming the random walkers by 2.5 percent, the debate is still heard among academics in virtually every business school.

It's hard for someone who witnessed the trending market of tech stocks in the late 1990s to fully subscribe to the notion that the market is too efficient to be timed. In fact, market timing became very popular during the last great bull run in stocks. The only problem lies in the fact that individuals had access to all the right information but didn't understand what they were looking at. Anyone who watched the action of the initial public offering (IPO) market for technology stocks during that period would have had to conclude that the outcome of a tech IPO was highly predictable.

RANDOM EVENTS CREATE THE TREND

There's an old saying on the floor: "The trend is your friend." Anyone who has ever been successful trading in the markets will tell you that trends do exist, and anyone not in tune with the trend, whether to follow or be a contrarian, is a fool. The late 1990s taught many people that there just might be something to market timing. This period saw an explosion of derivatives products such as the ETFs and other investment vehicles that made entering and exiting positions very easy.

One of the best examples of the randomness of events dictating the flow of the market was at the inception of the first Gulf war. As Saddam Hussein amassed his forces along the Kuwaiti border, the markets were looking ahead to the unemployment number that was to be released later, along with any data that would show the economy coming out of recession.

As I talked with the traders and portfolio managers available to me, no one seemed to care about what was happening in the Persian Gulf and they thought any aggressive moves by Iraq would be immediately stopped by the threat of U.S. intervention. History taught us that Iraq miscalculated the way the United States would respond and opened the door for decades of problems in the region. As the U.S. State Department negotiated with Iraqi diplomats, there was one trader from First Boston, Andy Elner, who suggested to me that this was a larger problem than originally thought. In hindsight, he was the only one who saw the storm coming.

In the days before the electronic marketplace, the pit used to explode with activity anytime there was a news item or event that would affect price action. Something big like a surprise move by the Federal Reserve would generate hours of frantic trading, with volume nearing capacity in the open outcry session. But since the creation of the S&P contract, no one had experienced the United States at war. More important, how would the market react to the country in a state of war? As the deadline for the Iraqis approached, everyone became a political science expert.

The talk across the floor was of the possibility of war and the ancillary implications for the entire market. I talked with many of the traders I was covering from First Boston and other institutions about the direction the market would take in the event of war. I painted different scenarios, from a long drawn-out campaign to a short in-and-out strategy. Without exception, everyone was convinced that the equity markets would decline significantly and the run into short-term Treasuries was assured. In other words, they were putting on the "economy deterioration spread."

One morning a press conference was announced with Jim Baker, secretary of state under President George H.W. Bush, in which he would talk about the ongoing dialogue with the Iraqi delegation. In a scene reminiscent of the movie *Trading Places*, in which everyone stops trading to listen to the crop report, the entire S&P futures market was silent, waiting for the headline or a hint of what was being said. At this time on the floor TVs were not allowed, nor were they part of the exchange landscape (a situation that has since changed now that large TV monitors have been placed on every corner of the exchange floor).

A local in the pit would look for what was referred to as the "leak" from a desk that would give them an idea of what was said and how the flow would trade off the information. As Baker approached the microphone, the order flow around the pit ground to a halt. Every trader off the floor within range of a TV set was watching carefully to get a clue about what was going to be done next. Being on the telephone myself, I asked the traders to turn up the volume so I could hear what the rest of the world was being told. Baker talked about the frustrating dialogue between the international community and the Iraqi government, then he mentioned Kuwait. Prior to the press conference, the understanding had been that the international community led by the United States had given Iraq an ultimatum to leave Kuwait (which they had recently invaded) or face the consequences.

Listening on the phone, I could hear Jim Baker talking, and then it happened: When Baker uttered the word "regrettably" in describing the Iraqi answer, the market erupted like a volcano! All I could hear on the phone from that moment on was "*Sell* me 100!" I had three traders yelling orders simultaneously. Sell! . . . Sell! . . . Sell! Unfortunately, there was not much bid when we tried to sell the futures—everyone had had the same idea. Finally, after a 10-point drop, the market found buyers and the orders were filled. The traders had put on the short position that they were convinced was a winner if the war started. The move in the S&P futures went from roughly 310 even down to 303. The market has never seen that level again. Not only was it the low of the move that day, it was also the low of the move for the rest of the decade.

VICTIMS OF RANDOMNESS

The traders had thought out their strategies very carefully and yet they became victims of the randomness of the market. The panic selling that took the trade down to the low was the result of completely miscalculated analysis. The logic that many apply to everyday life cannot be transferred to the market condition. In the words of Dennis DeCore, "The market is completely illogical!" And that makes sense—if the market were indeed rational, then everyone would be able to profit from the price aberrations. Understanding that futures trading is, in essence, a zero-sum game (for every winner, there is a loser), then we know that everyone can't make money all the time. I've always called it Bouroudjian's law: The market will do whatever it can to hurt the most people.

One of the most intense episodes of randomness to hit the market was in the mid-1990s when the Federal Reserve chairman at the time, Alan Greenspan was speaking at a conference during the evening hours and referred to the stock market as being in a state of "irrational exuberance." The overnight Globex session for the stock index futures went crazy. The futures began to sink and between the night trading session at the Chicago Board of Trade (CBOT) bond pit and the electronic S&P 500 futures contract, off-hour volume records were broken. Prior to Chairman Greenspan's speech, the stock market had been experiencing a period of growing euphoria during which portfolio managers were just beginning to discover the world of tech stocks.

This was the financial world that existed before the speed of information dissemination that we enjoy today. Greenspan's speech sent shock waves throughout the entire capital markets universe. Fixed-income securities, along with equities, experienced volatility that had not been felt for years. In fact, the last great test of volatility came during the start of the first Gulf war, and the market had steadily moved higher from that point.

Random events are the basis for random walk theory. The speed and efficiency of the marketplace don't allow anyone to anticipate an unexpected event. By definition, it's something that is out of the norm. One of the biggest arguments against random walk theory is the invention and evolution of the options marketplace. When random walk theory became all the rage in the early 1970s, the capital market structure was much different. Options, for example, were a new product line not understood by many traders. Furthermore, there were only call options for investors to trade; the concept of listing a put option contract on an equity came years later.

The use of these products gave traders who used the Black-Scholes mathematical models the ability to make winning trades consistently with little risk.Once the academic world began to see the power of quantitative analysis in pricing options, it became clear that random walk theory had faults. How could events drive the market randomly when traders were able to use the randomness for a calculated high-percentage trade? It becomes a dilemma for the devout random walker who feels the market is too efficient to allow traders to capitalize on such events.

AN EDUCATED OPINION

One thing that the average investor doesn't fully understand is that random walkers believe that an educated opinion is the only thing a person needs in order to invest. When other traders ask me how I feel about the market, I always tell them what I think, then follow it up by asking, "What do you think?" A surprised look usually crosses their faces when I ask that question, and they often respond by asking why I care about their thoughts on the market. I tell them that their educated opinion is as good as mine.

One of the best options traders I know is Greg Hadley, who is a longtime friend from the TKE fraternity house at Loyola. Hadley would ask me time and time again what I thought of the market, hoping to gain some insight and achieve a winning trade. He made me realize that a trader who does the due diligence necessary to risk capital has an opinion that is educated and should be taken seriously. After all, how many people put their money where their mouths are on a daily basis?

For some reason, this shocks many traders. The very idea that an average investor could offer an educated opinion that is as relevant as one from the professional trading community is foreign to them. One reason for this might be because people are inherently lazy. They want other people to do their work for them, and most prefer to sit back and have others tell them what to do with their money. If you do your homework and follow the geopolitical events of the day, then the opinion derived is based on solid information rather than a reading of the tea leaves. Experience is the big difference between a professional and an amateur. When nonprofessionals ask me about trading, I always tell them that it's important for them to understand that they are amateurs (what many call *retail investors*) in a professional world. Even with the same information the "market opinion" of a retail investor cannot be as insightful as that of the seasoned pro. It would be as if I went into a health care profession after reading about it for a few months, believing I could do whatever a doctor can. It takes years to fully grasp the nuances of the market to get a better understanding of the organized chaos that unfolds daily.

One of the advantages of having so many solid customers and reliable contacts in my network is that it enables me to see how the various business schools outside of Chicago approach the market condition. To many of us in Chicago, looking outside of the area for insight into the capital structure has always seemed unnecessary because of the amazing amount of intellectual capital produced at the University of Chicago and Northwestern.

But we forget that there are many other great business colleges and universities across the country and abroad that build a foundation for traders based on random walk theory. Talking with many of these individuals seems to indicate that most business schools teach this theory because academia has been dogmatic in its approach to the capital markets structure. One thing is evident, however: Graduates of these incredible institutions emerge with the ability to think in a clear and analytic fashion regardless of their belief or nonbelief in random walk theory.

One of the first stories I heard about the speed of market efficiency and randomness was during the 1967 war between Israel and its Arab neighbors. The event was well before I began to trade and since I was only six years old at the time, I can hardly remember it. Nevertheless, people who were there explained to me the chain of events. As hostilities began to escalate in the spring of 1967, futures prices for commodities began to rise. The logic behind a rise in commodity prices during hostilities is that demand will outstrip supply if the conflict is prolonged, which creates upside price pressure for most products. On June 5, the Israeli air force attacked airfields in Egypt, Syria, Iraq, and Jordan, acting in a preemptive strike before the anticipated attack.

The news of the attack sent the capital markets into a volatile whirl. Commodity prices began to surge at the CBOT, with grain prices going limit up (the most a price can move in a given day). The action was no different at the CME, where they were trading the meat markets. Over the course of the years, the two exchanges had found niches trading different types of agricultural products. The CBOT was trading the nonperishable commodities such as corn, soybeans, and oats, while the CME was trading perishable commodities such as pork bellies and live cattle.

The news of the war between Israel and the Arab nations moved the futures markets into states of limit-up days; that is, they raised the daily limit, then locked, with no trading and a growing book of bidders hoping to buy anything. There are many reasons why a trader would want to buy a market locked limit up if possible, but the most important one is that it gives traders the edge. A market that is locked limit has a high degree of probability to open higher the following day, maybe even another limit move. This was the case during the Six-Day War—all the markets moved up in unison, taking both the grains and the meats to limit move session after session.

After the third day, with the pork belly pit filled to capacity and locked in a limit-up position, the market found a large seller. It was Ralph Peters! He was holding his long grain positions, but he began to sell the huge holdings he had acquired in the pork belly market. After covering an enormous position for a large profit, he began to sell into a short position. When asked by one of his clerks why he would sell out a limit position then flip into a short trade, the answer was simple: Neither the Jews nor the Arabs eat pork!

Word of the trade started to spread across the floor, and within minutes the entire market was filled with frantic activity as traders came to realize what Peters had just understood: Not all commodities are the same. The events that trigger moves in one market can have an entirely different effect on another market, based on the fundamentals. The randomness of the trade took the price up with the other markets and then turned it lower in a split second. The market went crazy! Not only had the world been long the belly market, but there were spreads between the various commodities that turned into instant volatility.

Anyone who was caught in the whipsaw of the Six-Day War and lost money was a classic victim of randomness. The volatile nature of the events was a case study in the randomness of prices and constitutes a great example of random walk theory at work. Even in today's market, events will take the price of certain markets into artificially high price action only to fall back to the norm. The only difference is that today's market is filled with more participants and is saturated with information through the use of the Internet and access to professional trading techniques. What took a few days for traders to realize during the Six-Day War in 1967 would take only seconds today.

NON-RANDOM WALK THEORY

There is another school of thought that takes random walk theory and turns it upside down. In 1973, Andrew Lo, who holds a Ph.D. in economics from the University of Chicago, wrote a book called *A Non-Random Walk Down Wall Street*. The one thing that makes Lo much different from his predecessors is that he incorporated the use of technical analysis into the efficient market model. He had an attraction to technical analysis and tried, with some success, to disprove the effectiveness of random walk theory. Knowing that most of academia was subscribing to the theory, Lo concluded that most financial markets are predictable to some level. He went on to claim that the predictability of the market was not a problem based on inefficiency or irrational price action, but, rather, the predictability of the market is what makes the wheels of capitalism move. It's simple—if liquidity providers thought there was no way they could capitalize on the inefficiency of the prices, then there would be large problems in capital formation and the entire market structure would suffer.

Lo concluded that the markets can be efficient at times but participants can profit during these periods with ongoing research and constant innovation. Simply put, traders that do their homework can thrive in any market environment.

Lo maintains that beating the market is not easy, nor should people think they can walk into a market condition that is emotional and expect results without hard work. Lo says that finding above-average returns on an individual's portfolio is akin to a company trying to maintain a competitive advantage in a marketplace. If a company—any company—were to launch a new product line, the company would need to support the launch in every way possible. Management must be flexible and adapt to the ever-changing conditions, or else competitors will steal the market share.

Money managers and traders find themselves in much the same boat—if they don't remain flexible and innovative, then they will not be able to outperform the market. As dynamic as the market may be, a trader must be just as dynamic. Just because a market strategy worked yesterday and today does not mean it will work tomorrow. In an interview with *Technical Analysis of Stocks and Commodities*, Lo summarized his hypothesis:

> *The more creativity you bring to the investment process, the more rewarding it will be. The only way to maintain ongoing success, however, is to constantly innovate. That's much the same in all endeavors. The only way to continue making money, to continue growing and keeping your profit margins healthy, is to constantly come up with new ideas.*

I remember asking Merton Miller about Lo's work, and I found it fascinating that of all the economists' work that Merton had come across about the market condition, it was Lo he liked. He pointed to the fact that he was able to incorporate the changing world and the efficiency of the market into a cohesive approach to market structure.

An important conclusion of Lo's work is that innovation will always produce a high-percentage trade at times. More important, Lo's work foresaw the technological changes that allow the aberrations information to be disseminated with unimaginable speed and reliability. Even today, as we witness the evolution of the entire futures market into an electronic universe, the changes needed to maintain a trading edge are still very apparent.

But one thing is certain: The time frame used to study both approaches to investing has been short. Even though the last few years have seen the market timers effectively outperform the random walkers who use the buy-and-hold strategy, history dictates that there will be a reversion to the mean. Random walkers will tell you that eventually those who time the market will not be able to maintain above-average returns. They will end up as most mutual funds on Wall Street end up—underperforming the major market averages.

The only thing that would give investors a glimmer of hope is that information has become more readily available for those wishing to participate in the market. The widespread use of the Internet and electronic trading platforms gives the average investor the tools and the technology to compete in today's markets. The real question is whether the average investor knows how to use what is available. The last few years have seen an explosion in trading and investing, but little emphasis is put on education. Maybe it's because, in the words of Woody Allen, "Those who can't do, teach... and those who can't teach, teach gym!" Unfortunately, most of the new amateur traders in today's market are being taught by those who can't do... or teach... or teach gym!

As I think back on the many great traders and portfolio managers whom I've encountered in my career in the futures industry, it is clear that a majority are from the random walk school. I remember Bing telling me that I was giving him only half the story, and I realize now that he was a true product of the efficient market theory. He came out of Harvard Business School, where subscribing to something other than random walk theory was looked upon as economic heresy. He was telling me, in his unique way, that the charts are not the reason the market is moving higher or lower. The market is moving because of events that are unknown to us.

The same was true for Vinny and Denny, who called market technical work "voodoo" but still had a certain amount of respect for what they considered to be a self-fulfilling prophecy. Even Scott Weisblum, a product of Wharton, had a certain disdain for the technical work, relying instead on the fundamental analysis of the various stock indexes and the technological edge he created for himself. All of these remarkable individuals were great traders in their own different ways but they shared one important characteristic: They understood the basic concept of the efficient market theory but likewise understood the need to incorporate change and innovation into their trading techniques.

CHAPTER 8

The Psychology of the Marketplace

The Highs Are High ... but the Lows Are Lower!

My wife, Donna, aside from being a wonderful spouse and mother, is a great RN. Twenty years ago when we were first married she worked at a hospital on the north side of Chicago that was frequented by traders and their families. I had heard time and again how wonderful my wife had been and the tender bedside manner she showed in the postsurgical unit where she worked. One morning as I walked onto the trading floor I was approached by a clerk in the options pit who informed me that one of our brokers had left for health reasons. "Babe" was in his late 50s and sported a ponytail and an earring. He was a huge man in girth and had a laugh to match. As it turns out, Babe needed to go into the hospital for opens heart surgery (something I found out about later). Three months later I saw a man walking onto the trading floor who was barely recognizable ... it was Babe! He had shed half of his body weight, some 150 pounds, and was very frail in appearance.

I didn't recognize him until he came up to me and began to speak. Having seen Babe in action in the trading pits, I knew that he was one of the tough guys. He was old-school and the look in his eye reinforced the attitude. He was known as a trader and broker you did not mess with, but now, at least physically, he was half the man I remember, and he had a look on his face that confused me. He spoke slowly: "I thought I was dying. Your wife saved my life! She held my hand and told me it was going to be all right when I thought I was gone." As he was speaking to me, I could see that he was beginning to cry. His tears deeply affected me. "I don't think I would have made it if it wasn't for her," he continued. "God bless her," he said, and he walked away. I quickly called my wife and asked her if she remembered him. Donna had always been sympathetic to patients' need for privacy, even before the HIPAA rules, and she never shared tales from her work with me. But she knew exactly who I was talking about and asked me how he was doing. I told her that he looked frail but was feeling better. Then I shared with her the comments that he had made in regard to her care.

As I was telling her the story, it dawned on me that I could make a customer a billion dollars and I'd never get that type of response. I will never have any customers tell me that I saved their lives because of what I do for a living! I told the story to Bing and he commented that the traders around Babe would be affected by his experience. Not only did it force Babe to leave the pit, it also changed the way those closest to him approached trading. Market psychology made a delicate shift in the S&P options pit and especially in the minds of a few traders in Babe's circle. The appetite for risk was greatly diminished, and two of Babe's colleagues retired within the year.

THE MARKET PSYCHE

One of the first lessons learned about the markets by anyone wishing to participate is that the market has a psyche all its own. As a beginning trader, I didn't realize at first that certain external factors drive the attitude of the traders on both a micro level and a macro level. On a micro level, certain incidents and phenomena that are strictly local in nature have a direct impact on the way the local community treats daily trades. These include the death of a child or spouse or a near-death experience undergone by someone within the group. A macro event is more akin to the World Trade Center events of September 11 and the treatment of the markets not only by our locals, but by the entire capital markets universe. As market observers, we must try to understand the impact of market psychology.

In the summer of 1989, as the markets seemed to be back on track after the disastrous October of two years earlier, the S&P pit became more active. The order flow that had diminished started to grow again, along with the volatility that brings day traders and other players into the session. Feeling the market in all its euphoria allowed me to get caught up in the excitement. It's very easy to get wrapped up in the world around you, especially when there seems to be a celebration around the globe. The Berlin Wall was coming down, and on a personal note, my first child was due in the fall. It was a great time to be trading in the markets!

My work had taught me that we were about to experience what I would refer to as a "rally of biblical proportions." Why not? The United States was the leader in the world's technological revolution and possessed the greatest entrepreneurial spirit history had ever seen, and now we had won the Cold War. If there was ever a bullish scenario, that was it! I started to put on small positions, allowing my account to slowly grow to a level I felt was sufficient to take a shot at larger trades. I had worked the position up to a dangerous point where I was long too many S&P 500 contracts and had overlaid the position with a long call position. This is what many professional traders call a *Texas hedge*, which is having the same exposure with two different positions. I remember going home one night during this period thinking that I should lighten the number of contracts in my possession when I returned to the floor the next day—after all, it was earnings season and, as bullish as I was, anything could happen.

Walking onto the floor early the following day, I quickly ran to the CQG machine to get the levels I would use to slowly cover a portion of the large position I had pieced together. The market was called slightly lower but not so low that it would drastically impact the profit of the trade. Before the opening bell, United Airlines (UAL) announced a disaster in its earnings. The Street was not prepared for the disappointment. The opening call in the market began to get lower and lower until I realized that we might be in for a full meltdown when the market opened. The UAL news shook the entire stock market right down to its core.

What followed would be called the "UAL crash" because it was UAL's release of earnings that became the catalyst for the major break in stocks that year. My position got decimated! I had turned what was a winning trade into one of the largest losers I had ever faced. I walked off the floor, after covering the trade, and ran into my old friend Bobby Gault. Gault was a gifted filling broker in the S&P pit and he would play an important part in my life later. But on this day he could see the frustration and disappointment on my face. Knowing I was a relatively new trader, he took me aside and told me something that I have never forgotten. "Remember," he said, "it's only money, and we can always get more. Family is what is important!"

Bobby has been a big part of my life for the past 20 years, but it was that comment that I will carry with me forever. There was a shift in the psychology of the marketplace right before my very eyes (and trading account) and I hadn't been able to identify the change!

EUPHORIA IN THE MARKETPLACE

If anyone is looking for a case study to show the impact of market psychology, the late 1990s and early 2000s would be the perfect time periods to examine. The late 1990s were an extraordinary time when a tremendous amount of wealth was made and distributed among certain sectors of the economy that had never experienced it before. The entire market was celebrating, and the party was in full gear. Everyone was making money. I would get into a cab and the driver would tell me about the fortune he was making in a particular stock. Of course, this was followed by a period when the stock market bubble burst, sending many retirement accounts, along with many trading accounts, plunging to near worthless status. Trading arcades began to close, and any talk of brokering the markets was like selling snake oil. The year 2001 changed everyone forever—but more on that later.

In the mid-1990s when the markets were making new highs day after day, it was clear to those of us participating daily that we were experiencing something special. We felt we were part of a historic move in the markets, one that would be studied for years to come. As students of the market, we had read about and heard about major moves up and down in stocks, but none of us ever would have thought that the entire stock market would climb to the levels it did.

It was a perfect situation in which to examine a market that was going through the feeling of euphoria. The post–Cold War effect was in full force. The world of capitalism was experiencing the fruits of victory, having spread the seeds of industry and profit around the world. Everyone was turning into a capitalist—even the Chinese, who considered themselves communists, were really living with a suppressed form of capitalism based on an underground economy that was growing faster than the gross domestic product of some G7 nations. Those of us in and around the equity quadrant at the CME watched in amazement as the number of customers grew geometrically. Retail accounts were flocking to the stock index trade like never before, creating a period of prosperity for all segments of the membership—locals, brokers, salesmen, and futures commission merchants (FCMs).

A deeper look at the mid- to late 1990s is a great way to exam the euphoric psychology that was rampant among the investing public during that period. It was a time when anyone who had a stock trading account was buying the market on tips and finding that 75 percent of the time, they made money. The one thing to always remember is that making money is infectious. In fact, the most difficult thing to do is to go from a middle-class lifestyle to living like a rock star and then go back to that middle-class existence. It had reached a point where everyone I met was talking about the stock they had bought or were going to buy, and more important, these anecdotes about trading profitably were coming from nonprofessionals.

I was hearing these stories from cab drivers and grocery clerks. But how could I fade the crowd (be a contrarian), even when my gut instincts told me that I must? I looked at some of the fundamentals and began to stay away from some of the outrageously priced technology stocks, keeping my interest, and money, in biotech and exchange memberships. I would be a contrarian to the Nasdaq market by not participating at all except to put on an occasional day-trading position. I felt that even though I was bullish the market, the euphoric conditions surrounding the tech boom were making it difficult for me to hold anything long term.

One morning on CNBC someone asked me what chart points showed resistance in the Nasdaq index, and I replied, "The time has come to throw away the charts!" I borrowed this line from Bing to let the world know that charts had nothing to do with what was going on, and any seasoned professional looking at the charts would have to agree.

I wrote earlier that the life of a moneymaking local is a charmed life indeed! During the run in the stock market it seemed that everyone was leading a charmed life. It had reached a point that anyone buying a stock with four letters was making money. It's no surprise that the entire country was feeling the euphoria created by the rising market. The media even gave the phenomenon a name: *the wealth effect.* Not only were brokers and traders making money, but the boom time also had a large impact on the businesses and service industries around the nation.

Every day there were stories of people who had never traded equities in their lives finding a stock and holding it to the tune of millions of dollars. I was hearing these stories everywhere I went. One morning Dennis DeCore told me that his barber had just given him a stock tip. As a professional trader and a natural contrarian, Denny took the event as a signal that a top in the market was very near. His prediction was six months ahead of the start of the massive decline in equity prices—his gut feeling was absolutely correct!

FEAR AND GREED

It's been said that the market is driven by two basic human emotions: fear and greed. Each of these emotions has a way of changing the disposition of the market in a short period of time. In fact, it could be said that the emotions that drive market psychology are the lifeblood of trading. Both fear and greed have a way of taking the trader out of the trade. For traders to become successful, they must first find a way of detaching themselves from the raw feelings that accompany every position they put on. I have made thousands of trades in my career and there is always a little bit of fear that pulsates through my body every time I buy or sell the market. As much as you try to convince yourself that it's not money, that they're simply points in the market, you can't help but think about the monetary implications.

What we experienced during the late 1990s was an abandonment of fear in the marketplace. If anything, the fear seemed to be replaced by a certain complacency that led the investing public into a false sense of security when it came to the equities they owned. And why not? We were being told by the tech companies and the media that we were in a new paradigm. All the old rules about the way markets were priced and the way we were supposed to interpret their profits were being rewritten. We started to look at pro forma numbers and took them as gospel. The market euphoria had taken investing into a new age: the technological revolution.

Back with my floor brokerage operation, things were going better than ever. I had a wonderful crew made up of John Fiandaca and George Sereleas, along with their staff. The business had become so lucrative that it came to the attention of both Fiandaca and Sereleas that the pit brokerage coming off the customer order flow was lost revenue. They both came to the same realization: They could stay and work the brokerage business with me or they could go into the pit and pursue their fortunes.

John Fiandaca, a second-generation Italian from the northwest side of Chicago, was the first to try his luck in the pit. An all-state wrestler, which came naturally to the youngest of four brothers, Fiandaca is one of those rare athletes who was able to transfer the determination amateur wrestling requires into the right pit psychology. He decided he wanted to be a spread filling broker, which means he wanted to start his new venture in the most difficult part of the trading pit, the back month area, which is a fraction of the size of the rest of the pit. This was always considered prize real estate because the action of filling a spread requires two different legs to the trade—in other words, double commission.

Every broker group tried to put a body in the spread area so they could muster enough market share to justify a presence. Fiandaca was no different, except that he had captive business in hand when he entered the pit—namely, the spreads that were coming off the desk. This was enhanced by the promise of Adrian Byrne and John Scarnavac at CSFB to give Fiandaca an opportunity to compete for the business.

What happened next is pure CME at its best. Fiandaca stood at the heart of the pit with a look of unmistakable determination on his face. Where others were being shoved and tossed around like toy soldiers, Fiandaca was as solid as the Rock of Gibraltar. We began slowly making sure that the order flow was executed properly; after all, the business was taking a large risk in using an undercapitalized broker. I made a point of telling customers, and Fiandaca himself, that we would do whatever we could to protect him and his new brokerage business from the error risks associated with pit execution.

Before the rollover—the quarterly expiration period when the contracts are physically rolled from the expiring month to the next front month—was complete, we noticed something amazing. The service and the fills coming from Fiandaca were better than anything we had ever received before. Then it struck me—there was a lack of competition for the business in the back month configuration. One of the problems was that there was not enough room for everyone to stand, but even more important was that prior to Fiandaca's emergence there were only two groups that controlled the vast majority of the order flow in the area. Together, between the desk and Fiandaca, we had done something we never expected: We made the spread brokerage execution more efficient through competition.

Sereleas was a different story. The son of a Greek doctor, he came to work with me a couple of years after receiving his MBA from De Paul University in Chicago. His main responsibility was servicing Scott Weisblum in the S&P MidCap and the Russell 2000 markets. Earlier in this book, I mentioned the talent that Weisblum showed as a trader for the Cooper Neff BNP group, but he wouldn't have been so successful had it not been for the presence of Sereleas as his eyes and ears on the floor.

This was one of the largest customers on the desk, and it was thought that anyone handling the account would make sure that the smaller midcap and Russell pit (they are both located in the same area) were attending to the needs of our customer. After all, Weisblum had become the biggest user of these products on a daily basis in the world. A born thinker, Sereleas was not by nature an emotional zealot, which is what is required at times when covering customers. What he lacked in raw fury he made up for with pure intelligence, a fact that was obvious to everyone around him.

One morning, Nick Castrovillari, our filling broker in the midcap Russell pit and a close friend, told us that there would be an opening among the brokers in his group. He asked if we knew of anyone we would want to fill our orders. It was a smart suggestion on Castrovillari's part—he knew that we needed to be happy with the choice of broker that was going to be made. After talking it over with both me and Weisblum, Sereleas decided that this was a window of opportunity that could close fast. He quickly sprang into action, and began doing the homework necessary for both brokering and trading the smaller stock indexes. He started in the pit as a broker but found that he enjoyed trading. Not only did he become one of the best brokers in the pit, but he discovered his natural ability to feel the order flow and understand, through his days working with Weisblum, how the fundamentals of the market affected the daily trade.

Both Fiandaca and Sereleas are examples of the psychology of the marketplace at that time. Not only were everyday people making money though a rising equity market, but the prosperity accelerated to a certain degree the social mobility within the entire capital markets universe. What was happening at my desk was the norm throughout the floor. Coworkers were finding niches to fill as they were being created by the market and also finding incredible success along the way. Even though we are witnessing the explosion in volume caused by the proliferation of electronic trading, the late 1990s could be considered the golden age of the S&P 500 futures pit.

It was a wonderful time for anyone associated with the entire equity quadrant at the CME. Other areas within the exchange had experienced similar intervals. Agricultural products were the futures products of choice in the late 1960s and 1970s (primarily because there were no other products to trade). Then came the golden age of currency futures, which lasted about 20 years, until the consolidation among European currencies and the unregulated cash market shrank the CME market share to a fraction of the overall notional value of Forex traded daily.

The interest rate quadrant continues to experience quality order flow primarily because technology has not yet been able to take the back month spreads (the deferred months in the Eurodollar contract have thousands of combinations going out 10 years) or the options markets (which have thousands of strike prices) and transition them effectively onto the screen. But as far as the equity quadrant was concerned in the late 1990s, it felt like the party was going to last forever. And why not? We were in a growing industry with the best volatility a market had to offer. We had just launched a successful Nasdaq futures market and were finding continued success with the smaller midcap and Russell futures. But everyone knows a party can't last forever!

THE PSYCHOLOGY OF THE TRADING PIT

If there was any question about whether the good times might be over, it was answered in 2001. The previous year had seen the tech balloon pop and the ancillary impact of the shrinking wealth effect was beginning to show, with a slowdown in business and a lack of interest. I mentioned earlier that my old friend Aaron Reinglass is fond of saying that it's not drinking that causes hangovers, it's stopping drinking that causes them. Well, 2001 was the year the entire pit, as well as the nation, sobered up quickly.

It's been said that the psychology of an advancing market is much different from that of a breaking market. Where the advancing market is infused with feelings of euphoria and prosperity, the breaking market is characterized by fear and a loss of appetite for risk. In 2001, two very important things happened that shook the psychology of the marketplace, one on a local level and the other on a nation scale. Both events are worthy of having books written about them, but I'll share with you the way they affected the market's psyche and how they changed the lives of many of us who were involved.

The collective consciousness of the market is a very fragile thing that can be upset in many different ways. In February 2001, my filling broker in the S&P 500 futures pit and very close friend, Bobby Gault, was waiting for his family at a cabin they had built on Beaver Island in Lake Michigan between the Upper Peninsula and the mainland of Michigan. Gault had left early to open up the cabin, which had been secured against the harsh Michigan winter. Leaving for work that morning, I heard a story on the news about a family on a chartered plane out of Midway airport in Chicago who had vanished en route to Beaver Island. I wondered whether the Gaults knew this family.

Before that morning's meeting with Ed Arana, the CFO, to check on the firm's risk exposure, I received a call from the floor from Bob Nowak, who had taken over the day-to-day operations of the floor execution desk with his partner Steve Bauer. Nowak said, "There's a problem with Bobby's family!" After a few seconds of silence, I asked, "Were they on the plane that was heading up to Beaver Island?" Nowak said yes. I went numb. Gault was a gifted filling broker, but he had also done wonderful things for me on a personal level and our families had occasionally socialized.

I started shaking and paced the office, my mind racing. I made calls to see if we could fly up to the island or get close enough to help with the search that was getting under way. Later, Gault told us that he could see the plane was in trouble as it approached the small Beaver Island airstrip. He figured that the pilots were lost and that they had given up their approach, deciding to head to a larger, better-lit airport in Charlevoix, about 30 miles away. Bobby was wrong, however. The plane crashed in the woods a few miles from the airport, splitting in two and killing the pilots. Bobby joined the search, frantically looking for wreckage or a sign of survivors. At 2 AM, the Coast Guard suspended search and rescue efforts until daybreak because of poor visibility. They told Gault there was little chance of finding survivors at that point.

Back in Chicago, our thoughts were all with the Gaults. Winter conditions made flying difficult and flights to the Charlevoix area had all been canceled. The news stunned the trading pit. Bobby Gault was a great broker, and he was also one of the most personable members of the CME. Everyone knew him. In fact, he had met his wife, Mirth, at the CME years earlier when she worked in the Eurodollar futures pit. The news of the crash changed the market psychology for the week. The natural volatility of the market was subdued, with traders merely going through the motions.

As a community, the futures pits are competitive but they regard themselves as a big family. If a trader loses a child or a spouse, the entire pit offers support to the grieving member. But this was the first time we had collectively faced a situation where an entire family was lost. Even the most aggressive traders in the pit reacted to this situation.

In the Commerz offices, feeling helpless, I tried in vain to get Gault on the phone to offer my help. He and I had become very close; every day for an entire decade we had lunch together, during which we shared our thoughts on family and life. I knew that Mirth and the kids were more important to him than anything else.

Seeing I was troubled, Ed Arana came into my office to ask me what was going on. He, too, knew Gault and, as a father of three, felt the impact of the situation. He likewise suggested flying up there, but because of the horrible weather, all flights to northern Michigan had been canceled. I felt we simply had to get to Bobby. The entire pit showed its concern. Volume suffered a big hit that day—events had altered the pit psychology.

And so the community sprang into action. Kenny Johnson, a local and one of the largest liquidity providers in the S&P 500 futures pit, owned a share in a private jet and volunteered it to get us to the area faster than anything else available. As we prepared to leave for the Midway airport, word came from Michigan that there was a survivor . . . then we heard there were a couple of survivors. Finally, word came that Mirth and the three kids had survived, but unfortunately the pilots of the aircraft weren't so lucky.

Most people in and around the S&P pit felt the same emotions I did during those few troubling hours—horror and fear that an entire family had been lost, then the exhilaration of knowing they were all safe and back with Bobby. It was one of the most volatile emotional swings I had ever experienced in my life. The days that followed were filled with media stories about the Gault family and their miraculous survival, but the one thing I remember most is when Gault and his family visited the trading floor. As the entire CME equity quadrant rose and cheered, Bobby stood in the spot where he always conducted his pit brokerage business, holding his youngest son, Alec, high over his head. The crowd cheered even harder. The toughest traders I knew, people who seemed unable to show emotion, were wiping away tears as they watched this scene. I'll never forget it!

PANIC AND FEAR

One thing that many new traders do not understand about the market is the psychological aspects of trading. The study of the market psyche is a discipline in and of itself, but you don't need to be an expert to recognize the effects. Understanding that the market is driven by basic emotions is the first lesson in market behavior. Understanding what the collective investing public is thinking is a different art, but one that is likewise essential in learning about market behavior. The Gault family's experience demonstrates how such an event can change the pit psychology of the market. In that case, it was only for a day, but what happens when the entire nation is caught up in the same emotional roller coaster? Many books have been written about the behavior of individuals in terms of market psychology, but those who truly understand the nature of the market understand that it is nothing if not dynamic.

The mood of the market can be changed by months of sluggish action or by a single event. The market can go from a boring, low-volatility session to one that is full of price swings and action. It's been said that those on the floor really work just 10 percent of the time; the other 90 percent of the time is spent waiting for that 10 percent flurry of activity. Nevertheless, seasoned veterans know that you must remain alert for a change in conditions at all times.

It could be argued that events that drive the market in either direction are nothing more than catalysts and not true causes of the action. But remember, a trader's job is not to outthink the market; it's to profit from it! Although it might sound cold, trading is not altruistic. To be a good trader, you must see the market from two distinct perspectives: You must look at the smaller waves of emotion that drive the intraday volatility, but you must also always be aware of the much larger megawave of emotions that is driving the collective investing public. Smaller emotional events that might drive the market are such things as the fall of Enron and the impact of the loss of billions of dollars in market cap.

The ancillary effects of the event are much larger. The passing of the Sarbanes-Oxley Act, which could end up costing the business community millions of dollars, might create an environment that drives business overseas. This is a difficult subject that will be debated for some time. But every now and then a particular event changes everything. Such an event happened on September 11, 2001.

9/11

The events of September 11, 2001, will be written about for years to come. But rather than spend time writing about the causes behind the event, I will tell you what happened in my world during those difficult days. Many things happened behind the scenes at the CME, and much of what was done, directly or indirectly affected the entire market and the psychology that pervades it. I think of the event itself as the Kennedy assassination of our time. Everyone remembers exactly where they were that morning.

If any single event let the entire world know that the days of bull market innocence had come to an end, September 11 and its aftermath were it. In fact, the event constitutes a perfect case study of the changing of the collective psychology of the marketplace in a single day. No other news event caused more market disruption and confusion than that. Understanding the emotional impact of the event is important for anyone trading the markets today because much of the market psychology that surrounds today's trading was caused by 9/11!

For me, September 11 started like any other day with an early trip to the CME floor to do CNBC and Bloomberg TV before heading back to the Commerz offices. I was scheduled for a 9 AM TV appearance to talk about the economic releases coming out that morning. As I watched CNBC, I heard Mark Haines say something about a plane hitting the World Trade Center. My first reaction was to call Vinny and Denny, who were at the Nomura offices across the street from the WTC, at the World Financial Center. I asked them if they could see what was happening and if they were safe. They told me they were fine but it looked as if a traffic copter or something small had hit the tower. From their angle it was difficult to see the extent of the damage caused by the first plane.

Walking on the upper trading floor at the Merc, I saw my old friend Peter Yastrow, who had taken a position with Cantor Fitzgerald covering their proprietary traders and brokers. Cantor's New York offices were on a high floor in the tower that had been hit, and Peter and his colleagues at the desk looked concerned. Something was wrong—clerks were wiping away tears as they left the floor. When I asked what was happening, I was told that the traders and brokers on the other end of the phone in New York had realized they were not going to make it and had asked the clerks in Chicago to say goodbye to their families for them. Imagine being on the phone with people who know they're going to die, and there is nothing you can do!

Although the stock market had not yet opened, the electronic futures market began to break hard. As we watched the TV for details about the first tower, we all looked on in horror as the second plane hit the other tower. It was at this point that the event became world changing. People sensed the panic. Brokers began yelling that there were other planes in the air not accounted for and that the CME could be a possible target. I urged everyone to calm down, and allowed anyone to leave if they wanted to. I sent my whole crew home and had told everyone associated with my operation that I would call them with more information as it became available.

I was called to the control center adjacent to the S&P pit to confer with the New York markets on whether they would open. During the course of the teleconference, we all turned to the TV as Mark Haines announced that the first tower had collapsed. With that, it was decided that the stock market in New York City would not open and that the CME would close its futures market. I immediately called Vinny and Denny in New York. They had fortunately left the building after the second plane had hit. Later they would tell me that they could see the second plane as it sped along the river before hitting the second tower. At that point they evacuated the World Financial Center and the island of Manhattan.

Everyone else was vacating the CME floor, but I felt that I should stay to help with any disaster recovery that might be necessary. Aside from being on the CME board of directors, my responsibilities also included a seat on the Commerzbank Futures board. The U.S. headquarters for the bank was located in the World Financial Center a few floors above Vinny and Denny. By the time I called, the entire banking division was out of the building and setting up shop in a warehouse some 25 miles away in New Jersey. I knew that Frankfurt would ask about the situation and how the exchange was dealing with the catastrophe.

THE FUTURES INDUSTRY'S FINEST MOMENT

I went up to the office of Scott Gordon, who was then chairman, and asked if I could be of any assistance. As it turns out, the CME had sprung into action immediately and within hours had prepared a plan to get the New York commodities markets up and running on Globex, the CME's electronic platform. The hours that followed showed cooperation at its best. Never before had rival exchanges come to each other's aid! The New York exchanges faced two large problems: First, it was difficult to physically get humans in and out of lower Manhattan, and second, it was presumed that there would be a liquidity problem. Most of the largest end users of the capital markets are based in the New York area.

What happened next might be one of the proudest moments of the CME and the entire industry. At the same time rescuers were searching through the rubble for survivors of the carnage in Lower Manhattan, the CME clearinghouse and technology departments, headed by Phupinder Gill and Jim Krause, created, virtually overnight, a system that would allow the New York Mercantile Exchange and the New York Board of Trade to list their products and clear them at the CME if necessary. This kind of cooperation among the exchanges was unprecedented. Up until this event, the relationship between the various futures exchanges had been much like a sibling rivalry. Never before had one exchange offered the use of its infrastructure to another exchange. I watched in amazement as former competitors extended a helping hand to each other. Although the New York exchanges decided to decline the CME offer, it nevertheless thrust the CME into the limelight as the exchange that could replicate an entire market overnight if needed—a difficult thing for any competitor to match and something that would not be forgotten later when the CME would trade as a public company.

Not only did we see cooperation among the different trading floors, but we also witnessed a cooperative effort to help clearing operations based in the New York area. FCMs offered their back-office services to those who had lost their operations. A good example is the cooperative effort to help Carr Futures, a division of Indo-Suez Bank in France, re-create a back office and assist with customer positions. The industry had come together like never before. The psychology of the market had been changed, but how? The stock market was closed for days, and the reopening of trading brought forth uneasy feelings of confusion and fear.

A few days later, New York officials determined that they would reopen the stock market. Many of the specialist firms had relocated to disaster recovery sites and had regained control and functionality of their trading and order entry systems. The open of the market was greeted with a big cheer by the trading community, as well as an unexpected phenomenon—low volatility. Even though the market was poised to open significantly lower, the opening was accompanied by a strange mood of reserved activity. It is not well known that trading desks of the major proprietary operations were asked not to be aggressive. In other words, the largest traders, which included the index arbitrage community, were asked to be patriotic with their trading. I had witnessed other events that had brought out the predatory instincts in some traders—those hoping to profit from a catastrophe. This was evident, for example, when the space shuttle *Challenger* crashed and sellers plunged the market and made a fast profit on the national disaster. But this was different. I had never seen the collective psychology of the market change so dramatically as the result of a single event!

The same traders who were normally sharks were as tame as dolphins as the first day of trading commenced. It was a widely felt that anyone who tried to profit from the attack was simply unpatriotic! The entire country had come together like never before in modern history. Even the members of Congress stood on the steps of the Capitol to symbolize unity during a time of deep national need. The days that followed in the market brought subtle price swings, but no one attempted to plunge the market. If we, as students of the market, are to learn anything about market psychology from the events of September 11 and the days that followed, we must understand what happened to market pricing during that period. With hindsight, one thing is clear: Whenever there is a terrorist attack (including that of 9/11), it is a wonderful buying opportunity for stocks!

Dealing with the media throughout that experience was very trying. I was accustomed to talking about the direction of the market, but I had never been asked to comment on social issues or voice an opinion about current events. But now things had changed. Every interview I did on CNBC and Bloomberg TV would eventually work its way to asking about the feelings and thoughts of traders. I started every interview by saying, "Our thoughts and prayers go out to all our friends in New York," but that just didn't seem like enough. We were trying to get on with our lives, but it was impossible.

How could we? We would watch the rescue workers digging through the rubble on big-screen TVs set up around the floor and were trying to maintain a focus on the market at the same time.

Emotions were running high, and I knew that anytime I was going to appear in the media I needed to act responsibly and say the appropriate things. Like everyone else, I too felt angry! I knew people who died in those towers and wanted to tell the world that I thought these terrorists were nothing more than animals. The Islamic fanatics had hit too close to home. I couldn't help but think that the same fanaticism that took down the towers was responsible for the killing of millions of Armenians (including 30 members of my family) and other Christians at the hands of the Turks less than a century ago. The same problems that my grandparents had faced and survived had followed me and my little family to the United States. But I understood, as the de facto face man for the CME on TV, that it was my job to make sure I came off as professionally as possible, keeping in mind that national security might be at stake. I also knew that I was partially responsible for setting the tone and mood of those watching the broadcasts.

The one thing I reiterated in these appearances was the fact that I was very proud of my fellow traders and the entire trading community for not trying to profit from the carnage and confusion that ensued in the wake of the attacks. Those of us in the financial markets industry do not see ourselves as doing something that is meaningful in scope. We aren't doctors or nurses and we're not teachers or social workers, but the way the entire industry conducted itself during that time made me very proud to say I am a member of the trading community.

EMOTIONS DRIVE THE MARKET

The events that surrounded the stories of Babe, the Gault family, and September 11 reveal how market psychology can be affected at different levels. Babe's story showed the effects on a small group of traders experiencing an indirect result in the form of a less liquid product for a short period of time. The Gault family accident showed how a single incident within the trading community can have a tremendous impact on daily volatility. And the events surrounding 9/11 showed market players demonstrating a willingness to work together like never before. Each of these different stories is useful to help traders understand that market psychology is all about the study of basic emotions.

These are the basic emotions that drive our daily lives and that must be understood for someone to be a great trader. Whether the event in question takes place on a single day or consumes a prolonged period of time, getting a handle on the emotional side of the market as it reacts to the event is a must for every trader. Unlike the arguments that surround random walk theory, basic human passions never change. People will always experience fear and greed, and it is those two raw human emotions that always drive the market. The feelings that drove tulip bulb prices to ridiculous levels in Holland hundreds of years ago are the same basic emotions that more recently drove tech stocks to unsustainable prices.

Many investors will put capital at risk based on the market psyche. Some of these investors are mistaken for technicians who chart the market, but they are really a kind of market sociologist looking for recurring patterns of human emotions that work in cycles. Both euphoria and fear come in waves. It's up to the individual trader to recognize, much like a surfer, which wave to ride and which wave to let go by. The feelings that surrounded the rising market—the wealth effect—created an atmosphere of prosperity and happiness worldwide. But as high as the highs of the bull market were, the lows that followed were even lower. The decline in the Nasdaq market followed by the events of September 11 transformed the euphoria into fear within a year. The wealth effect was now replaced by a global war on terror and the new enemy was the ideology of hate. The fear that became a part of the investor consciousness has stayed with the marketplace to this day.

We often hear about a "war premium" being built into pricing. This is especially true in the crude oil and gold markets. The war premium is, in effect, the market psychology quantified. Computer programs have priced the emotional aspects of trading and come up with formulas and models to describe pricing instability. But this emotional pricing creates two problems: First, the technology used in pricing raw human feelings is programmed by a human being, limiting it, by definition, to the emotions understood by the creator. Second, technology itself has limitations that must be realized, making the human factor a necessary part of any emotional analysis.

Another reason to understand and study the psychology of the market is that it gives traders a better understating of themselves as individuals. Traders and investors can better focus on finding the right opportunity when they're able to identify the psychological factors that are driving prices one way or another. Traders who get caught up in the feelings of the trade can no longer be objective in their analyses. To remain disciplined and profitable, it becomes essential to eliminate the surrounding noise. In other words, you must focus on the opportunity at hand rather than the event itself. Understanding the true nature of the raw energy that is responsible for pricing the markets is a never-ending discipline.

As students of the marketplace, we need to observe the way raw emotion plays a part in every trade that is made. There should be a certain amount of fear and greed associated with every trade you make. It's finding the right balance between the two that is essential to becoming a good trader. I'm reminded of something Bing once said to me when I first started trading: Always have a little fear of the market but never lose respect for it. He was trying to teach me to live with the fear while remembering that the market can always take me out. Never, ever lose respect, and don't get caught up in the greed!

CHAPTER 9

Demystifying Economic Releases

A few years ago, well before Hurricane Katrina destroyed the city, my wife and I went to New Orleans for a weekend away without the children. Never having been there we were both taken by the wonderful food and the nonstop revelry. Being of a conservative nature, my wife and I loved the food but found the dedicated debauchery to be something that passed us by years ago. Nonetheless, we decided to go out to Bourbon Street and enjoy the Big Easy, hitting the watering holes and listening to great jazz along the way. Having found a comfortable club with a crowd that appeared to be the appropriate age to include us, we agreed to sit and people-watch.

As we sat and enjoyed the sights and sounds of New Orleans, a gentleman walked into the bar in an obvious state of intoxication. He looked to be in his mid-50s and his pants looked like expensive dress slacks that had been cut with a pair of scissors recently. I noticed that he was working his way around the bar, talking to every female in the establishment. The ridiculous-looking pants coupled with a glare that would take days of nonstop drinking to acquire rendered his attempts at finding female companionship for the evening futile.

As he worked his way through the room, I saw that he had a Rolex watch on his wrist—and it was real. It had a sweeping second hand (the sign of a real Rolex) and was laced with diamonds all across the face. It was a beautiful timepiece worth well over $25,000 but one that you would not expect to see on such an individual. After being rebuffed by half the women there, he spotted my wife and me sitting on the other side of the room. He staggered toward us, and as he did, I looked at my wife and said with a smile, "It's your turn, honey!" At that moment, he walked straight up to me and said, "You look just like that guy from Chicago that reports on the business channels." Cautiously, I responded with a pleasant "thank you" and hoped he would continue on his way. Before resuming his quest for company, he turned to me and said, "You know, you and Santelli are the only ones on TV who explain the numbers so I can understand them. I like you guys!" I looked at my wife, who was trying very hard not to laugh out loud. She said, "There you go, Jack. There's your audience!"

As amusing as that story might sound it proved to me that I had been able to properly communicate the potential market impact of the economic releases. As drunk as that investor might have been, he was able to identify me and knew I had taught him something.

Instant analysis is perhaps the most difficult thing to do on live TV. I think the only reason that people like Rick Santelli and others are able to do it so effortlessly is that they take the instant analysis that you need when you are a market participant and transfer it to the TV screen.

I asked Rick to do an interview for this book because I know of very few individuals like him who understand the market condition and convey it properly to the investing public. In fact, I find myself listening to his commentary more than any other on business television because of his talent for breaking down the daily activity into a clear and concise form.

INTERVIEW WITH RICK SANTELLI

Bouroudjian: Rick, you've been in the public eye for a few years; tell us a little bit about your background. How you actually got into the market, and how you ended up getting on TV.

Santelli: Well, in terms of getting into the market, I went to the University of Illinois, and since a very young age, I thought I was going to be a lawyer. It's what I always wanted to do. After graduating from Champaign, I came to visit a friend at the Chicago Mercantile Exchange, the CME. His father was a pork belly broker and before that, going back to the '50s, prior to the existence of the present CME Exchange building [he] began his career when the CME was in the Franklin Building.

I was so fascinated with what was going on down there. He tried to explain to me . . . some of the intricacies of the meat market, and that's all it took! I guess I fell in love with it from day one, and never proceeded to go to law school. I took a job with Lehman Brothers—back then it was called Shearson—and then took a job with Shearson when they acquired Lehman. I believe I was making $68 a week and my train pass, which was on a monthly basis, cost about $35 per month, so there wasn't much to live on at the end of the month, but I think it was probably the best move I ever made.

Bouroudjian: How'd you get on TV? Was it an accident or is it something you wanted to do?

Santelli: Well, TV is another crazy story altogether. You talk about how life throws curve balls. I started trading around '79 and caught the great gold market at the CME when prices shot up close to a thousand dollars an ounce. The Iran/Iraq conflict started in January of '81 and that was the peak. Gold, instead of going up, started to come down. The Hunt brothers got stuck trying to corner the silver market, which helped drive prices lower. But I traded at the CME until about '84, then went to the CBOT around 1993 or 1994. It was during this time that the exchanges all pretty much unilaterally started to look at the media in a more affectionate fashion. Instead of keeping the media out of the turnstiles, they decided, "Hey, let's let the media on the trading floor." But since that was really never allowed, there wasn't a big pool of experienced traders that had dealt with the media.

I had a friend who was working for media-relations for CBOT at the time, and it was one of the local channels, channel 26, which grabbed me and threw me on the air for the first time. I wasn't very good at it in the beginning. I look at some of those old videotapes and think, oh my god, I was so rough around the edges. And we were on this little catwalk on the old CBOT floor, which was originally the 1930s grain room. When the grains moved into the addition in 1981, all the financials moved into the old grain room. I remember doing an interview on that two-foot catwalk, and it was an experience! It was me, a cameraman, a young lady holding a mike. It was kind of dangerous now that I think about it. Looking back on the shot, we all looked green, because the green light from the boards cast a shadow; it was kind of eerie. It was like Halloween TV. But I liked doing it, and I started becoming a guest for Reuters TV, which is no longer in existence.

Back then, getting to be an occasional guest on CNBC was about as cool as it ever could get. I started doing a few spots on CNBC, and lo and behold, I became the guy for Unemployment Fridays. Every first Friday of the month, I was the guy who broke down the numbers. They didn't have individual shows back then; it was one giant show all day long. Jimmy Rogers used to always be on the first Friday along with me. I think Cramer became the regular when Jimmy stopped doing it before Kudlow took his place. So I appeared on TV for the better part of five years. Now it's 1999 and we found ourselves on a new trading floor. The CBOT opened up that big monster floor in '97. I remember I was having issues with one of my bigger customers at the time, and at that time in my life, I was with Sanwa Bank.

Unemployment reports still had really big movement in the marketplace—it's been a lot more tame of late. One customer was driving me crazy! I executed the orders, ran up and did my spot on CNBC with a lot of issues on my mind. Mumbling half-heartedly, I said into the microphone, "God, I should just do this for a living!" You got to be careful what you wish for—all of a sudden the wheels started turning. The next thing I knew I was flying out to CNBC headquarters; at that time they were in Fort Lee, New Jersey.

About seven months after that, we worked out a deal. I stopped trading, gave up my memberships, and went to work for GE/CNBC full-time. I remember my wife and parents looking at me as if I were crazy: "Are you out of your mind?" This all happened when I was having a great year. 1999 was a great year for brokerage—the clients were trading, it was profitable and still, for me, fun! I left it all, and thought to myself, there are so many changes taking place in the industry!

Whether it's brokerage rates coming down, or even the disappearance of the edge, things were changing. Traders like me looked at the markets and thought the edges weren't as big as they used to be. My god, if you look what the edges are now, it makes the edge in '99 look rather gigantic. I made the move and now I'm going on eight years with CNBC, almost thirteen if you include the time I was a guest. I think it's probably the best career decision I ever made. I think I do a couple of things in life well. I can fix an old Lincoln with my eyes closed, and I love talking about the market. When you get paid to talk about something you love, it's an added bonus!

Bouroudjian: You've been a successful trader and you've been a successful broker. How do you get your information, and better yet, is there anything you do differently now than you did before?

Santelli: I guess the first part is, when I really started to get into the fixed-income markets, it started in the Treasury bill and Eurodollar futures contracts in the early '80s. I met a gentleman named Richard Sandor. And anybody who understands the history of this business we're in, namely futures, knows that there're two names that always crop up—Leo Melamed and Richard Sandor. And I think, until the end of time, those two gentlemen, will always fight over who is the father of financial futures. Personally, I think they both should get the title. Anyway, I met Richard, and I ended up working for him. And back then, I was a market technician.

I was an avid technician from my first moments on the floor in '79. Richard Sandor was an economist drumming the praises of a menu of new financial futures products to conservative bankers and institutional end users. Richard told me, "Listen, if you're going to work with me, we're going to deal with servicing institutions. You must learn about hedging, you're going to have to learn the language of bankers." You can look at a chart, and get an idea of what you think is going to happen, but when you make your presentation to your client—whether it's on the phone, it's an order, or in person—when you travel, you have to convert your market predictions and observations into their dialect. So I started to learn about the fixed-income market. I guess what I tried to do at that point was to embrace, understand, and follow the fundamentals. The charts would tell me the direction of the market.

I tried to marry the two concepts together. And I think, as time progressed, I found the economic side of it really fascinating. You know, back then, if the Fed changed interest rates, the information didn't reach the traders quickly. There wasn't transparency. CNBC didn't have a show devoted entirely to the statement or the announcement. There wasn't even a statement issued on the air. If you wanted to know what the Fed did, back in the '80s, you had to look at your Quotron screen and you had to watch where Fed funds actually traded, and figure out if they moved or not. At this time the trading activity in the 30-year bond was huge. The contract started in '77, but it didn't really get legs, and really start to get aggressive, 'til around '84, '85. I just thought that this is an area that not only would enhance technicals, but in many ways become a common metric for such new contracts, especially after coming off of double-digit inflation and interest rates in the early part of the decade. So I tried to marry these two market methods together. I guess what's changed today, versus back then, is that this very metamorphosis is now the cornerstone of computer trading. So now we have a proliferation of large players coupled with a huge amount of liquidity and a global stage that has altered all aspects of trading. The force of the GDP powerhouse from the likes of China, India, or different parts of the Pacific Rim and Asia with their inexpensive labor costs and pockets full of export bounty in the form of lots and lots of U.S. dollars is changing decades of economic rules on the fly. Many economists will debate me on this issue, asking, "Is it really different this time?" Yet I stick to my opinions that comparing major data points like inflation, jobs, or trade imbalances is a dicey proposition. To assume these types of comparisons are "apples to apples," considering such dramatic and profound global change, will be debated for years to come.

I think when it comes to the global explosion of economies and capital markets, it truly is different this time. We're never going to put China back in the box. You're never going to change the global forces that have been unleashed. I think Mr. Greenspan figured it out at a very early time, that all of a sudden, in the '90's, you have this productivity miracle going on, but in many ways, the ability of the U.S. economy to power through levels of employment, and GDP, that normally, in the past, would bring on horrible inflation and a raft of other negative consequences, is amazing. And now, years later, we have Ben Bernanke, talking about productivity in the same fashion, that it will help the U.S. economy increase its capacity. I think our productivity, like so many new and improved economic theories, is more than partially due to what's going on in China and the other new large global players.

If you have a factory that makes widgets, and you can outsource the factory, and have lower labor costs, and make a profit without fighting the global labor market realities, everybody seems to walk away a winner. So what have I done differently? I now question how you interpret all of the data today, and all of the issues that move the market in the context of history, because I think we're writing a new set of rules. I think in 10 or 20 years, when you go to the biggest business schools in the country, they will look at the period from about 2001 on as defined by a couple of different major issues.

Terrorism—September 11th. Changed the markets, really cemented the notion that we all learned in '87, that when things get nasty, the credit market picks up the slack. You know, it's the old-fashioned "flight to quality." The other big notion is that the global economy is probably in its infancy now, and I think for many years to come it's going to change every measurement of how we trade the market, and if I could leave readers with one notion, the question I now ask myself, before I ever use an economic statistic or pattern on a chart, is "What's the money doing? Follow the money." Because I think, with the push of a button, all the electronic platforms, the speed and efficiency in money, capital, trading . . . it's now instantaneous, you can move everything quickly.

I also think one must realize that there are so many things that have changed—it's very dynamic! Maybe one of the biggest things to have changed is the role of central bankers. In this global setting, any given country's central bank has a much shorter reach with much less efficacy to imprint their will. Central bankers now are starting to have summits on globalization, and behind closed doors, I'm sure they're discussing the very issues that we all are.

Bouroudjian: I'm going to switch gears on you a little bit. You do an amazing job, breaking down economic releases. I do it once in a while, but you do it all the time. Is there anything special that you do, to be able to break down these numbers, so that the average investor can understand them?

Santelli: Being prepared is the biggest factor. I'll always be cognizant of what data is coming out, where it has been and where expectations place it currently. For argument's sake, let's say it's CPI [Consumer Price Index]. I will look at the way the market has behaved the last several releases, and see what parts of the report the market moved on. What was the year-over-year core inflation, and what was the headline number? What part of the overall data did the market concentrate on? And then I will try to put down on paper all the extremes of that series; in other words, let's say we're talking about core inflation CPI. What's been the lowest or highest read? So that as the data's released, I can put the important component in some type of structure to see whether it's in the top part of the range, or a new high, or is it in the bottom part of the range, or a new role for the series, or is it in the middle? Then I get to what I commented on earlier, follow the money. What I will do is keep one ear tuned to the noise level on the trading floor and both eyes glued to the news boards as the information is released. I'll see what the number is, and I will try to scan all the sectors, span the interest rates, the equities, and the foreign exchange as each of these important sectors relates price to the data that is unfolding in real time. Is the trading on the floor getting louder and more aggressive, or is dimming down? Is the market moving up or down aggressively, is it moving up or down with big volume or with small volume?

I guess I've gotten this to the point where I tease some of the guys in the pits; I will sometimes not look at all the data, as I'm on TV, but I can tell you what it is. Because you get to the point where you know the markets and the reactions so well, that you can just get a sense of the data purely from the activity, or lack of, on the trading floor. Although sometimes there's a delayed response. Many times as of late we find traders digging deeper into the subtext of the numbers. It seems as if we're all turning into economists . . . trying desperately to get to the market-moving aspects of the report. As important as the data is, the price movement of the market is studied more than the actual numbers. This is why I feel that the technical study of the market can be viewed as all-inclusive, with data points just a subset of the charted activity.

So, I guess, my motto in that regard is "Prepare, and know exactly what the data has been." Because you've got to know where you've been to know where you're going. The most important thing is to make the market the star. Whatever the market does is always right. I learned an important life lesson early in my career. You can change CPI data. You can revise unemployment data. You can pretty much revise everything in life, even election returns, as we learned in 2000. But there's one thing you can never change and never revise, and that's yesterday's prices in the market. It can never be changed. Once they're on that chart, once the Dow Jones Industrial Average closes for the day—that's the price. And that will be the price forever. For the markets are the star. Everything else is relative, and the only constant is the price structure.

Bouroudjian: One more question. If you had a new trader come to you and say they wanted to start trading or investing, what one or two points, aside from "Follow the money," which is an excellent point, would you give them? Would you like to share a secret that maybe the floor has, or maybe the professional community has, that the average investor doesn't know?

Santelli: Oh, I think that's the easiest question of all. The market is the aggregate vote of all the players. So at any given moment, the price that you see on the board, or on your screen, represents a consensus. People—in this case, investors—are biological organisms, which makes them very predictable on a number of levels in terms of their behavior. To that end, I love playing little games; I do this with my kids. I'll say, "Okay, get on the other side of that door. And I want you to come and see if I'm home, so knock on the door." They always knock three times. It's a Fibonacci number. Certain behavioral traits, like how many times we knock or ring a phone, are comfortable to us as humans. One finds Fibonacci numbers a somewhat magical metric in nature, astronomy, art, and even in the origins of the present-day calendar. How many times, Jack, have you talked about retracements in the markets? Much of the methodology is based on the Fibonacci numbers and the golden mean. The intermingling effects of time and price on our decision making process are some of the cornerstones of technical analysis.

Why are there always charts in a trading room? Well, I'll tell you why. Because people under certain conditions have a certain amount of behavior that's always consistent. So I guess what I would tell a new trader is that the market is not the "random walk," as some economists might have us believe. People under many different circumstances, whether it's under pressure, or whatever, always seem to have some constants in how they assimilate information. And I think you have to carry that notion into the marketplace. And you have to try to understand the group dynamics, and also realize that there's a lot of constants to understand, and even count on. A great example of this large-scale behavior is the market bubble. There have been bubbles going back, anecdotally to the beginning of trading. What I find interesting is, there will always be bubbles. And it isn't because people are stupid, it's because they can't help themselves. They're a biological organism that is put together in a certain fashion, that no matter how hard we try, we can't escape the fact that we're human. There're certain things [that] affect us in certain ways. Tops and bottoms in markets, for example, tend to be accompanied by a series of recognizable patterns.

Many times you look for that capitulation trait. That's such a human dynamic. Sometimes logic and common sense justifiably keep savvy traders from getting involved in markets that seem to transcend wisdom in how they are priced. Yet many times, even level-headed investors reach a point where they just can't resist the temptation to get involved. Those are the trends in the marketplace that you have to pay most attention to. Beginners or novice traders should open to the possibilities of the markets. Even if one has never looked at a market, taken an economics or futures class, the learning curve may not be as steep as professionals would have you believe. I tell friends and others trying to learn the markets to spend a couple of months looking at charts of the major sectors such as interest rates and equity indices. Specifically, daily, weekly, and monthly charts. After a couple of months of observation, you'll know exactly what I mean; there are certain characteristics that are repetitive, over and over. It's like an EKG of the market. And once you get tuned into that, everything else will fall in place. You might even find that it will hook you as it has me.

Bouroudjian: Is there anything you might add? Anything else you can think of that you'd want somebody to either know, that you want to say?

Santelli: Well, I think that the markets are the most interesting Rubik's Cube puzzle in the world. Some people like soap operas or sporting events. But I think that the markets encapsulate everything that's challenging and fun. It's a great puzzle that can be peppered with a profitable, monetary aspect. It has everything to offer, and anybody who thinks markets are unexciting, or boring, ought to put a little flesh in the game. They will realize that that feeling that they get in their stomach is very addicting. And, Jack, as you well know, whether traders are profitable or not doesn't seem to matter much because in either case they always seem to come back for more.

ECONOMIC RELEASES

The following are the economic releases that I believe move the market the most. It is my intention to give you a feel for what the number means to traders and investors alike. Much of the analysis is common sense, but the thing to keep in mind is that there are times in the economic cycle that turn good news into bad and bad news into good. A great example is the recent move in the short end of the yield curve in interest rates. As the economy grew stronger and stronger, the Federal Reserve decided it should act as a pin in the balloon and slowly let the air out of an overheating economy. During the cycle of Fed tightening, any good news about the economy seemed to give the Fed more reason to be aggressive in the tightening mode.

Unemployment

Unemployment—if ever there was an economic report that was the mother of all numbers, this is it! The employment release is a set of labor market indicators. The unemployment rate measures the number of unemployed people as a percentage of the labor force. Nonfarm payroll employment counts the number of paid employees working part-time or full-time in the nation's business and government establishments. The average workweek reflects the number of hours worked in the nonfarm sector. Average hourly earnings disclose the basic hourly rate for major industries as indicated in nonfarm payrolls.

The anticipation on Wall Street each month is clear, the reactions are usually volatile, and the information for investors helps determine investor confidence. By looking past the headline unemployment rate, investors can take a more strategic look at their portfolios and even take advantage of unique investment opportunities that often happen in the days before and after the release. The employment data gives the most complete report on how many people are looking for jobs, how many have them, what they're getting paid, and how many hours they are currently working. These numbers are the best way to measure the current state as well as the future course of the economy. Nonfarm payrolls are categorized by various sectors. This sector data can go a long way in helping investors determine in which economic sectors they intend to invest. The employment statistics also provide insight on wage trends, and wage inflation is high on the list of enemies for the Federal Reserve. Fed officials constantly monitor this data, watching for even the smallest signs of potential inflationary pressures, even when economic conditions are weak. If inflation is under control, it is easier for the Fed to maintain a more accommodative monetary policy. If inflation is a problem, the Fed is limited in providing economic stimulus. By tracking the jobs data, investors can sense the degree of tightness in the job market. If wage inflation threatens, it's a good bet that interest rates will rise; bond and stock prices will fall. No doubt, the only investors in a good mood will be the ones who watched the employment report and adjusted their portfolios to anticipate these events. In contrast, when job growth is slow or becomes negative, then interest rates are likely to decline, boosting bond and stock prices in the process.

Retail Sales

Retail sales is one of the most volatile numbers month to month. It is the measure of the total receipts at stores that sell durable and nondurable goods. Everyone talks about consumer spending, but what they don't know is that consumer spending accounts for more than two-thirds of the economy, so if you know what consumers are up to, you'll have a pretty good handle on where the economy is headed. This is the information edge that traders and investors are searching for. The pattern in consumer spending is often the foremost influence on stock and bond markets.

For stocks, strong economic growth translates to strong corporate profits and higher equity prices. For bonds, the focal point is whether economic growth goes overboard and leads to inflation. In an ideal world, the economy walks that fine line between strong growth and excessive growth that causes inflationary pressure. This balance was achieved through much of the 1990s. For this reason alone, investors in the stock and bond markets enjoyed huge gains during the bull market of the 1990s. Retail sales growth did slow down in conjunction with the equity market in 2000 and 2001, but then rebounded at a healthy pace in the last few years. Retail sales gives the investors a sense of the big picture, as well as the trends among different types of retailers, both high and low end. There are times when auto sales are especially strong or apparel sales are showing exceptional weakness. These trends from the retail sales data can help you spot precise investment opportunities, without having to wait for a company's numbers.

Producer Price Index and Consumer Price Index

The Producer Price Index (PPI) and the Consumer Price Index (CPI) are the best indicators of inflation in the economy. Both numbers move the market for obvious reasons but have much more impact when the Federal Reserve is in the market. For example, when the Federal Reserve is at the end or the beginning of a cycle of tightening or easing, then the numbers have a much larger impact than at times when the Fed is out of the picture. The PPI is a measure of the average price level for a fixed basket of capital and consumer goods paid by producers, while the CPI is the measure of prices that have been passed along to the consumer. The PPI measures prices at the producer level before they are passed along to consumers. Since the PPI measures prices of consumer goods and capital equipment, a portion of the inflation at the producer level gets passed through to the CPI. By tracking price pressures in the pipeline, investors can anticipate inflationary consequences in coming months. Investors need to watch inflation closely. Individual traders or investors who understand the process of inflation and how inflation influences the markets will benefit over those who don't understand the consequences of inflation. Inflation is an increase in the overall prices of goods and services.

The relationship between inflation and interest rates is the key to understanding how data such as the PPI and the CPI influence the markets and everyone's portfolios. If someone borrows $1,000 from you today and promises to repay it in one year with interest, how much interest should you charge? The answer depends largely on inflation, because you know that the $1,000 won't buy the same amount of goods and services a year from now as it does today. If you were in a country where prices doubled every couple of months, you might want to charge 500 percent interest for a total payoff of $5,000 at the end of the year. In the United States, the PPI tells us that prices were rising about 4 to 5 percent a year through the summer of 2005. While the CPI was rising less rapidly during this period, you would want to take into account the higher inflation rates evident at earlier stages of processing when you were determining what interest rate to charge simply to recoup your purchasing power within the next 12 months. You might want to add in one or two percentage points to cover default risk and the opportunity cost, but inflation remains the key variable in what interest rate you would charge.

Inflation (along with default risk and opportunity cost) basically explains how interest rates are set on everything from your mortgage and auto loans to Treasury bills, notes, and bonds. As the rate of inflation changes and as expectations on inflation change, the markets adjust interest rates accordingly. The effect ripples across stocks, bonds, commodities, and your portfolio, often in a dramatic fashion.

Housing Numbers

The explosion in real estate prices across the country and their connection to the investing public are key to understanding the impact of numbers related to housing. Housing starts measure initial construction of residential units (single-family and multifamily) each month. A rising (falling) trend points to gains (declines) in demand for furniture, home furnishings, and appliances. This narrow piece of data has a powerful multiplier effect through the economy, and therefore across the markets and your investments. By tracking economic data such as housing starts, investors can gain specific investment ideas as well as broad guidance for managing a portfolio.

Home builders usually don't start a house unless they are fairly confident it will sell on or before its completion.

Changes in the rate of housing starts tell us a lot about demand for homes and the outlook for the construction industry. Furthermore, each time a new home is started, construction employment rises, and income will be pumped back into the economy. Once the home is sold, it generates revenues for the home builder and a myriad of consumption opportunities for the buyer. Refrigerators, washers and dryers, furniture, and landscaping are just a few things new home buyers might spend money on, so the economic ripple effect can be substantial, especially when you think of it in terms of more than 100,000 new households around the country doing this every month.

Since the economic backdrop is the most pervasive influence on financial markets, housing starts have a direct bearing on stocks, bonds, and commodities. In a more specific sense, trends in the housing starts data carry valuable clues for the stocks of home builders, mortgage lenders, and home furnishings companies. Commodity prices such as lumber are also very sensitive to housing industry trends.

Productivity

Productivity measures the growth of labor efficiency in producing the economy's goods and services. Unit labor costs reflect the labor costs of producing each unit of output. Both are followed as indicators of future inflationary trends.

Productivity growth is critical because it allows for higher wages and faster economic growth without inflationary consequences. This is a hot topic these days with the economy so strong, the labor market so tight, yet inflation so well-behaved. Some Wall Street experts state that dramatic productivity advances are allowing the economy to continue a much faster pace of growth than previously thought possible. Former Fed chairman Alan Greenspan and the present chairman Ben Bernanke have expressed skepticism about those statements, however. In either case, the productivity data gives investors important clues on how stocks and bonds can be expected to perform, and the market reactions to these releases show the true importance of productivity growth.

Durable Goods

Durable goods orders reflect the new orders placed with domestic manufacturers for immediate and future delivery of factory hard goods. The first release, the advance, provides an early estimate of durable goods orders. About two weeks later, more complete and revised data is available in the factory orders report. The data for the previous month is usually revised a second time upon the release of the new month's data. Investors want to keep their fingers on the pulse of the economy because it usually dictates how various types of investments will perform. Rising equity prices thrive on growing corporate profits—which in turn stem from healthy economic growth. Healthy economic growth is not necessarily a negative for the bond market, but bond investors are highly sensitive to inflationary pressures. When the economy is growing too quickly and can't meet demand, it can pave the road for inflation. By tracking economic data such as durable goods orders, investors will know what the economic backdrop is for these markets and their portfolios.

Orders for durable goods show how busy factories will be in the months to come, as manufacturers work to fill those orders. The data provides insight into demand for items such as refrigerators and cars, as well as business investments such as industrial machinery, electrical machinery, and computers. If companies commit to spending more on equipment and other capital, they are obviously experiencing sustainable growth in their business. Increased expenditures on investment goods set the stage for greater productive capacity in the country and reduce the prospects for inflation. Durable goods orders tell investors what to expect from the manufacturing sector, a major component of the economy, and therefore a major influence on their investments.

Consumer Confidence

The Conference Board compiles a survey of consumer attitudes on present economic conditions and expectations of future conditions, surveying 5,000 consumers across the country each month. While the level of consumer confidence is associated with consumer spending, the two do not move in tandem each and every month. The pattern in consumer attitudes and spending is often the foremost influence on stock and bond markets. For stocks, strong economic growth translates to healthy corporate profits and higher stock prices. For bonds, the focal point is whether economic growth goes overboard and leads to inflation. Preferably, the economy walks that fine line between strong growth and excessive (inflationary) growth.

This balance was achieved through much of the 1990s. For this reason alone, investors in the stock and bond markets enjoyed huge gains during the bull market of the 1990s. Consumer confidence did shift down along with the equity market between 2000 and 2002 and then recovered in 2003 and 2004.

Consumers became more pessimistic in 2005 and 2006 when gasoline prices surged. Consumer spending accounts for more than two-thirds of the economy, so the markets are always dying to know what consumers are up to and how they might behave in the near future. The more confident consumers are about the economy and their own personal finances, the more likely they are to spend. With this in mind, it's easy to see how this index of consumer attitudes provides insight into the direction of the economy. Just note that changes in consumer confidence and retail sales don't move in tandem month by month.

Gross Domestic Product

Gross domestic product (GDP) is the broadest measure of collective economic activity and encompasses every sector of the economy. GDP is the all-inclusive measure of economic activity. Investors need to closely track the economy because it usually dictates how investments will perform. Investors in the stock market like to see healthy economic growth because robust business activity translates to higher corporate profits. Bond investors are more highly sensitive to inflation, and robust economic activity could potentially pave the road to inflation. By tracking economic data such as GDP, investors will know what the economic backdrop is for these markets and their portfolios.

The GDP report contains a treasure trove of information that not only paints an image of the overall economy, but tells investors about important trends within the big picture. GDP components such as consumer spending, business and residential investment, and price (inflation) indexes illuminate the economy's undercurrents, which can translate to investment opportunities and guidance in managing a portfolio.

Although there are many other economic releases that drive the market in one direction or another, it's not imperative to get caught up in every number. Some numbers, such as the retailers or the car sales figures, can give investors and traders a feel for what the health of the consumer might be, but the overall impact is minimal. The only times the market acts in a volatile manner following the release of a minor number is if the release is unexpectedly good or bad. A car sales figure that is a surprise to the upside, for example, could lead to a rally in both carmakers and suppliers alike rather than finding strength in just one concentrated group of stocks. The only other very important part of the economic release cycle is the institution that has the final word: the Federal Reserve.

The Federal Reserve

The Federal Reserve is a mystery unto itself. Many have tried to study the Fed and the actions of the Federal Open Market Committee (FOMC), which meets regularly to forge monetary policy, but few really understand its true nature and responsibility. There have been dozens of books written about what it does, and better yet, what it's supposed to do. Chartered on December 23, 1913, it is the nation's central bank. Many investors don't realize that the responsibility of the Fed has changed slightly over the course of its existence. It was created by an act of Congress with the mission to formulate monetary policy for the country's economy. It seems that those who created the institution never thought they would have the power that they clearly have in today's market.

The concept, at the time, was to help relieve the cycle of boom and busts that shook the nation's banking system to its core. The situation had reached a point, primarily because of the Industrial Revolution, that boom and bust markets seemed to be almost expected. Prior to the creation of the Fed, a great run in the stock market was always followed by a panic that closed banks and created depression-like conditions for years. Unfortunately, 16 years later the country suffered the worst depression in history, with very little guidance from the nation's central bank.

Things seemed to change after World War II, when bankers began to see the need for a strong central bank in the wave of the massive rebuilding efforts put out by the Marshall Plan. Billions of U.S. dollars began to pour into the ravaged European countries, with the Federal Reserve cautiously adding liquidity to the system. As the U.S. economy began to be the world's leader, the importance of the nation's central bank began to grow to unimaginable levels. In fact, the actions of the Federal Reserve are so important to the global economy that every equity and fixed-income market in the world is affected by them.

The Fed really started to morph into the institution it is today after Jimmy Carter's administration. When Paul Volcker became the chairman of the Fed, he inherited double-digit inflation and growing unemployment. The interest rates were at an all-time high and the constant fear of stagflation made owning U.S. equities very risky. As Ronald Reagan took office and started to push the supply-side theory, Volcker and the Fed, unilaterally, began to tighten the money supply and contain inflation at a manageable level. Prior to Volcker, the Fed was a political organization answering to the whims of the executive office instead of maintaining a desired course. The Carter administration had created a mess. Not only were they taxing the most profitable American citizens at ungodly high levels, but the constant printing of dollars was helping fuel the inflation scenario.

Everything changed with the Volcker Fed. The institution stopped acting as if it was political and began to function as a central bank. It contained inflation through very aggressive tightening and helped pave the way for the supply siders to help stimulate the economy. Of course, much of the success of the Volcker Fed lay in the hands of the Reagan administration, with its promise to lower taxes and expand the economy. The rest is history. Under Carter, smart money was looking to shelter income from the government. Investors were looking for capital preservation instead of capital appreciation! Traders were searching for three-to-one write-offs on investments. The word on the Street was not how much an investment could make you but rather how much one could write off and shield income!

When Reagan lowered taxes and eliminated tax loopholes, investors began to make constructive investments that made the economy grow. It's no coincidence that the capital that was freed from the vise of the Carter tax policies launched some of the great companies that we trade today. Many of the technology companies started in the late 1980s and early 1990s were seeded with capital that would have otherwise gone to unproductive investments. I have always had a warm spot in my heart for Volcker and Reagan because I started at Loyola in the fall of 1979. The year Reagan ran was my first presidential election and I will forever be convinced that his leadership helped save our economy at a crucial point in history.

Today the Fed has slowly matured under Alan Greenspan's leadership. As he turned over the gavel to Ben Bernanke recently, we were all reminded of the marvelous job he did in the years he spent in office. Sometimes we forget that the economy experienced a stock market crash only months after Greenspan's appointment. At that time he was able to orchestrate the leadership needed to guide the economy to safety. Although the jury is still out on Bernanke, it's clear that he intends to follow the legacy set by Volcker and Greenspan to be a vigilant inflation hawk with sensitivity to the marketplace. Never has it been more important for investors and traders to listen to every speech made by Bernanke and other Fed governors. The first few years of a new Fed, when nine members have less than three years on the board, are critical. This is the time when leadership is earned! This is also the time when the astute Fed observer can find an information edge— something every trader wants!

CHAPTER 10

Information Is Gold

I n the summer of 2004 my wife Donna and I decided to take the children on a family vacation to London. It was always our hope to be able to show our children how others lived in the world and give them something neither one of us ever had—childhood memories of a vacation abroad. As students of history, both Donna and I were always looking to find vacation spots filled with archeological ruins or historical significance. The trip to London accomplished our objective. Not only did we live in a London flat for a week, but we spent our days riding the Tube and working our way through the many layers of history. On our way back, we encountered the necessary preboarding ritual, which included a trip through customs, where we were asked to declare anything of value.

The trip back from London to Chicago always seems a bit shorter because of the time difference that makes it earlier when you arrive in the United States, as opposed to the jet lag that follows when you land there. Not one to be social on airplanes, I have been known to put on my earphones and keep to myself—out of the fear of sitting next to someone who won't shut up! This trip was a little different; Donna and the kids were sitting across the aisle and I ended up sitting next to a gentleman in his late 30s whose name escapes me (hopefully, he'll read this book and contact me).

About an hour into the flight, the man turned to me and started to talk, and I broke my unwritten rule and responded. I figured, what the heck, it was a long flight; it would be nice to have an intelligent soul to talk with for the duration. My hope was to find someone to engage in, in the words of Chicago columnist Irv Kupcinet, "the lively art of conversation."

The gentleman began by asking about my occupation and whether I was in Great Britain on business or pleasure. I told him I was traveling with my family, but that I had been to London on business trips in the past. I explained my role in the financial services industry as best I could to someone who seemed clueless about it. After I gave him the "Readers Digest" version of my career, the conversation turned to his occupation. He told me that he was an engineer by training but had crossed over into research and development for the auto industry. In short, he was an inventor!

He related to me the many different inventions that he had helped develop or had patented, among which were the capless gas cap and a special screw containing an alloy mix, which made it invaluable in modern auto production. I sat in awe as he went on for roughly an hour talking about the many wonderful things that the future holds because of creative individuals such as him. I remember thinking how great it must feel to dream on paper like that and then turn it into the real thing. This man was actually making something out of nothing!

After the eight-hour flight, we exited the aircraft and waited in line to go through customs. I stood with my family and he stood directly in front of us, waiting for the next available agent. As he went through, the customs agent asked him if there was anything he wanted to declare, to which he answered no. A British national coming into the United States is required by law to declare anything over a certain value. It occurred to me that he was walking through customs declaring nothing, which was probably correct, but in reality he was entering the United States with perhaps hundreds of millions of dollars in ideas! The information stored in his brain was like gold. This man could enter this country with very little in the way of material resources, yet he would produce ideas that could potentially generate unbelievable profits. Intellectual capital, or information, is often priceless!

WHERE DO PROFESSIONALS GET THEIR INFORMATION?

One of the questions most asked of me when I speak at conferences or to a group of clients is "Where do you get your information?" It's a question I asked as a new trader and one that should be on the lips of every participant in the marketplace. There are many ways to acquire the information needed to remain competitive, but the effectiveness of the information is determined by the type of trader the person is. There are three distinct types of traders when it comes to the need for information. The first type could not care less about anything other than the bid and offer and the flow of orders in the market. The second type keeps up on current events just enough to get a feel for the macroeconomic landscape. But the third type is my favorite—the information junkie.

What kind of trader could not care less about the surrounding world when trading? It would surprise many average investors and retail-based traders that some market participants would risk capital without looking for the guidance offered through information and research. In fact, some of the most successful traders and investors on the floor of the Chicago Mercantile Exchange (CME) have made fortunes by understanding the nature of the edge rather than basing trading decisions on information. I've met traders who don't read a thing before they enter the trading pit, relying instead on pure gut feeling rather than any information from the newspaper or the Internet. Average investors tend to perceive professional traders as being in the know about what is going on.

In other words, professional traders are on the inside, whereas all other market participants are on the outside. Nothing could be further from the truth, however. The reality is that the average informed individual has a better understanding of both geopolitical events and macroeconomic trends by staying informed. The average scalper standing in any pit at any exchange could not care less which direction the market moves as long as the edge is in his or her possession.

A trader who has a tendency to stay mildly informed usually relies on technical work to guide trading decisions. I know many traders who look at the world through the eyes of a technician with no desire to understand the geopolitical nature of the market; instead, they base every position on technical analysis of the market. There are very few people who fall into this category, although some have been very successful. Usually scalpers, who also hold long-term positions, find themselves staying somewhat informed, but not to the extent of the information junkie.

I always thought it must be very difficult to put on a position in the market without doing as much due diligence as is humanly possible. It's been my experience that traders who fall into third class, for the most part, fail. The problem lies in the fact that it is very hard to be both a scalper and a position trader at the same time. Usually, a scalper who turns into a position trader got stuck on one leg of the scalp, which renders a scalper useless. Once a position has been established, the trader can no longer remain objective and flexible—he or she now needs the market to move a certain way, period!

As I said, my favorite kind of trader is the information junkie. When I first arrived on the floor back in the early 1980s, information was very hard to obtain. This was in the days before the Internet and even prior to the pro-liferation of the personal computer. All information was received through TV, print media, and word of mouth. I immediately realized the importance of having adequate information when it became clear that knowledge was the key to profitability. I'm not talking about insider trading; I'm talking about having the network and the resources available to filter out the noise and find the truth. Many of the things I have discussed so far in this book, such as the 2:40 PM order imbalances and the days of the month when capital flows are committed, were considered a few years ago to be information that was available only to professionals. But as information becomes more readily available to the general public, the effectiveness of the information is somewhat diluted. Today's information junkies are addicted to the Internet and have found that technology has infiltrated every aspect of their lives. Between the BlackBerry phenomenon and the advent of the cell phone, staying in touch with the world around you has never been easier.

I've always been fond of reading the newspaper to get my daily dose of information and opinion. I rely on the *Chicago Tribune* and the *Wall Street Journal* for guidance. Occasionally I read the *New York Times* but only when there are larger political issues that I want to understand. For those of us who rely on information for everything, the Internet has been the saving grace. It's hard to imagine a world without being able to Google any topic you could think of. This phenomenon has turned everyone who has access to the Internet into a semiexpert on any given topic. Recently when oil prices began to drift higher and higher, the traders with open crude oil positions started to watch certain things such as the rig count in the Persian Gulf and other obscure data that they had never followed or even looked at before. Even today the media has become very familiar with terminology that once was the exclusive domain of wildcatters and oil service employees.

BUSINESS TV

When I talk with traders and reporters who appear on TV, I'm often surprised at how little they really know. There are certain individuals who have my utmost respect, such as Rick Santelli, but there are others who seem to be trying to justify their opinions rather than give an accurate read on the market. I find that at times I might be a little too bullish for the market condition, but I have my own rationale for being bullish and find very little reason to change my long-term view. I will always give a reasonable argument for any positions I have about the market condition and do the necessary homework before I go on the air. But there are others who don't qualify what they are saying. People who appear on business television or radio broadcasts and tell the audience that they are bullish or bearish better have sound reasoning to back up their opinion. They don't necessarily have to be right; after all, we've learned that calling the market is an art not a science. But it is a responsibility to listeners and viewers that public financial commentators use sound fundamental logic to support any analysis they offer.

One of the interesting things to watch for is the way the different reporters feed off the information received by other reporters. Sometimes when I'm watching an interview on one business channel, I find the other business channel commenting about what's being said on the first channel. One reason for this might be that there are only a handful of media outlets, outside of the Internet, that give anyone reporting on the market the needed background. With only two major business television stations, CNBC and Bloomberg, the world is collectively watching the same thing.

When I go overseas, I'm amazed at the number of traders who recognize me from my appearances on CNBC or Bloomberg TV. I'm surprised because these are European traders trading European markets, not dislocated Yanks trading from abroad. Many of these traders and portfolio managers see me via the Internet, keeping a close eye on the markets in the United States along with their positions at home. With the world becoming a much smaller place through globalization, the incestuous relationships among the global markets cannot be ignored.

Traders in Chicago and New York are strange in that they think the world revolves around them and the products that they trade. Whether it is commodities, equities, or bonds, traders making the market think they are the center of the universe. It really wasn't until the ruble meltdown in 1998 that traders in the United States realized that what happened on the other side of the world while they slept was just as important as events that occurred while the U.S. market was open. Forex traders had known this for years, but the rest of the U.S. financial services industry was slow to catch on. This period forced traders to begin paying attention to the movement of both the Asian markets and the European markets in order to gauge what would happen when the U.S. market opened. It used to be that the U.S. market set the trend for the entire world, but that is no longer the case. The size of the various markets around the globe and the amount of U.S. capital invested in those economies forced the close-knit relationships among all the major equity markets around the world.

Back before business television became as popular and widely accepted as it is today, the most important tool for any trader looking for information was the newswire. The most famous wire services are Reuters and Dow Jones, both of which are still used today by the majority of the trading population. In fact, if you were to go to the floor of any major exchange, you would see a large TV monitor strategically placed somewhere around a trading pit or post. There are traders who, even today, cannot trade unless they are staring at a newswire in search of information that might move the market. These traders have turned the gathering of information into an art form.

Some of the greatest traders in history have been information junkies who were absolutely addicted to the newswires and now have found solace in the use of the Internet. It's the information junkie who follows the obscure releases that the average trader ignores. If I were to ask the average S&P trader what the car sales figures are, or what the retailers are showing for any given week, I would be met with a puzzled look and a shrug of the shoulders. But the information addict knows every detail that is moving the market. In fact, I find that these traders are the best sources to have when preparing for the day ahead.

ORDER FLOW

The most profitable type of information comes from people who understand the nature of capital flows and how they affect the market. The importance of watching capital or order flow is one of the best-kept secrets among traders. Many traders have made untold fortunes because they understood the market condition and the nature of the order flow. Again, I'm not talking about insider trading but, rather, a true understating of what makes the market tick. When the Hunt brothers were trying to corner the silver market in the late 1970s and early 1980s, it was knowledge of order flow that made traders huge sums of money.

Back in 1973 Nelson Hunt and his brother William Hunt, the sons of a rich Texas oilman, along with a group of Arab investors, decided they would try to corner the world's silver supply. When they began to buy the commodity, it was trading at roughly $1.95. In 1973 President Nixon had recently taken the country off the gold standard and politically the country seemed to be falling apart. As the decade moved on, the price of silver moved steadily higher until late 1978 and early 1979, when the price started to reach the $5 mark. It didn't happen overnight but the move was nonetheless amazing for any commodity at that time. As 1979 progressed, the price began to skyrocket until it peaked in early 1980 at $49.95 an ounce. The trading in the pits in Chicago and New York was frantic, with life-of-contract moves happening in a day. What used to take a year to complete in terms of price movement was now happening in a day's time. The volatility was absurd. Information was at a premium—but what kind of information?

The Hunts used a certain broker in the New York market (the primary silver futures market). Despite having a presence in Chicago and in London, the New York broker seemed to have a large chunk of the business that was generated from the attempted cornering of silver futures. Traders paid clerks to do nothing but stand by the elevator waiting for this broker to emerge and walk toward the trading floor. I have heard the story from a handful of veterans who got their start by standing next to the elevator and running into the pit to tell their employers that the Hunt brothers' broker was walking into the pit. The natural course of action would have been to immediately buy the market, knowing full well that this broker was about to buy everything in the pit and take the market limit up. Some clerks were told to not even bother getting to the trader; instead, they were instructed to run to the pit and place an order to buy as many as 50 contracts if they saw him walking toward the pit. This is one definition of understanding order flow. The traders who made a fortune on the back of the Hunt brothers' attempted corner were shrewd enough to understand the nature of the market and order flow and capitalize on the price aberration they knew was coming.

The exchanges, realizing that there was an attempt at a corner of the silver supply, changed the rules, making any transaction "liquidation only." That is, no one was allowed to establish a new position in the futures market. This was done for a variety of reasons, the most important one being that the members of the exchanges were the ones taking the other side of the trades. As the Hunts were taking delivery on the silver contracts, it was the market makers and liquidity providers who were getting squeezed. The Hunts were highly leveraged in their strategy and began to look for assistance in maintaining the price at an artificially high level. They decided to collateralize further purchases of silver futures with silver bonds, which they would issue.

The story is that they were meeting with a group of Swiss bankers on or around March 26, 1980, asking for capital to cover margin calls generated by a break in the price of silver down to $21.62. The previous few months had seen the price move sharply lower, creating a financial dilemma for Nelson and William Hunt and their partners. They presented a plan that collateralized the loan they were requesting with silver certificates they would structure and offer to the institution. The Swiss bankers listened to the presentation, asked the Hunt entourage to step out of the room, and proceeded to sell silver futures. If they were planning on using silver to back a margin call, what would happen if the price continued to decline? The following day, March 27, was known as Silver Thursday. Silver moved from $21.62 down to $10.80, a whopping 50 percent decline in one day! Traders who continued to follow the strategy of buying the market every time the Hunt brothers' broker emerged found it to be a costly lesson.

INFORMATION CAN BE DANGEROUS

Squeezes and attempted cornering of markets have been around as long as markets have traded. The key is to be able to identify the move and, more important, understand when it might be over. There are a number of traders who still look at the world in a myopic way. They feel that the only good information is the type that revolves around the ego gratification that is the basis of any attempted corner. They are constantly on watch for a buyer of pork bellies or sugar, hoping to find a pattern that would suggest a squeeze. As narrow-minded as that type of thinking might be, these are the traders who have been around for decades and understand the power of good information. But there is one thing that all of them will agree on: A little information can be a dangerous thing!

There are times when having a little bit of information can be a recipe for disaster. In the early 1960s, the commodities markets were hit with a number of squeezes and attempted corners. This was before the regulatory scrutiny that exists today, and many of the commodities traded were at the mercy of a few individuals who controlled the pricing. One such commodity was salad oil, which traded in Chicago. The Allied Crude Vegetable Oil Refining Company was controlled by a man named Tino DeAngelis. He was the president of the company and had formed the entity in order to buy surplus vegetable oil from the government and sell it as an exported product overseas.

Allied was borrowing millions of dollars, which it used to speculate on vegetable oil in the futures markets. DeAngelis was securing the loans with the salad oil that Allied had in its possession, much like what the Hunt brothers tried to do years later. According to the American Bureau of Statistics, the reported amount of salad oil in Allied's possession was larger than the country's entire production! But even with all the noise around them, no traders understood what was happening, except one: Ralph Peters!

As I mentioned earlier in the book, Ralph Peters had the one of the greatest information networks ever created by any Chicago trader. His sources ranged from high-level diplomats to the lowest maintenance workers. As Allied continued to buy salad oil, Peters put the network to use. He found out that the loans that were being issued to Allied were being collateralized with the salad oil holdings at a facility deep in the South. He quickly took a trip to the facility to see for himself that the salad oil was there and that the position he was in—namely, long salad oil futures—was correct.

He took some comfort in the fact that the bank examiners were there at the same time checking on the tanks and making sure they were full. They did this by opening the top of the tank and dipping a stick 6 to 12 inches down to make sure the oil was there. Ralph located a man named Jimmy who worked the yard and became his contact for the grounds. He asked Jimmy to keep an eye on the place and if he noticed anything out of the ordinary—anything at all—to give him a call immediately.

Peters flew back to Chicago feeling good; he had identified a squeeze and had checked on the product, which gave him all the confidence that he was in a highly profitable position. A couple of days later, the phone rang and it was Jimmy warning him that something didn't seem right. He said that he had been employed at the facility for over 20 years and had a habit of banging on the tanks as he made his rounds. Being a musician, he realized that the pitch of each tank was a little different than it had ever been before. The tanks didn't sound empty, just different. Where others might have disregarded this as insignificant, Peters sensed a problem and sprang into action. He flew down to see Jimmy immediately. He had a large chunk of his net worth tied up in the position and anything out of the ordinary was enough to warrant an inspection.

He met Jimmy at the tanks and they discussed the situation. They walked around the lot and banged on the tanks together. Jimmy said that the only other time he could remember hearing a sound like that come from a tank was when they once filled it with water for cleaning. Peters smelled a rat. He asked Jimmy to open the tank so he could see the product for himself. Jimmy, realizing that the $50 a week he was getting for supplying information to Peters might not warrant losing his job, refused. After a couple of minutes of negotiations (it was very difficult to say no to Peters), the price was $200 to open the tank for an inspection.

Looking into the tank, they saw the same thing the bank examiners had seen—oil! They dipped the sticks down 6 inches, then 12 inches, and still nothing but salad oil. Then Peters had the idea to use a longer stick, a yardstick, to dip into the tank. As the stick came out of the tank, they looked at each other in disbelief. Below the top 12 inches of oil was nothing but water. Allied had put the salad oil on top of the water, knowing that it would float and create the impression that the tank was full of oil. The hoax had even fooled the banks and investment houses that offered credit to DeAngelis and Allied so they could maintain their positions in the futures markets. Peters jumped from the tank and flew back to Chicago. He had information that no one else had . . . at least not yet. He knew that he had just uncovered one of the largest scandals to ever hit the commodities markets, but was he the only one who knew?

When the market opened the following day, Peters dumped the entire position to the eager buyer—Allied. Peters sold his long position and began to get short slowly. Then the news hit. The tanks that were being used to secure the loans for further purchases of futures contracts and physical oil were filled with water. The loans were secured with nothing at all!

News of the scandal drove traders into a frenzy. The market began to lose all the momentum created by DeAngelis's attempts at a corner, and Allied went under. DeAngelis went to prison for the crime, and it nearly took down two major brokerage houses of the day. But Peters had the right information. He had the network to tap into and, more important, knew when to use it effectively. Peters had known that a little information can be a dangerous thing. He was shrewd enough to identify when an apparent squeeze was taking place and had the network to let him know it was all a hoax. Peters's advice all those years ago was right on the money: Know your market!

THE INFORMATION NETWORK

Building a network for information is, perhaps, the most powerful tool traders can create for themselves. Everyone wants to know the right people, but how does one get to know who they are—and how to get them to talk! This is a question I ask everyday as I talk to portfolio managers and brokers searching for a hint of what might lie ahead. I usually walk the floor, tapping into sources for information that I know are reliable. It's easy to get information; it's hard to get reliable information. I try to find individuals who have a vast understanding of market structure and know what it feels like to risk their own capital. It's better to talk with individuals who risk their own capital rather than an analyst or a technician because the emotions aren't the same. In order to get a feel for why a trader puts on a particular position in the market, it's important to understand the fundamental emotions behind the trade. Using logic and doing homework are necessary tasks in forming a high-percentage trade, but it's basic human emotion that drives the actual decision.

The question that all new traders should ask themselves is "How does one create this network of information?" After all, not everyone has access to portfolio managers and brokers to talk with on a daily basis. The reality is that everything you might need in the way of information is available at all times. It's more a question of filtering out the noise and finding the essential truth, As traders, or simply as human beings, we are all searching for the truth. Whether it be metaphysically or financially, the search for the truth never ends—rather, it's a dynamic part of human behavior. But we're taught to think critically—don't trust everything you read! The empirical theory of knowledge posits that man by definition is fallible; therefore, any knowledge attained is subject to fallibility. If that's true, then how do we know what to believe and what to discard as rubbish?

At a certain time in every trader's career, the person is asked to take a leap of faith. The ultimate leap is when you put on the first position in the market knowing that your capital is now at risk. Information sources are no different. After doing the necessary due diligence, such as mentally monitoring performance, then it becomes necessary for a trader to take a quasi leap of faith and rely on a source for information. This source might be a reporter on television (keeping in mind that, like Rick Santelli, many reporters are former traders and brokers) or it might be less obvious, for example, your local banker. It should come as no surprise that bankers often maintain a conservative outlook on the economy but can be insightful in their understanding of the retail public. In all honesty, your information source could be anyone in the financial services industry. I take that leap everyday when I get the information I need from my sources. If I find that someone is consistently wrong, I'll still keep the person in my loop as long as the person's logic is correct. Having a devil's advocate in every group is an important part of the process. In order to truly understand the beast, then all sides of the story must be known.

Coming from a liberal arts background, the thought of searching for the truth brought back fond memories of the philosophy and theology courses that were a huge part of my Loyola curriculum. The Jesuits trained us to realize that there is one absolute truth and the quest to find that truth should never end. When I encountered traders with pure mathematical minds, I began to realize that there are different types of truth. The metaphysical truth I was trained to search for was much different from the absolute truth derived through pure mathematics.

What I mean is that in the market, there are many truths. The market will go up! The market will go down! Every day there is a new truth that unfolds. This concept is an inherent part of looking for the right information. The most common misconception is that information is different depending on when and where you are when you receive it—nothing could be further from the truth!

One thing that everyone must understand is that stories can change, but numbers can't. Once a trade is made in the pits or on the screen, it goes out to the rest of the world and is recorded for all time. People often see the market information they are getting as tainted statistics or they might even question the authenticity of the numbers, but one thing is sure: If the numbers reflect recorded price history on a listed product, then they are bound to be accurate. Prices that have been disseminated to the rest of the world cannot be altered. That is a truth. The last trade of every commodity, stock, or bond is where the market was at that time.

When I first began doing early morning shots on CNBC and Bloomberg TV, the question concerned how relevant the futures are to the opening of the equity markets later in the morning. My response was always the same: The markets are reflecting what traders are thinking at that moment in time. Neither reporters nor viewers seem to understand the true nature of the market: that market pricing is extremely dynamic.

NUMBERS AND TECHNOLOGY ARE UNIVERSAL

I realized that numbers don't lie when I encountered a young woman at the exchange who worked as a guide in the gallery showing groups around and explaining the workings of the CME. Kristine Martino would lead a group of foreign visitors and speak to them in their own language. As someone who was taught rudimentary Armenian at an early age, I've always been fascinated with anyone who could speak several languages. Kristine had the ability to carry on a series of conversations in various languages without missing a beat, and many visitors even told her that her accent and pronunciation were perfect.

It became a habit of mine to wander up to the visitors' gallery before my shots to chat with Kristine. Occasionally she would ask me to speak to a group of visitors or answer questions that were a bit more detailed than she was prepared to answer. She was, after all, trained in languages, not in trading. I would listen to her translate the conversation and was never quite sure whether the meaning of my comments was being expressed precisely, but when it comes to market prices, the language is universal. The language in which you receive information on the markets doesn't matter—numbers don't lie! The story itself might have lost something in the translation, but the numbers that we were all looking at were understood by everyone. For example, I've met officials from the Central Bank of Armenia and found that I could not understand a word they were saying. Their Eastern Armenian dialect was so strong that I asked them to speak English. But through all the misinterpretations of conversation there stood the truth of the numbers.

One of the interesting things that has happened over the course of the technological revolution concerns the way people look for information. It used to be that traders or investors could not be islands unto themselves and hope to find success in the financial markets—on the contrary, the most important thing any trader could have was a network of people. Humans were the information pipeline that allowed traders to get an edge. Today the situation is much different. Traders can lock themselves in a room and isolate their trading from other people and find that it's still possible to turn a profit. The human factor has evolved into a technological variable. Now it's a question of knowing where to look in cyberspace for the needed information, as opposed to knowing the right person for the right information.

But one thing remains constant: Good information must be kept a well-guarded secret. Having worked with the Japanese at Nikko, the French at Credit Agricole, and the Germans at Commerzbank, I came to understand that information is a precious commodity. The Japanese would fly traders into the United States so that they could spend days with us to pick our brains and get a better understanding of our capital market structure. It was astounding how they would ship people around like clockwork every three years from Japan in order to give as many employees as possible the needed experience in the U.S. markets.

One reason for this, as I found out years later, was that many of the Japanese workers who came to this country ended up staying here and renouncing their Japanese citizenship. It had gotten to the point that the executives began to fear a flight epidemic among Japanese nationals working in America. The solution for the futures group was to maintain a cultural barrier between U.S. personnel and our Japanese coworkers. Regardless of this attempt to keep us separate, I went to extremes to acquire the trust of my Japanese colleagues. Emulating them, I worked long hours, went out drinking with them, and most important, I took them to play golf! This kept me in the loop as far as any vital market information was concerned, and I still have contact with many former colleagues who are now living back in Japan.

As I look back on the various institutions that I have worked with, I find that they were all very different in their approaches to garnering market information. The Japanese were meticulous in the way they researched every aspect of the capital markets universe. In fact, my Japanese friends had a very annoying habit of asking the same question in several different ways, drilling for a new take on a given subject. Their style was intensely interrogative, and they usually ended up getting the information they wanted. Anyone who works with the French, however, realizes that when it comes to the financial services industry, the French know it all. In fact, during a managerial meeting, I asked whether I should throw out every book in the office that had been written on the markets. When they asked me why, I responded, "Because you guys obviously know it all!" The stereotype of French arrogance aside, culturally they understood the need for proper information dissemination, and they, like the Japanese, found what they needed most of the time. Both the Japanese and the French digested the changing landscape around them and adjusted accordingly. They both started managed futures divisions, which kept the profitability of the futures FCMs intact for years.

The Germans were a completely different story. The overbanked and entrenched middle bureaucracy of the German system made the process much more cumbersome. I came to the conclusion that they just did not get it! The German philosophy was to maintain a presence without a plan. I found it absolutely extraordinary that a country that produces some of the finest and most efficient exports is lost when it comes to understanding the nature of the marketplace. Much of that might be cultural. The entrenched German hierarchy makes individualism a problem. Unlike the Japanese, who stress the collective in place of the individual, the German management philosophy is more dictatorial. Many of the German banking institutions have floundered, however, making way for a wave of modern German portfolio managers who are revolutionizing the investing landscape of the entire country.

As far as I'm concerned, there are only a few places I trust for good information. Having come of age in the 1960s and 1970s, I am a TV addict. Maybe that's why I find it so easy to go on TV and voice an opinion or break down an economic report. Television is where I get the bulk of my information. Between Bloomberg and CNBC, there isn't much left to cover. If I don't know what is happening abroad, all I need to do is turn on cable TV and find the Bloomberg or CNBC feed from Europe or Asia. Sometimes I'll be watching the Asian market report and see myself talking on tape about the U.S. markets earlier that day, and I reflect on the fact that people are basing market opinions on the information I provide. At a certain point I feel that I have a fiduciary responsibility to the audience of any show to give them accurate and useful information. Business TV has become so much better over the last decade that it has moved from being pure after-the-fact analysis to being an intricate part of every trader's day. Traders risk capital because of the comments made or not made by someone on one of the broadcasts.

SEARCHING FOR THE TRUTH

There's a fine line between the entertainment of business TV and the search for market truth within all the confusion. It can be difficult to keep in mind that business TV is in show business, not the capital markets structure, which means it is constantly probing for accurate and fresh information. A great example is when Maria Bartiromo of CNBC interviewed the new chairman of the Federal Reserve, Ben Bernanke, at a dinner in New York. During a live broadcast from the media booth of the CME, Bartiromo told the world that Bernanke had commented to her on the economy. As she talked about her meeting with Bernanke, whose comments to her had been hawkish, the market began to tumble. In this case, TV had scooped the rest of the media universe. In an age when anyone can claim 15 minutes of fame using a camera and the Internet, the information provided by Bartiromo proved profitable. Anyone watching the broadcast knew that the market was breaking and understood the catalyst behind the break.

Whenever I search for the real story behind a market move, I'm always reminded of Bing telling me that I was giving him only half the story. I came to understand, years later, that information was the other half. If you're going to make an educated investment or trade in the market, then it becomes imperative to have a combination of both price action and information. The speed at which information is now disseminated makes split-second decision making a more important variable in trading. Information that used to take days to come out of the Fed or corporate America now comes within seconds of the event. Whistle-blowers and disgruntled employees can now get on a Web site and explain the reasons for their displeasure with a corporation.

Many investment decisions have been altered over the last couple of years due to the explosion of the weblog, or *blog*. Today, if there is any question about the efficacy of a corporate product or a problem with one that has already been released, more than likely there is a blog out in cyberspace ready to expose and describe the problem.

The power of information is nowhere more evident than in the history of traders charged with insider trading. Those unethical individuals who let greed dictate their actions have realized how powerful and profitable the right information can be. Insider trading has been around since the inception of the market structure. How many real estate fortunes have been made because the property purchased by an insider ended up being worth multiples of the original purchase price? Today, insider trading is looked upon as the crime that it is. Anyone considered an insider who has information that might alter the price of a commodity or equity cannot act on that information—period. There are no exceptions. It's one of the reasons for the dual trading restriction in many of the trading pits at the CME. How can a broker fill customer orders and trade his or her own account without the appearance of impropriety? It was a necessary step taken unilaterally by the CME to show the rest of the investment universe that self-regulation works.

As the years have gone by, the exchange has done a remarkable job at maintaining the integrity of the marketplace. Every rule change that helped dispel the appearance of impropriety has contributed to the foundation on which the CME built a multi-billion-dollar corporation.

After taking into account the various methods by which traders attain the information necessary for making their investment decisions, it becomes fairly obvious that information itself is a commodity. The commoditization of information makes it that much more difficult to separate the cream from the milk. It becomes a quest to find the needle in the haystack, and for the lucky few who know where to look for the needle, trading becomes less complicated. Having the right knowledge makes the landscape of trading very different from trading without a real understanding of the condition of the market. And having the technology needed to retrieve the information is just as important. The worlds of information retrieval and technology have never shared a closer relationship than they do presently. The speed and reliability of the portable handheld computer makes the retrieval and transport of any type of information very easy. Maybe one day we'll all be like the inventor I met on my way back from London—we'll have nothing to declare, but we'll have millions of dollars worth of information stored on a microchip in our brains. Anything is possible!

CHAPTER 11

Risk Management

Managing Exposure and Uncertainty

I t's been said that risk has two basic characteristics: exposure and uncertainty. Without either one, there can be no risk. Two of the biggest myths in the capital markets are that institutions assume risk and that all risk flows to those entities that are well capitalized and positioned to assume that risk. Nothing could be further from the truth! All risk flows down to the individual, regardless of the institution in question. A good example is an event that took place in 1994 and 1995 that shook the investment world right down to its core.

In the summer of 1994, the Nikkei futures pit at the Chicago Mercantile Exchange (CME) became very active. The dollar-denominated Nikkei contract that was trading in Chicago was different from the yen-denominated contract traded in Osaka, Japan, or at the futures exchange in Singapore, which is called the Simex. Logistically, the Nikkei futures pit was placed directly behind my desk, making my operation a great access point for customers wishing to trade the product. One of the customers I handled was a firm out of London that was a conduit for trades done by Barings, a firm from Singapore.

I had taken orders from a group of traders whom I had met when I spent some time with the late Tom Mallon, a former New Yorker who transplanted his family to the Chicago area and ended up running the Merrill Lynch futures office in Chicago. He introduced me to two men based out of London who were working as introducing brokers with a mixture of retail and institutional execution business. As a two-dollar broker, I would charge $2 for every contract that my desk would fill. The billing method was referred to as *third-party billing*. In other words, we were not clearing the trade—another FCM, a futures commission merchant, was doing that. We were simply executing the orders they gave us.

I didn't think much of the lead because the Nikkei contract was not a very actively traded product and the chance of making a great deal of profit was slim. Besides, the product was difficult to service, there were only a handful of brokers and locals in the pit, and the bulk of the business was done on the open. My hope was to find a way to get the other execution business that was being done in the S&P 500 and the Eurodollar pit, which would generate much more in the way of commission dollars.

As we entered the summer and fall of 1994, the Japanese stock market as measured by the Nikkei 225 was trading around the 21,000 level. This was a move down from the unsustainable levels that the Nikkei had been looking at some five years earlier; nonetheless, the 21,000 level seemed to be an area of value. I began to receive orders every morning from the group in London. Buy 100 on the open and keep buying throughout the day until 1,000 contracts are accumulated. Wow! I realized that would be half the daily volume. After executing the order, and knowing the liquidity problems that I might face, I quietly moved the size into the pit with little market impact.

The orders came once a week; then after November they started coming almost daily until the end of 1994. The size varied from 200 to 1,000 contracts, but the side of the market never changed—they were always buyers. Everything seemed fine—the customers in London were happy, the pit loved the new business, and my guys on the desk were getting great bonuses because of the account.

I knew something was wrong when, as 1995 rolled around, the business out of the London investment banks slowed to a trickle. An account that had once generated $30,000 to $40,000 a month in commission had reached a point that the call to London on a daily basis was costing more than the revenue flow. But I maintained the relationship, thinking that they would again become the leviathan in the Nikkei pit that they once had been.

In February, I received a call from the account in London. The business they were doing was agency business for a third party. As a conduit, they were not sure who the end user really was, but they had a feeling that there might be a problem. News had just hit the markets that Barings, Britain's oldest merchant bank, had uncovered over 800 million pounds in losses. This was one of the most prestigious institutions in the world, having financed the Napoleonic Wars, the Louisiana Purchase, and the Erie Canal. Barings was known as the Queen's bank.

I immediately raced to the offices, then at Nikko, and looked through all the boxes of documents we had saved, hoping that everything was in order in case investigators came to examine our records. My compulsion to save everything paid off; the records from all the trades made in the Nikkei pit for the account in London were all there.

Nick Leeson, a single trader, had accumulated losses that surpassed 800 million pounds sterling. The problem had been uncovered. The losses were hidden in an account that was floated around the global market time zones and collateralized with Barings's customer funds. It was the largest scandal to hit the British banking system. On February 23, Leeson jumped on a plane to Kuala Lumpur, hoping to hide from the world. Within days, the bank went from being one of the strongest and most stable to failure. It was astounding; a combination of an atrocious trader and equally bad risk management techniques caused one of the greatest failures in banking history. The positions Leeson accumulated had spanned various time zones. Futures and options contracts in the United States, Japan, and Singapore were all booked on the Barings ledger. What was supposed to be an arbitrage methodology between the various exchanges turned into speculative excess that was simply wrong in direction.

In short, Leeson had made a huge bet with house money, and not a single supervisor understood what he was doing. There was no real risk management or accountability that would have seen the concentrated futures and options positions and stopped the bleeding before the institution failed. The Nikkei went from the 21,000 level in June 1994 down to 15,720 by March of the following year. The index lost a whopping 25 percent of its value, and Barings had enormous exposure, being long the market.

News of the incident hit the Chicago markets like a hurricane. Not only was Barings in trouble, but so were the exchanges that handled the bulk of the transactions, Osaka and Singapore. The institutions collectively created the collateral that guarantees every trade made through the exchange. Together, they are the clearinghouse. The CME and the Simex have always shared a close relationship, from the inception of the Simex. Those of us who did business on both exchanges realized that the clearing mechanism at the Asian exchanges might be in jeopardy if Barings were to fail. The Nikkei pit in Chicago went crazy!

Over the course of the next week, a huge chunk of open interest was moved from Singapore and Osaka to the Chicago markets. There was only one big problem—the Chicago Nikkei futures market was denominated in U.S. dollars, while the Simex and Osaka products were denominated in yen. Any positions that were moved from the Asian exchanges to Chicago had inherent currency risk associated with them. So along with every Nikkei position that was moved over to Chicago, there needed to be a currency hedge constructed to protect against a fluctuation in the yen-dollar relationship.

RISK MANAGEMENT

Those traders who were able to understand and decipher the events of
the day put on high-percentage trades, being short the market, knowing
full well that Barings would have to liquidate the huge long positions established by Leeson. Traders made a fortune selling Nikkei futures in anticipation of large orders covering the concentrated long position. Many
seasoned traders had come to realize what Barings was painfully learning
firsthand: Without the proper risk management, anyone, and any position,
can carry you out. I was always taught to respect the market because it
is much bigger than I could ever be. This was a lesson that Leeson had
forgotten. For Barings, it became the perfect storm—a trader with in-
credibly bad luck, a shortsighted risk management methodology that allowed improper trading, and upper-level managers who had no clue what
was happening. Traders have known that they can, without the proper
management of their market positions, lose everything very quickly. But
what people don't understand is that the public eventually paid for the
entire debacle. One way or another, whether it is investors in the bank
or shareholders of the institution, the problem trickles down to the average investors. It's inevitable—they are on the bottom of the financial food
chain!

The ideas and concepts that surround risk management are as old
as time. From the first insurance policy written in Greek antiquity to the
modern-day electronic marketplace, the notion of managing exposure has
been fundamental. We all learn to manage risk in our lives on a daily basis
without really knowing it. We invest our money in savings accounts, which
are insured by the good faith of the U.S. government, and we pay insurance premiums for everything from our health to our cars and homes. By
nature, humans instinctively want to protect themselves against exposure
and uncertainty—and uncertainty is nothing more than ignorance of future
events.

If we were not ignorant of what might lie ahead, then what need would
we have to manage the unexpected? Every lesson learned by traders and
investment professionals around the world centers around the principles
of risk management. Each dollar invested by an individual is accompanied by a certain amount of risk embedded in the investment. For example, people who feel secure investing capital in traditional fixed-income
assets run the risk of missing big positive returns they might have gotten if the same capital had been invested in equities. Many times over
the years, bonds have consistently underperformed the equity markets.
Even a fixed return on an investment might look negative if it doesn't
outpace inflation.

UNDERSTANDING RISK

Risk is very easy to understand. Everyone has taken some sort of risk in life, whether it was rolling dice in a board game as a child or deciding what job to take. There is a certain amount of risk in every aspect of our lives. Consider that every day we take a calculated risk when we leave the comfort and security of our homes. I'm sure many of the residents of New Orleans felt the same as Hurricane Katrina approached—confident and secure in the safety of their houses. As human beings, there isn't a day that goes by when we don't take a series of risks. The severity of the risks depends on the individual appetite for risk. The risk in walking across the street and perhaps getting hit by an automobile doesn't seem to be in the same category as putting on a position in the market and looking to find a winning trade. Yet we must conclude that the abstract nature of risk is constant—it's the degree of risk assumed that is dynamic.

When people ask me about the markets, they usually want to know what they can read or study to become better traders. I tell everyone that the best traders I have ever encountered understand the nature of risk. Risk is the heart and soul of everything that is done in the capital markets. It is the oil that lubricates the machine we call capitalism. It is the essence of the market. I have made understanding risk a professional mission throughout my career. Whether it is executing customer orders or trading my own account, understanding the essence of the market forced me to take a certain amount of calculated risk. The bottom line is that in order to start the journey toward understanding risk, it's imperative to put a certain amount of capital at risk.

The only way to learn is by experiencing the feelings associated with the application and registration of risk on the rest of the basic human emotions. Only by having a gut-churning first trade will anyone experience the real market essence. But that doesn't mean jumping into a trade without the proper guidance or homework. Think of it like swimming: You can read about it all you want, but eventually you must get into the water and feel what it's like to be wet. I see trading in much the same way. I can read and prepare myself all I want, but eventually I must get wet—very wet!—to understand the market.

UNDERSTANDING REWARD

The concept of reward is, much like risk, one that everyone easily understands. A certain amount of greed is inherent in human nature; it's a basic instinct. The idea of reward, or profit, has been a motivating factor throughout the history of humankind. From antiquity through modern times, profit has been responsible for every major advance and achievement in every civilization. Even the art of the ages, in many cases, was motivated by profit. I'm fortunate to have the Chicago Art Institute directly across from my office. Occasionally, when I have some time, I wander through the halls marveling at the wonderful Impressionist collection and the array of masters on display. Whenever I look at these masterpieces I realize that there is a high degree of probability that the work was commissioned by a wealthy patron of the times. Even the glorious sounds of Beethoven and Mozart were the result of artists willing to create in exchange for reward—the one main difference being that, unlike the exploits of traders, art lives forever!

Many in the industry refer to the *risk-to-reward ratio*, which implies that the amount of risk taken should be in proportion to the amount of reward that is possible. To some, risking capital on trades is unacceptable, so they turn to brokerage, which is commonly called the "sell" side of the business (trading is considered the "buy" side). Those who end up on the sell side have an entirely different appetite for risk than the end users of the products. The brokerage community transfers risk and has an implied risk in execution built into every transaction.

The average individual is under the misconception that brokers assume no risk. Again, nothing could be further from the truth. I have known countless brokers who have had their net worth disappear because of an error made by a clerk. Imagine losing everything you own in trying to execute an order that generates $2 per contract! During the heyday of the Nasdaq bubble, the dollar volatility of errors made being a broker or servicing the contract a near-death experience. It was very common for my desk to take $50,000 swings on orders that were on 10 contracts for which I received $20 in commission. It was obvious to everyone, including myself, that the risk-to-reward ratio was completely skewed. It was hard to justify servicing the contract; in fact, it had reached a point where the brokers began to charge extra for any flow in and out of the Nasdaq 100 futures pit.

For the locals who were in the Nasdaq pit at the time, nothing could have been better. The contract had a wide bid and offer, and any edge in the market was very profitable. My concern, as the chairman of the equity index committee at the time, was that brokers would quit selling the product, destining it for mediocrity at best. The S&P market had just started to trade the smaller e-mini version of the product with growing success, and many of the exchange leaders understood that a migration to the electronic platform would help save the Nasdaq contract. The risk-to-reward ratio was so severely skewed in the direction of the end users that neither the brokers nor the exchange reaped the benefits. The contract had a daily volatility that other contracts never experienced. It had become, as many on the board heard me say, the equivalent of selling Cadillacs for $1,000 apiece. In short, we had a wonderful risk management vehicle but had completely miscalculated the effect of a bubble on the contract. We were selling a highly leveraged product that was going through huge intraday dollar volatility and found very little in the way of commission dollars generated.

You cannot separate the concept of greed from that of reward—they are intertwined. A person cannot seek profit unless there exists a bit, even if it is very small, of greed at the root. It might sound odd, but even those who are altruistic or do volunteer work seek a higher spiritual reward. They are working through metaphysical greed as opposed to the materialistic greed that drives capital markets. We have been taught from childhood that greed is a bad thing. The mantra "Greed is good" originated in the 1987 movie *Wall Street.* My view is a little different. I feel that greed is neither good nor bad—it just *is.* Greed exists in our daily lives, regardless of whether we recognize it, and it's up to the individual to use greed for good or for bad purposes.

Traders whose greed takes them from being calculating market participants looking for high-percentage trades to raging maniacs are an example of greed turned upside down. Insider trading and other violations of securities laws are extreme examples of greed gone awry. But investors whose greed drives them into the capital markets with investments that create businesses and jobs help strengthen the economy and make society better as a whole. In this case, greed is used for something good. Every tax break and policy change that has legislated capital back into the hands of the individual has, on anecdotal evidence, proved to serve the country better in the long run. This was clear when President Kennedy lowered rates in the early 1960s and it was clear again when President Reagan did the same in the early 1980s.

The problem is that high taxes force investors into unproductive investments. No longer are traders looking for profits; a high tax base forces them to look for shelters. During the Carter years, the high tax base, coupled with an anemic market condition, made capital preservation the most important thing among investment professionals. No longer was it important to find returns in the equity markets; keeping up with inflation was more important. Preserving the capital at hand was more important than taking risks in a sick market. With inflation out of control and interest rates at record highs, Reagan came into office with a fresh idea—give the money back to the masses and see what happens. Supply side!

Whether you are a Republican or a Democrat, you can't ignore that once tax rates were reduced to lower acceptable levels, the ancillary effect was to free up capital that launched the tech boom a decade later. The unproductive investments and tax shelters of the Carter era were legislated out of existence. The idea was simple: Give investors a chance at reward from investments made in the capital markets. I think it's no coincidence that the bull market that changed history began in 1982 during Reagan's administration. Supply-siders understood it best; use greed to help generate the largest recovery the economy has seen since the Great Depression. The redistribution of capital from the government into the hands of the private sector gave investors hope and confidence in the economy—enough confidence to become sufficiently greedy to invest billions of dollars in the stock market and create stock ownership by the general public in record numbers.

IS THERE ANY PLACE FOR LUCK IN INVESTING?

If everything we do is a calculation of risk and reward, is there any place for luck in the equation? I've heard many traders say they would much rather be lucky than good. This implies that no matter how good you might be as a trader, there needs to be a certain amount of luck involved. It's a known fact that traders can be correct in their opinion on the market direction but lose every dime because of timing or, even worse, an error that ruins them. It's safe to say that I fall into the same camp as many of my fellow traders who feel that there has to be a bit of luck involved when navigating the rough waters of the capital markets. Too often I have found myself on the wrong side of an error minutes after I should have known, only to realize that the market had come back and changed what would have been a huge financial loss, if it had been caught immediately, into a scratch. That's what I mean by luck.

I don't want readers to get the impression that you can throw a dart at a stock table and pick a winning stock, although some might suggest that it's as good a strategy as any, but all investors need to have chance working to their advantage at one time or another. I would venture to guess that outside of the financial services industry, and perhaps in every profession globally, success depends on a combination of hard work and a little bit of good luck.

Traders know better than anyone how luck and risk are intertwined. One interesting fact about most traders I have described in this book is that they are all, with the exception of Steve Helms, gamblers. This is not to imply that all traders are gamblers or that gambling and trading are in any way connected, but the fact that the ones I've mentioned here are gamblers leads me to a few conclusions. Every great trader I have met who gambles—Bing Sung, Dennis DeCore, Don Sliter, or whoever—is a *great* gambler. Each has had a history of winning in casinos and has, at times, competed in tournaments hosted for high rollers. Each plays one game that he has mastered. Bing plays baccarat, Dennis plays blackjack, and Don is a craps player.

If there is any connection whatsoever between the two worlds, it's the fact that great traders understand risk but are also good at money management. The discipline it takes to be a great trader is the exact same that is needed to recognize when to walk away from the tables in a casino. It really boils down to one common denominator—smart money management.

They all understand that casino gambling, by its nature, puts the player at a mathematical disadvantage. The odds are always in the favor of the house. How, then, do some individuals consistently make out better than others?

Smart money management is not something that comes naturally to many people, but it must be learned by anyone who wants to succeed as a trader or investor. Money management is what investing and trading are really all about. The first lesson in trading is to limit your loss. Why is it then that so many traders are carried out of the marketplace because of a loss gone wild? The reason is that trading is one thing, and managing money and positions is entirely different. The reason the greatest traders in history are remembered is because they ended up profitable. No one remembers the traders who once made it big, only to lose their net worth later. Yet many great traders have found themselves on the wrong side of the markets after years of profitable trading, only to come to the conclusion that smart money management would have been a much better alternative.

One problem is that traders who make large sums of money trading a certain size cannot go back to trading in smaller increments. A trader who normally trades 10 contracts at a time, which would be worth $2,500 per S&P point, finds it very hard to go back to trading one-lots, worth $250 per point. The trader no longer thinks of it as making $250; he or she now thinks of it as losing $2,250. A trader who can avoid the trap of market ego can survive a long career. It becomes a balancing act—the ability to manage wealth in an intelligent fashion without letting ego or emotion interfere.

SMART MONEY MANAGEMENT

Money management—or wealth management—is a topic, like most topics covered here, that is worthy of an entire book. There are many ways to manage wealth that are both easy to understand and effective. I first learned how easy proper asset allocation can be when Bing taught me the methodology behind a properly balanced portfolio. Coming from a liberal arts background, I was much more comfortable debating the merits of Kant or Hegel than learning about proper portfolio diversification; nevertheless, I listened and learned. Bing told me how Harvard's endowment fund had allocated its assets. A certain percentage was in bonds, another in equities, and the rest in alternatives that had no correlation to the rest of the Harvard assets.

Bing would say that a portfolio needs to be adjusted according to the world around you. He taught me that it was very important to maintain controlled exposure and allocate properly into the different asset classes. He showed me how a bond portfolio allocated a certain amount into municipal, corporate, and U.S. Treasuries, creating a field of duration of yield that could extend as far as the trader wished. The most important thing is that he made me conceptualize the management of money.

A basic tenet of wealth management is that the more you have, the more you can lose. There's no way around it. Therefore, learning how to manage the exposure that you create for yourself becomes vital. But it's also important to remember that risk comes in many guises. Some risks are hidden, such as the unexpected risk of a geopolitical event, while other risks are expected, such as taking a futures position with a stop-loss order to limit the loss. Both risks need to be managed, and both risks *can* be managed. The long-term geopolitical risks can be addressed in a number of ways, such as options strategies, that give traders and investors downside protection with full upside potential. The smaller nanorisks that a trader or investor encounters daily can also be addressed by products in the marketplace that are less complicated.

A trader with exposure in one sector of the equity market can use the other sectors as a way to manage the risk of the trade. For example, if a trader is stuck in a long position in the Russell 2000 futures but realizes that the MidCap 400 futures are at a historic high in the spread between the two, then the trader may opt to sell the MidCap futures against the Russell position instead of covering the trade. This flexibility gives the trader the option to spread into a position in order to cover extreme exposure or leg out of the spread when the market allows.

SIX SIGMA

During the 1990s a new method for managing risk was adopted. It was called *six sigma*. I first heard the term from friends working at General Electric during the reign of Jack Welch, and I soon came to realize the importance of the method when Jim McNulty, former president of the CME, discussed the topic with the board of directors. The exchange was considering demutualization at the time, and effective and efficient management was needed to make the CME more appealing. McNulty embedded the methodology into the corporate culture. In statistics, a *sigma* refers to the standard deviation from the mean of a population. Standard deviation describes the likelihood of your next data point deviating from the mean of the whole data set. Six sigma is all about variance reduction. The sixth sigma refers to the likelihood that only 3.4 out of every 1 million data points will appear outside the sixth standard deviation. That translates into fewer than four errors per million transactions.

Technology and math had taken risk management three full standard deviations in either direction, something that was unheard of less than five years earlier. What had been a methodology for training management teams in the corporate world was now the rage in the trading rooms all across the globe. Risk management had reached a new level; it helped create what we have today—comfortably controlled exposure.

Six sigma thinking went far beyond the boardrooms and the trading desks of the global institutions; it became a way of thinking for an entire age group. An whole generation came of age listening to the gospel of six sigma as preached by corporate America. But what can the individual learn from an abstract management theory that seems out of date today? The answer lies in the fact that numbers never change. As long as you can imagine a move three standard deviations in either direction of the present market price, then it becomes important to have a methodology to cover exposure all the way through. What good is knowing the problem unless you propose a solution to whatever it might be?

I believe that the introduction of six sigma thinking forces the practitioner to think analytically. The same logic and reasoning that give a trader the courage and confidence to put on a trade are found in six sigma methodology. In short, it produces the high-percentage trades and helps maintain controlled risk in the portfolio.

DISCIPLINE

There are four basic elements that you must fully understand in order to be a good trader or investor. We've discussed the first two, risk and reward. The third is discipline. Traders and investors can at some point lose the discipline that had led them to a certain amount of success. I have seen too many former traders think they had enough wealth to retire, only to realize years later that they didn't have nearly enough to last the rest of their lives.

A good example is the windfall in CME stock that many members received upon the demutualization of the exchange. Depending on the type of seat you owned, you were allocated a set amount of stock in the newly formed public company. The CME seat, which allowed the owners and lessees to trade everything at the exchange, was given 18,000 shares. The IMM seat, which allowed owners and lessees to trade the fixed-income and equity futures and options, was given 12,000 shares, while the IOM seat, which gave rights to the equity and options markets only, was allocated 6,000 shares.

After the initial public offering (IPO), many of the traders decided that the allocation of stock was an extension of their trading as opposed to the investment in the exchange. Some of the best locals in the business couldn't understand the difference between the speed of trading, which helped them acquire wealth, and the long-term investment in the exchange, which served as more of an annuity. There were some full CME seat owners who were given 18,000 shares of stock and sold everything at the IPO price of $35 a share. As of the writing of this book, shares of CME were priced around the $450 level. The idea that the equity in the exchange was used as a bankroll to trade made no sense whatsoever. Traders who understood the business plan of the CME and saw the vision being created by management and the board held on to a large portion of their positions, only to find a windfall profit years later.

There have been many seminars and lectures by market experts trying, mostly in vain, to explain how traders and investors become disciplined. Why is it that some individuals have a difficult time with discipline? After all, are we all not subject to discipline of one type or another over the course of our lifetimes? Whether it be school or a job, the discipline of doing something well day after day can be hard work. I find that discipline is learned over the course of time. I have a hard time explaining my concept of discipline to my children, but I am absolutely sure that one day they will understand what it's all about. Maintaining a focus on any subject, let alone the markets, is nearly impossible in a society laced with distractions.

Even traders have found that sensory overload can be an obstacle to trading. It is way too easy to put on a baseball game or ESPN during the trading session while watching the markets with one eye. Traders who lose focus lose their discipline. When traders lose discipline, the next step is usually a losing trade—it's inevitable! Of course, there's always the chance that a trader will not be completely concentrating on market conditions and will still come out a winner. But those are the exceptions rather than the rule.

When I reflect on the qualities that the best traders seem to share, discipline and courage are the two that stand out. It's unfortunate that the retail public doesn't understand the need for fiscal discipline when trading the market. It pains me to see retail-based accounts lose day after day, only to send in more hard-earned money in an attempt to recover the losses they endured. It can become a vicious financial cycle. The missing ingredient in most of the retail accounts that end up consistently losing money is a compete lack of discipline. To put it bluntly, how many times does one need to get hit in the head with a hammer before realizing that it hurts? What's ironic is that many of these account holders are very successful in their chosen professions. More than likely it was a disciplined effort that made them reach their goals, yet when it comes to the markets, discipline seems to escape them.

COURAGE

The final element that a trader must understand in order to be profitable is courage. There are different types of courage. It's hard to use that word and not think of the men and women in uniform fighting wars and risking their lives for a better America. I have found that the meaning of the word *courage* has changed in my mind over the last 22 years. I was told that you need a combination of fear and courage when entering a trade. I have always looked upon large traders as having a great deal of courage. After all, they were taking huge financial risks and making it work. It's obvious to anyone who has ever traded that courage cannot be taught—it must be experienced. You cannot teach other people to be courageous; either they possess courage or they do not! I have seen great traders who could not muster the courage to trade larger size. It amazed me how some of the most gifted members of the exchange never seemed to feel comfortable trading anything more than one contract at a time.

I used to think I knew what courage really was, then the entire world changed. A combination of events made me ask myself, "Do I really know what courage is?" When the country went through the trauma of September 11, courage took on a whole new meaning. The definition of courage that I was using to describe traders who were trading large size could not be used when describing the heroics of the firefighters and workers who perished in the towers. Nor could I use the same definition to describe the courage needed to go to the Persian Gulf and fight for our country. Dan Scarnavac, a friend and colleague on the floor of the CME, fought in the first Gulf War. When he trades, he does so with little fear. Where others are terrified of losing money, Scarnavac has quiet courage when he establishes positions. It only makes sense—how courageous do you have to be to put on a trade when you've faced enemy fire in a hot battle zone?

I've tried to teach what I think are the most important characteristics of being a trader. Mostly young interns—those who listened and understood the importance of risk, reward, discipline, and courage—usually went on to successful careers either in the capital markets or in other professions. The best student I ever encountered was Derek Buending. Derek was a natural. Although I call him my nephew, he's my cousin Ani's son. His uncle on his father's side was a great options trader, and between me and the rest of our family, Derek was well-versed in the ways of the capital markets.

Upon graduating from high school, he decided to leave Houston and come to Chicago to work in the markets before going on to college. He hit the CME floor like a dynamo! He soaked up information like a sponge and seemed to easily grasp every concept I discussed with him. He would call me at the end of a day and ask about the session—about the fundamentals moving the market and the news events that seemed to affect the entire trade. After a month he told me that he was interviewing for a job with Kingstree, a proprietary trading group in Chicago.

Kingstree was no ordinary prop shop. It was the premier trading group in the city, with a waiting list a mile long of hopeful traders looking for employment. When Derek told me about the interview, I made sure I lowered his expectations by disclosing that he would be up against not only college graduates but MBAs looking to learn from the best. Derek was introduced to the firm through someone he had met on the train. As luck would have it, this turned out to be the person who was responsible for the psychological evaluations that are an important part of hiring any trader for the firm. It was no surprise to me, but according to the evaluation, Derek was almost perfect for the job. The only drawback was his age—Derek was only 18!

I received a call from Kingstree's company psychologist, who told me how impressed he was with Derek and how he thought Derek would, one day, become a great trader. It was a very proud moment for all of us—his parents, his uncles, and the rest of the family! We all knew that this was a tremendous achievement for Derek at such a tender age. He was able to land a job that MBAs were dying to get! He took to trading just like he took to everything else he attempted in his life: with vigor and enthusiasm. Derek began trading the fixed-income market with an eye toward trading the equities at a future date. His trading, at first, was very spotty. He had a difficult time mustering the courage to trade. He had understood every other element needed to become a good trader except for the courage it takes to trade. He called me one evening to talk about the issue.

I remember spending a great deal of time talking about the various characteristics that I thought were needed to be a great trader. I told him to avoid the obvious land mines, such as adding to losing positions or cutting winning trades short, but the bulk of the conversations I had with Derek centered around the human behavior and basic emotions that drive the market. He understood the fundamentals of the trade, but he was lacking the human experience needed to fully understand the emotional side of the game. Over the course of the next few weeks, Derek began to understand the true nature of the market. He grasped the emotional side more quickly than anyone else I have ever met. He focused himself on the various elements that drive investment capital and started to make winning trades. His trading career had begun, but he was putting college on the back burner.

I expressed to him how important it was to go to school while he was trading in order to learn more about the macroeconomic factors within the economy. His youth caught up with him during the course of a couple of sessions, and he started to lose money for the firm. We talked about the fact that he was struggling, and I reiterated that he was playing in the big leagues. As Dan Frishberg of BizRadio is fond of saying, there is no minor league on Wall Street! Finally, after a meeting with his mother, Ani, and calls from his father, Steve, in Texas, he decided to go back to school. Before he left I told him what I would have wanted others to say to me under the same circumstances. The markets will always be here. No matter when you come back, there will always be a market to trade. I told him that he understood risk and reward, but life would teach him about the rest. I explained to him that courage is the key to everything, and that I thought I understood what that meant. I wished him luck when he decided to go back to Houston for college.

In February 2006, Derek was in a horrible car accident. Six years earlier, his sister, Stephanie, had died in a car accident at the age of 16. As I got word of Derek's accident, my thoughts immediately went to his parents, Ani and Steve. They were reliving a nightmare! After two weeks of fighting for his life, Derek died. I flew to Houston to pay my respects to his parents and be with the rest of the extended family. It was dreadful to be burying another of Steve and Ani's children. I met many of the doctors and nurses who worked desperately to help Derek pull through. Anyone who wasn't working at the hospital at the time came to the funeral home and attended the service.

One nurse spoke about my cousin Ani. It so happens that at the same time Derek was in the hospital, another family was there with a child who was struggling to survive an accident, and that child died. When Ani heard this, she went to comfort the other family. She told them how she had already lost one child and would likely lose the other one, too. She assured the parents that, slowly, day by day, the pain lessens, although it never completely goes away. When I looked at my cousin Ani and her husband, Steve, I realized that everything I had ever thought about courage was nonsense! This was courage personified! We buried Derek on a rainy February morning, and a piece of us all died with him.

I tell this story because I ended up learning much about a subject I thought I knew well. The courage that I talk about when discussing trading is nothing compared to the real courage it takes to live with some of the horrors in this world. There's an old saying on the floor of the exchanges: It's only money; we can always get more. This is another way of saying that there are more important things in the world than making a winning trade; life is precious, but money is replaceable. I never understood the full meaning of that—until we lost Derek.

In loving memory of my nephew, Derek Buending.

Index

A

ADM. *See* Archer Daniels Midland
Advancing market, psychology, 126
After-the-fact analysis, 101
Allied Crude Vegetable Oil Refining
    Company, 162
  scandal, 163–164
Alternative investments, efficient
    frontier (relationship), 58–61
Anti-futures rule, 84
Anti-random walk, 108
Arana, Ed, 127–128
Arbitrage. *See* Index arbitrage; Risk;
    Statistical arbitrage
  execution. *See* Goldman Sachs
    Commodity Index; Nasdaq;
    Russell arbitrage; Standard &
    Poor's
  opportunity, creation, 82
  out of bullets, 43
Archer Daniels Midland (ADM),
    marketplace involvement, 10
Asian order, completion, 38–39
Asset allocation, 37–39. *See also*
    Foreign exchange
  collection, 54
  instruction. *See* Sung
  order, execution. *See* Nikko
    Securities
  strategic model, 37
Asset class, status. *See* Managed funds
Assets, noncorrelation, 64
Athletes, trader ability, 22–23
Averaging down, process, 23–24

B

Back-office services, offering. *See*
    Futures commission merchants
Baker, Jim, 111–112
Bank National Paris (BNP), CN
    acquisition, 45
Barings
  customer funds, usage, 173
  long positions, liquidation, 173–174
  losses, 172
  trades, 171
Bartiromo, Maria, 168
Bauer, Steve, 127
Bernanke, Ben, 152–153
  Bartiromo interview, 168
Bifurcated market, creation, 108
Bingisms, 11
  learning, 12
Black, Fischer, 3
Black-Scholes mathematical models,
    usage, 113
Black-Scholes model, usage, 3
Blog. *See* Weblog
Bloomberg TV, 130, 165
  market commentary, 37
  TV appearances, 11, 159
BNP. *See* Bank National Paris
BOD. *See* Chicago Mercantile
    Exchange
Bond portfolio, allocation, 179–180
Boom/busts, cycle (relief), 151
Bouroudjian, H. Jack (1987 crash,
    impact), 12
Bouroudjian's law, 112

Brokerage community, profit
    (decrease), 75–76
Brokerage houses, product
    structuring, 68
Brokers, selection, 125
Brosowski, Fred, 93
Brown, Stephen, 110
Buending, Derek, 183–185
Buffett, Warren, 14
Bund futures contract. *See* London
    International Financial Futures
    Exchange
Bush, George H.W., 111
Business cycles, understanding, 94
Business programs, report, 42
Business television, popularity, 159
Business TV
    truth, search, 168–169
Business TV, usage, 158–160
Buy program, 41
Buy-and-hold strategy, incorporation,
    109
Byrne, Adrian, 20, 124

C
Capital
    flows, 49–50
    management, 40
    redistribution, 177
    risk, 134
    taxes, impact, 177–178
Capital markets
    September 11, impact, 99
    structure, 96
        approach, 114
Capitulation trait, examination,
    144–145
Cargill, marketplace involvement, 10
Carter, Jimmy, 152
Castrovillari, Nick, 125
CBOE. *See* Chicago Board Options
    Exchange
CBOT. *See* Chicago Board of Trade
CFTC. *See* Commodity Futures
    Trading Commission
Charting price action, 102

Charts
    examination, 100–102
    points
        DeCore/McLaughlin, opinion, 103
        usage. *See* Nasdaq
    presence. *See* Trading
    problems. *See* Technical analysis
Chicago Board of Trade (CBOT)
    commodity prices, increase, 114–115
    competition, 80
    Dow Jones
        deal, 73
        futures contract, 72–73
    FBI, impact, 74
    fixed-income pits, 55
    founding, 2
    impact. *See* Equity futures franchise
    media relations, 139
        improvement, 139
    momentum, 74
    nonperishable commodities, trading,
        115
    runner, experience, 19
Chicago Board Options Exchange
    (CBOE)
    OEX/SPX options, 31
    OEX/SPX pits, involvement, 27
Chicago Mercantile Exchange (CME //
    Merc)
    agriculture markets, 30
    board of directors (BOD), 72
        meeting, 105
    ED options market, 32
    equity index committee, 46
    FBI, impact, 74
    founding, 2
    history, 76–77
    liquidity providers, impact, 8
    matching engine, 83
    membership, interests (balance),
        71–72
    metamorphosis, 82
    Nikkei futures pit, 171
    problems, 74
    runner, experience, 19
    September 11 events, 131

S&P futures pit, 55
S&P options pit, 31
stock, 181
trades, 87
upper trading floor, 98
Closing orders, impact, 49
CME. *See* Chicago Board of Trade
CN. *See* Cooper Neff
CNBC, unemployment numbers
    (release), 98–99
CNBC TV, 130, 165
  appearance, 11, 159
  Santelli guest, 139
Commerz Futures, 4, 57, 59
  Bund traders, responsibility, 83
  capital, repatriation, 82
  competition, 68
Commodity broker, Fisher (meeting),
    93
Commodity exposure, seeking, 64
Commodity Futures Trading
    Commission (CFTC), creation,
    15
Commodity prices
  housing industry trend sensitivity,
    148
  increase. *See* Chicago Board of
    Trade
Commodity Research Bureau (CRB),
  8
Commodity trading advisors (CTAs),
  59
  database, 66
  portfolio, 63
  strategy, 60
  track records, 61
Conference Board, consumer attitude
    surveys, 150
Consumer confidence, economic
    report, 150
Consumer Price Index (CPI)
  data
    change, 143
    usage, 142–143
  economic report, 147–148
  increase, deceleration, 147–148

Cooper Neff (CN), 27–28
  acquisition. *See* Bank National Paris
  statistical arbitrage, usage, 45
Cooper Neff/BNP proprietary trading,
    79
Corporate events, importance,
    44–45
Corporate profits, 146–147
  relationship. *See* Equity prices
Courage. *See* Investors; Traders
  types, 182–183
CPI. *See* Consumer Price Index
CRB. *See* Commodity Research Bureau
Credit Agricole Futures, 74, 166
Crude oil markets, run-ups, 51
CSFB, 124
CTAs. *See* Commodity trading advisors
Currencies
  differentials, 26–27
  futures, 126
  volatility, increase, 64–65
Customers, importance, 67–69

D
DeAngelis, Tino, 162–163
DeCore, Dennis, 15, 178
  inactivity, 43
  index arbitrage career, success,
    27–28
  market observations, 112
  opinion. *See* Charts; Markets
  strategy, trading, 40–41
Default risk, 148
Deflation, impact. *See* Stocks
Delta-neutral traders, 6
Derivatives, trading. *See* Harvard
    Endowment Fund
Deutschmark/yen, differential, 26–27
Diawa, 38
Direct allocation method, 66
Discipline. *See* Investors; Traders
  importance, 181–182
Distan, Ralph, 94
Diversification. *See* Real portfolio
    diversification
  gaining, 57

DJIA. *See* Dow Jones Industrial
    Average
Dollar-denominated Nikkei contracts,
    171
  trading, activity, 172
Double commission, usage, 124
Double-digit inflation, 141
Dow Jones 30, examination, 47
Dow Jones deal. *See* Chicago
    Mercantile Exchange
Dow Jones futures contract. *See*
    Chicago Board of Trade
Dow Jones Industrial Average (DJIA),
    changes, 84
Due diligence, 61, 66
Duffy, Terry, 78
Durable goods
  economic report, 149–150
  orders, 149–150

E
Earnings, importance, 47–49
Economic activity, health, 150
Economic Contrarian (radio
    program), 99
Economic growth
  amount, 150
  translation, 146–147
Economic releases
  categories, 145–153
  explanation, 137
Economic uncertainty, impact. *See*
    Stocks
Economy
  deterioration spread, 111
  Fed, impact, 145
ED. *See* Eurodollar
Efficient frontier
  relationship. *See* Alternative
    investments
  understanding, 58
Efficient market theory, product, 117
EFP. *See* Exchange for physical
Electronic futures marketplace,
    creation, 76
Electronic futures trading (EFT), 74

Electronic markets, growth, 82
Electronic platform, usage, 85
Electronic trading, increase, 96
Electronically traded products,
    popularity, 81
Elliott Wave Theory, 90, 99
  impact. *See* Fisher
Elner, Andy, 111
E-mini
  announcement, 76–77
  concept, 73
    growth, 79–80
  product
    growth, 84
    proliferation. *See* Futures
      commission merchants
      community
  volume, increase, 78
  version. *See* Nasdaq; Russell 2000;
    Standard & Poor's
Emotions, impact. *See* Markets
Equity futures franchise, CBOT
    impact, 75
Equity Owners Association (EOA), 74
Equity prices
  corporate profits, relationship, 149
  increase, 146–147
Equity-fixed income AA, 39
Error risks, 124
Escape to the Futures (Melamed), 76,
    87
Eurex, impact. *See* London
    International Financial Futures
    Exchange
Eurodollar (ED) futures
  contract, margin, 86
  establishment, 79
  pit, Aranas work, 127
Eurodollar (ED) options
  market. *See* Chicago Mercantile
    Exchange
  pit, trades, 4
European bourses, closure, 38
European currency
  consolidation, 126
  creation, 39

European order, completion, 38–39
Exchange for physical (EFP), 40
  activity, 42
    occurrence. *See* Index arbitrage
Exchange-traded funds (ETFs), 50–52.
    See also Standard & Poor's
    Depositary Receipts
  introduction, 76
  market relationship, 32
Exposure, management, 171

F
FASB 133 definition, 65
FCMs. *See* Futures commission
  merchants
Fear
  greed, relationship, 123–126
  relationship. *See* Panic
Federal Open Market Committee
  (FOMC), 151
Federal Reserve (Fed)
  actions, 141
  central bank behavior,
    152
  cycle
    easing, 147
    tightening, 145, 147
  economic report, 151–153
  funds rate, 95–96
  impact. *See* Economy
Fiandaca, John, 124–126
Fibonacci numbers, usage,
  144
Fidelity Magellan (Lynch
  management), 13
Financial futures, Melamed (impact),
  73
Financial markets
  economic backdrop, impact,
    148
  success, 166
Fisher, Ted Lee, 91
  approach. *See* Technical analysis
  concept. *See* Structural analysis
  discipline, 94

Eastern philosophical precepts,
  incorporation, 98
Elliott Wave Theory, impact, 94
  examination. *See* Soybeans
  interview, 92–98
  speculation, 97
Fitzgerald, Cantor, 130
Flight to quality, 142
FOMC. *See* Federal Open Market
  Committee
Foreign exchange (Forex)
  Forex-related asset allocation, 39–40
  futures, establishment, 79
  market
    spreading, 26–27
    U.S. dollar demand, impact, 53
  traders, 159
Forward rate agreement (FRA)
  traders, 10
FRA. *See* Forward rate agreement
Friedman, Milton (impact). *See*
  International Monetary Market
Frishberg, Dan, 184–185
Fund managers, selection, 66
Fundamentals
  definition, 14–15
  discussion, 91
Futures
  contract. *See* Chicago Board of
    Trade
  definition, 2
  FCMs, profitability, 167
  industry, highlight, 131–133
  managers, power/proliferation, 62
  trading
    Holy Grail methodology, 67, 100
    revolution, 77–79
  usage. *See* Managed futures
    reasons, 2–3
  users, definition, 2–3
Futures commission merchants
  (FCMs), 57
  back-office services, offering, 132
  competition, 59
  impact, 86–87
  platforms, offering, 86

Futures commission merchants
   (FCMs) community
   change, 78
   e-mini products, proliferation
      (desire), 79
   evolution, 85–86
   limited liability, 82
Futures market. *See* Stock indexes
   creation, 2
   daily price movement, 50
   long/short positions, 59

G
Gambling, 178–179
Gamma long, instruction, 5
Gann methodology, 90, 99
   examination, 94
Gault, Bobby, 121, 126–128
Gault, Mirth, 127–128
GDP. *See* Gross domestic product
General Electric, 180
German hierarchy, impact. *See*
   Individualism
Gill, Phupinder, 131
Global futures exchanges, growth,
   96
Globalization, impact, 159
Globex
   creation, Melamed (impact), 73
   session. *See* Stock indexes
   stock indexes, trading, 83
Goetzman, William, 110
Gold markets, run-ups, 51
Goldman Sachs, involvement. *See*
   Markets
Goldman Sachs Commodity Index
   (GSCI), 8
   arbitrage, index, 9
Google, addition. *See* Standard &
   Poor's
Gordon, Scott, 131
Grasso, Dick, 84–85
Greed, relationship. *See* Fear
Greenspan, Alan, 31, 112
   appointment, 153
Gretzky, Wayne, 22

Gross domestic product (GDP)
   economic report, 150–151
   foreign countries, 141
GSCI. *See* Goldman Sachs Commodity
   Index
Guaranteed fund, 67–68

H
Hadley, Greg, 113
Hager, Kent, 28
Haines, Mark, 44, 130
Haircut, 86
Harvard Endowment Fund
   control, 11
   derivatives trading, 56
Hedge fund
   concept, 48
   investments, money flow, 59
Hedging, 9–10
Helms, Steve, 178
   movement. *See* Standard & Poor's
      500 futures
   position trader, 30
Holy Grail methodology. *See* Futures
Housing, economic reports, 148
Housing starts
   impact, 148
   rate, change, 148
Hughes, George, 22
Human factor, technological variable,
   166
Hunt, Nelson, 160
Hunt, William, 160
Hunt brothers, impact. *See* Silver
   market
Hurricane Katrina, 137

I
IMM. *See* International Monetary
   Market
Index arbitrage, 40–42
   nuances, 42–43
   strategy, 41
   universe, EFP activity (occurrence),
      43

Indexes
    examination. *See* Russell Index
    rebalancing, 43–44
Individualism, German hierarchy
        (impact), 167
Inflation
    impact. *See* Stocks
    interest rates, relationship, 147–148
    rate, change, 148
Inflationary pressures, signs, 146
Information
    availability. *See* Investors
    danger, 161–164
    location process. *See* Professionals
    network, 164–165
      creation process, 164
    obtaining. *See* Markets
    power, 169
    retrieval, technology (relationship),
      169
    universality, 165–168
    value, 155
Initial public offering (IPO), 181
    market, action, 110
Institutional asset allocation order,
        execution. *See* Nikko Securities
Institutional customer base, impact, 68
Institutional orders, usage, 85
International Monetary Market (IMM)
        creation, 73
    Melamed/Friedman, impact, 2
Internet, usage, 158
Intraday price aberrations,
        randomness, 109
Intraday volatility, driving, 129
Intramarket spreader, 26
Investments
    decisions, alteration, 168–169
    disappointments/opportunities, 71
    efficient frontier, relationship. *See*
      Alternative investments
    luck, usage, 178–179
    three-to-one write-offs, 152
Investors
    courage, 182–184
    discipline, 181–182

    information, availability, 117
    portfolio, correlation diversification,
      65
    security, false sense, 123–124
    taxes, impact, 177
IPO. *See* Initial public offering
Irrational exuberance, 31
    state, 112

J
Japanese candlestick charting
      methods, 90
Japanese stock market, Nikkei 225
      measurement, 172
JDSU, addition. *See* Standard &
      Poor's
Jobs Creation Act (2004), 53
Jobs data, tracking, 146
John Labuszewski, involvement. *See*
      Nikko Securities
Johnson, Kenny, 128
Jones, Paul Tudor, 48

K
KC-CO, 28
Kellogg School of Management,
      107–108
Kingstree, 183–184
Krause, Jim, 131
Kumar, Alok, 110
Kupcinet, Irv, 155

L
Late-day phenomenon, 52
Leary, Timothy, 92
Leeson, Nick, 172–174
Lefèvre, Edwin, 94
Legging the spread. *See* Spreads
Lehman Brothers, 138
Lemming mentality, 15–16
Lemmings, jumping, 15
Leverage, 8–9
Liddy, G. Gordon, 72
LIFFE. *See* London International
      Financial Futures Exchange

Lintner, John, 58–59. *See also* Potential
    Role of Managed
    Commodity-Financial Futures
    Accounts in Portfolios of Stock
    and Bonds
Liquidation only transaction, 161
Liquidity, 6–8
    addition, 152
    characteristic, 41
    migration, Bund trader
        responsibility. *See* London
        International Financial Futures
        Exchange
    providers. *See* Standard & Poor's 500
        futures pit
      squeezing, 161
    providers, impact. *See* Chicago
        Mercantile Exchange
Live cattle market, involvement, 26
Lo, Andrew, 116
    work, importance, 117
London International Financial
        Futures Exchange (LIFFE)
    Bund futures contract, Eurex
        (impact), 77
    liquidity, migration (Bund trader
        responsibility), 83
Long Term Capital Management
        (LTCM), leverage ratio, 61
Long-term positions, holding, 157
LTCM. *See* Long Term Capital
        Management
Lynch, Peter. *See* Peter Lynch method
    management. *See* Fidelity Magellan

M
Malkiel, Burton, 106
Mallon, Tom, 171
Managed Accounts Report, 62–63
Managed funds, asset class (status),
        63–65
Managed futures
    fund, concept. *See* Multistrategy,
        multiadvisor managed futures
        fund
    stocks, 64

    structures, 65–66
    usage, 55
Margin calls (coverage), capital
        (request), 161
Market psychology, 120
    driving, 123
    impact, process, 133–134
    understanding, 134–135
Market trading
    homework, 12–13
    knowledge, 10–11
    lessons, 11–12
Marketplace
    euphoria, 121–123
    psychology, 119
Markets
    average, underperforming, 117
    capitalization, 69
    change, September 11 (impact),
        142
    collective consciousness, 126–127
    condition, contrary opinion, 102
    efficiency, 116
    emotions, impact, 133–135
    equalizer, effect, 80–81
    exposure, downdrafts, 110
    fundamental aspect, 91
    geopolitical nature, 157
    Goldman Sachs, involvement, 7
    historic move, 122
    information, obtaining, 167
    knowledge, 35, 54
    Merrill Lynch, involvement, 7
    mood, change, 129
    move, story, 168
    opinion, 114
    orders, flow, 156–157
    outthinking, trader job, 129
    pricing, 134–135
    psyche, 120–121
    small investor, involvement, 69
    technical work, DeCore/McLaughlin
        opinion, 117–118
    technician, 140
    timing, 110
        incorporation. *See* Portfolio

transparency, 85–86
truths, existence, 165
Markowitz, Harry, 58–59
Marshall Plan, rebuilding efforts,
    151–152
Martino, Kristine, 165–166
M&As. *See* Mergers and acquisitions
McLaughlin, Vince, 15
    inactivity, 43
    index arbitrage career, success,
        27–28
    opinion. *See* Charts; Markets
    strategy, trading, 40–41
McNulty, Jim, 180
Melamed, Leo
    advice, 71
    Anti-Defamation League honor, 80
    impact. *See* Financial futures;
        Globex; International Monetary
        Market
    leadership, 74
    Santelli, meeting, 140
    understanding, 80
    visionary, 73
Merc. *See* Chicago Mercantile
    Exchange
Mergers and acquisitions (M&As),
    45
Merrill Lynch
    futures, 171
    involvement. *See* Markets
Micron Technologies, 105
Microsoft dividend payment, 44
Mid-Cap 400 contracts, trading. *See*
    Standard & Poor's
Miller, Merton, 84, 105
    influence, 108
    opinion, 106. *See also* Random walk
        theory
Mistakes, importance, 17–18
Modern portfolio theory (MPT), 56–57
Momentum trading, 60–61
Money management, 179–180
Money supply figures, release, 52
Monieson, Brian, 71
Monthly timing, impact, 51–52

Multistrategy, multiadvisor managed
    futures fund, concept, 67
Murrey, T.H., 100
Murrey Math, 100
Murrya, Troy, 22

N
Nasdaq
    arbitrage, execution, 9
    averages, 62
    bubble, 176
    contract, saving, 176
    e-mini
        success, 79
        version, 77
    futures market
        examination, 89–90
        success, 126
    index, 31
        resistance, chart points (usage),
            123
    market, level, 79
Nasdaq 100 Trust (QQQ), product
    example, 51
Nature and Trading methodology, 99
New York Board of Trade, 131
New York Mercantile Exchange, 131
New York money banks, funding
    desks, 95
New York Stock Exchange (NYSE), 47
    averages, 62
    floor, market makers (impact), 52
    system, computer glitch, 43
Nikkei 225 measurement. *See* Japanese
    stock market
Nikkei contracts. *See*
    Dollar-denominated Nikkei
    contracts
Nikkei futures pit. *See* Chicago
    Mercantile Exchange
Nikko International, creation, 67–68
Nikko Securities, 37, 166
    institutional asset allocation order,
        execution, 38
    investment vehicles, need, 67–68
    John Labuszewski, involvement, 1

Nixon, Richard, 160
Nomura, 15, 38
Noncorrelated asset classes, concept, 64
Nonfarm payrolls
    categorization, 146
    employment, count, 145–146
Nonperishable commodities, trading. *See* Chicago Board of Trade
Non-Random Walk Down Wall Street (Lo), 116
Non-random walk theory, 116–118
Norman, Mike, 99–100
NYSE. *See* New York Stock Exchange

O
O'Callaghan, Jack, 22
October 1987 crash, 12–13
OEX. *See* Standard & Poor's 100 index
Off-hour volume records, 112
Oil embargos, 61–62
Open outcry session, 54
Opportunity cost, 148
Options, 3–4
    premium/volatility, 4–6
    relationship. *See* Spreaders
    traders, 31–33
Order flow, 160–161
Osaka exchanges, 173
Out of bullets. *See* Arbitrage

P
Panic, fear (relationship), 128–129
Parkinson, Ward, 105
Peter Lynch method, 13–14
Peters, Ralph, 35–36, 115
    information network, 162–163
Pits. *See* Chicago Board of Trade
    involvement. *See* Chicago Board Options Exchange
    market trading, 97
    psychology, 124
    status quo, change, 84–85
Pit-traded product, migration, 81
Plantery, Mark, 22
Point-and-figure charts, 90

Pool operators, 66
Pork bellies
    market, involvement, 26
    pits, 115
Portfolio
    above-average returns, 116
    diversification. *See* Real portfolio diversification
    managers, market timing (incorporation), 109
Position traders, 29–31. *See also* Helms
Post-cold war effect, 122
Post-IPO exchange politics, 78
"Potential Role of Managed Commodity-Financial Futures Accounts in Portfolios of Stock and Bonds" (Lintner), 63
PPI. *See* Producer Price Index
Pre-IPO exchange politics, 78
Price fluctuations, MBA knowledge, 107–108
Price movements
    impact, 64
    randomness, 107
Price pressures, tracking, 147
Pricing instability, 134
Producer Price Index (PPI), economic report, 147–148
Productivity
    economic report, 149
    growth, importance, 149
Professionals, information (location process), 156–158
Profitability, key, 158
"Proof that Properly Anticipated Prices Fluctuate Randomly" (Samuelson), 106
Proprietary trading houses (prop shops), 78
Prosperity, creation, 122
Purchasing power parity, 97
    maintenance, 98

Q
QQQ. *See* Nasdaq 100 Trust
Quant jocks, 28

Quotron
  quote boards, 30
  screen, usage, 141

R
Racom Prize, 92–93
Random events
  basis. *See* Random walk theory
  impact. *See* Trends
Random walk, existence, 144
Random Walk Down Wall Street, A
    (Malkiel), 106
Random walk theory, 105. *See also*
    Non-random walk theory
  concept, 107
  domination, 108
  introduction, 109
  Merton opinion, 106–107
  random events, basis, 113
  technology, relationship,
    109–110
Random walkers, opinions
    (importance), 113–115
Randomentalists, 108
Randomness, 115
  impact, 112–113
Reagan, Ronald (tax lowering), 152
Real portfolio diversification, 61–63
Reinglass, Aaron, 101
Relative strength index (RSI), 101
Reminiscences of a Stock Operator
    (Lefèvre, Edwin), 94
Residential units, construction, 148
Resistance levels, usage, 102
Retail houses, problems, 79
Retail investors, 114
Retail sales
  economic report, 146–147
  growth, deceleration, 147
Reward, understanding, 175–178
Reward/risk enhancement overlay
    strategy, pursuit, 65
Risk
  arbitrage, 45
  compensation, 109
  understanding, 174–175

Risk management, 173–174
  absence, 173
  impact, 171
Risk-adjusted returns, 109
  production, 58
Risk/reward concept, 110
Risk-to-reward ratio, 63
  shift, 58
  usage, 176
Rollover conditions. *See* Standard &
    Poor's 500 futures
RSI. *See* Relative strength index
Rubik's Cube puzzle, analogy, 145
Rule 80-A, impact, 84
Runner, experience. *See* Chicago
    Board of Trade; Chicago
    Mercantile Exchange
Russell 2000
  contracts, trading, 7
  e-mini version, 77
  futures, 46, 180
  markets, 125
  measurement. *See* Small-cap stocks
  weakness, 50
Russell arbitrage, execution, 9
Russell Index, examination, 52–54
Russell stocks, supplier
    representation, 53

S
Salad oil, trading, 162
Samuelson, Paul, 106
Sandner, Jack, 78
Sandor, Richard, 140
Santelli, Rick, 138, 158
  interview, 138–145
Sanwa Bank, 139
Sarbanes-Oxley Act, passage, 129
Scalpers, 21
  long-term positions, holding, 157
  quality, 25
Scarnavac, John, 20, 124
Scholes, Myron, 3
  formula, creation, 5–6
Segal, Joe, 26
Sell program, 41

September 11 (9/11)
disaster recovery sites, relocation, 132
emotions, 133
events, 134. *See also* Chicago Mercantile Exchange
impact, 95–96, 129–131. *See also* Capital markets; Markets; Stock market
media, interaction, 132–133
Sereleas, George, 124–126
S.G. Warburg, Swiss Bancorp (merger), 38
Shearson Lehman, 138–139
Shepard, Bill, 75
genius, 76
Short-term Treasuries, run assurance, 111
Sigma, 180. *See also* Six Sigma
Silver market, Hunt brothers (impact), 160–161
Silverman, David, 74
Simex. *See* Singapore International Monetary Exchange
Simon, Paul, 80, 105
Singapore International Monetary Exchange (Simex), 173
Six Sigma, 180–181
Six-Day War, 115
Sliter, Donald, 24–25, 178
trader, ability, 25
Small-cap stocks (impact), Russell 2000 measurement, 52
Small-cap universe, representation, 53
Soros, George, 48
Soya Beana, 36
Soybeans
Fisher examination, 97–98
market, creation, 35
S&P. *See* Standard & Poor's
S&P500. *See* Standard & Poor's 500
SPDR. *See* Standard & Poor's Depositary Receipts
Sports, trading (relationship), 21–23

Spreaders. *See* Intramarket spreader
options, relationship, 27–29
personality, search, 27–28
Spreading, 26–27
Spreads, legging, 42
SPX. *See* Standard & Poor's 500 Index
Squawk Box, 44
Standard & Poor's 100 index (OEX), 27
options, 31
pit, involvement. *See* Chicago Board Options Exchange
Standard & Poor's 500 Index (SPX), 27
options, 31
pit, involvement. *See* Chicago Board Options Exchange
Standard & Poor's 500 (S&P500)
contracts, long position, 121
e-mini, success, 79
index, 47
mutual fund outperformance, 107
strength, 50
Standard & Poor's 500 (S&P500)
futures, 22, 31
purchase orders, 38
Standard & Poor's 500 (S&P500)
futures contract
electronic trading, 81
splitting, 72
version, size reduction, 75
Standard & Poor's 500 (S&P500)
futures pit
Helms, movement, 30
liquidity providers, 128
rollover conditions, 33
Standard & Poor's Depositary Receipts (SPDR)
ETF, 44
product example, 51
Standard & Poor's (S&P)
arbitrage, execution, 9
contract, 33
creation, 111
value, 86
Google, addition, 44
JDSU, addition, 44
market, involvement, 26

MidCap 400
  e-mini version, 77
  futures, 46
  Mid-Cap 400 contract, trading, 7
  MidCap market, 125
  options pit. *See* Chicago Mercantile
      Exchange
  pit activity, 120
Statistical arbitrage, 45–47
  usage. *See* Cooper Neff
Statistical index arbitrage, 45
Stock indexes
  futures, Globex session, 112
  futures markets, settlement
      (end-of-the-month anomaly), 49
  trading. *See* Globex
Stock market, 60
  closure, 130
  reopening, 132
  September 11, impact, 130
Stock prices,
      inflation/deflation/economic
      uncertainty (impact), 64
Strategic planning committee, 75
Structural analysis, 94–95
  Fisher concept, 95
Structured product approach,
      66
Sung, Bing, 11, 30, 178
  1987 crash, impact, 12–13
  advice, 34
  asset allocation instruction, 56
  lessons, 54
  trader, ability, 100
Support levels, usage, 102
Swiss Bancorp, merger. *See* S.G.
      Warburg
Swiss franc/Deutschmark, differential,
      26–27
Synthetic market exposure, 49

T
Technical analysis, 89
  charts, problems, 100–102
  education, importance, 102–103
  Fisher approach, 93–94

  problems, 106–107
  usefulness, 90–100
*Technical Analysis of Stocks and
      Commodities* (Lo), 116
Technicians, work, 92
Technology
  history, 76–77
  relationship. *See* Information;
      Random walk theory
  universality, 165–168
  usage, 75–76
Technology stocks (tech stocks)
  breakdown, 16
  usage, 112
Terminal value, acceptability,
      65–66
Terrorism, impact, 142
Texas hedge, 121
Third-party billing, 171
TPS. *See* Transactions per second
Traders. *See* Delta-neutral traders;
      Options; Position traders
  ability. *See* Athletes
  characteristics, 33–34
  competition, inability, 101
  courage, 182–185
  discipline, 181–182
  edge/advantage, loss, 81–84
  examples, 24–26
  experience, 19
  faith, leap, 164–165
  greed, 177
  qualities, 20–21
  sensory overload, 182
  shock, 113–114
Trading. *See* Market trading
  approach, 95
  art/science, contrast, 1
  disappointments/opportunities,
      71
  edge/advantage, loss, 81–84
  pit, psychology, 126–128
  relationship. *See* Sports
  revolution. *See* Futures
  room, charts (presence), 144
  textbook advice, 109

Trading Advisor Qualified Universe
    Index, 62
  positive gain, 63
Transaction costs, 64
  impact, 108
Transactions per second (TPS), 77
Trends, random events (impact),
    110–112
TV shots
  See Bloomberg TV; CNBC
  execution, 20–21

U
UAL crash, 121
UAL earnings, 55–56
Uncertainty, management, 171
Unemployment
  economic report, 145–146
  rate, measurement, 145
  reports, movement, 140
  Wall Street, anticipation, 146
Unemployment Fridays, 139
University of Chicago Graduate School
    of Business, 107–108
Upstairs screen trader, 34
U.S. dollar
  demand, impact. *See* Foreign
    exchange
  differentials, 26–27

V
Volatility. *See* Options
  curve, flattening, 57
  driving. *See* Intraday volatility
  impact, 126
  increase. *See* Currencies
  test, 113
Volatility index (VIX), creation, 13
Volcker, Paul, 152

W
Wage inflation, impact, 146
Wage trends, insight, 146
Walking casino, reference, 17
Walsh Greenwood, 15
War premium, usage, 134
Warburg. *See* S.G. Warburg
Wealth
  effect, 123
  management, 179–180
Weblog (blog), impact, 168–169
Weisblum, Scott, 46, 79, 125
Welch, Jack, 180

Y
Yastrow, Peter, 130
Yen/British pound, differential,
    26–27
Y2K phenomenon, 31